Love Vision
and
Debate

By the same author

The Pearl: an Interpretation (1967)

The Poet Reading to an Audience

Chaucer and the Making of English Poetry

Volume I

Love Vision
and
Debate

P. M. KEAN

University of Oxford

Routledge & Kegan Paul
London and Boston

First published 1972
by Routledge and Kegan Paul Ltd
Broadway House, 68–74 Carter Lane,
London EC4V 5EL
and 9 Park Street,
Boston, Mass. 02108, U.S.A.
Printed in Great Britain by
The Camelot Press Ltd
London and Southampton
ISBN 0 7046 2

Contents

Plates

Preface

It will be obvious to anyone who reads this book that the debt it owes to previous writers on Chaucer is a very great one. It is easy to acknowledge particular obligations, but there remains a large and nebulous area, of which I can only say that the shape of these chapters would have been different if other critics had not been in the field before me. I have tried to keep the detailed tally of agreements and disagreements with other writers to the minimum – without, I hope, failing to acknowledge direct debts – because, where footnotes are in any case all too numerous, the piling up of such references can become irritating. I must, of course, add that not all agreements are necessarily plagiarisms; nor are all omissions of references which might have been useful deliberate. My copies of the voluminous bibliographies of works on Chaucer could well have Isidore of Seville's lines written on their fly-leaves:*

> Mentitur qui totum te legisse fatetur,
> Aut quis cuncta tua lector habere potest?

I have tried, too, to keep annotation within bounds by referring to the best starting point for further reading on any topic, where other references will be found collected. In the process, of course, I have necessarily omitted individual reference to many important books and papers. In dealing with quotations from Latin authors I have used English translations where the content only is of importance, but I have usually given the Latin text when the exact

* Inscribed above the cupboard containing the works of St Augustine in the library of Seville (Migne, *PL* 83, 1109).

wording is of interest or in cases where Chaucer knew, or might have known, the work. It will be appreciated that I have not been able to use work on Chaucer which has appeared since this book was sent to the press.

I owe a special debt to various friends who have made numerous suggestions and corrections, to say nothing of pupils with whom I have discussed many of the ideas. Miss E. G. W. Mackenzie and Mrs D. R. Sutherland have both helped me greatly by reading parts of my typescript, and by patiently answering innumerable questions. I also owe a great, but less definable, debt to the late Dorothy Everett. Here I can only acknowledge a pervading influence – I do not think that without it I should write about Chaucer as I have done. None of these friends, however, is to be held responsible for my mistakes – I must say, with Chaucer, that 'what I drye, or what I thynke, / I wil myselven al hyt drynke',* and the responsibility for the final form of the book, and for all its deficiencies, is my own.

My thanks are due to the Houghton Mifflin Company of Boston for permission to quote from *The Works of Geoffrey Chaucer*, edited by F. N. Robinson; to the editor of *Medium Aevum* for permission to use parts of a paper which originally appeared in that journal, in chapter 4; and to the following institutions and libraries for permission to use photographs of manuscripts in their possession as illustrations: Corpus Christi College, Cambridge; the Bibliothèque Nationale and the Bibliothèque de l'Arsenal, Paris; the Metropolitan Museum, New York; and the Fitzwilliam Museum, Cambridge.

* *House of Fame*, 1879–80.

Abbreviations

CT	*Canterbury Tales* (passages quoted from F. N. Robinson, ed., *The Works of Geoffrey Chaucer*, 2nd edn, 1957, Houghton Mifflin Co., Boston)
EETS	Early English Text Society (O.S. = Old Series; E.S. = Extra Series)
ELH	*English Literary History*
MLN	*Modern Language Notes*
MPh	*Modern Philology*
OED	*The Oxford English Dictionary*
PL	J.-P. Migne, *Patrologiae Cursus Completus . . .* Series Latina
PMLA	*Publications of the Modern Language Association of America*
RES	*Review of English Studies* (N.S. = New Series)
SATF	Société des Anciens Textes Français

Introduction: Chaucer and the English tradition

A question which inevitably arises concerning a poet placed, as Chaucer was, within a period of change, is how far he helped to mould the course of events in his own day, as well as how far future developments were influenced by him. What is most important, without doubt, about any individual poet is his particular and individual achievement. Indeed, it is only through this particularity that he is in any position to exert an influence on the literary traditions of his country. It is to the examination of this special achievement that this book is mainly devoted, but not without some attempt to answer the question of what Chaucer's place is in a tradition which stretches a long way before and behind him. It is in both these senses – of individual achievement and historical position – that 'the making of English poetry' is to be understood. The English language is the chosen medium of Chaucer's poetry, in a period when he could as well have selected French or Latin – his friend Gower used both for major works. It would hardly be conceivable that he should thus choose to write in English without any reference to the fact that a long established tradition of the use of the vernacular for poetry lay behind him; and, in fact, he does show obvious knowledge of the work of some of his predecessors, especially in the fields of romance and lyric. If my interpretation of the *House of Fame* is accepted, it is also the case that he gave deliberate consideration to the problems posed by the use of English to a poet working on his scale, and with his particular interests. This, indeed, is the point at which the other sense in which we can regard Chaucer as a 'maker of English poetry' becomes important. It is evident that it is in these two respects – the scale on which he builds and the kind of content which he finds appropriate for poetry – that he has least in common with any English predecessor. There is nothing in English before him which is at all like, for example, the *Troilus* or the *Knight's Tale* in scope, and this means that there is nothing in English before him which poses just those problems of organization and presentation. For Chaucer's solutions, and the degree to which he draws on foreign models, as well as the degree to which he still feels the attraction of the older type of English romance narrative (especially in the case of the *Knight's Tale*), I must refer the reader to later chapters.

Chaucer is, thus, a maker of English poetry in the sense that he not only uses English for poetry and so, to an inescapable degree, looks back; he also makes it, in the sense that he adds to what he found, with the result that, after him, poets could base their work on a way of writing which was unlike anything that had existed before. The differences included a new kind of organization in large, clearly articulated works, which replaced a narrative structure that was largely episodic; and also a new kind of subject-matter derived from the world of learning. Philosophy, morals, the 'newe science', all become suitable material for poetry. But – and this was the real novelty – they were not expounded in verse treatises, but integrated into narrative structures in such a way that the work as a whole gained a new brilliance and a new depth of meaning; and this without sacrificing its validity as narrative to the demands of exposition. Finally, the approaches to language which had been adequate to earlier writers needed modification, if English was to become a suitable vehicle for the expression of this wider range of meaning. It had to be moulded into a fuller and more flexible medium, yet without ceasing to be English or losing contact with what had gone before, since much of the earlier poetry in English was still, even to an audience well-versed in contemporary French literature, a familiar and popular form of entertainment.[1]

It is this paradox of the 'new' poet, who is yet essentially linked to the past by the fact that he is also the 'English' poet, which is insisted on again and again by the writers who immediately followed Chaucer in the fifteenth century. They are never tired of singing his praises as the 'first finder' of English as a language fit for poetry: as 'sours and fundement / On englysshe tunge swetely to endyte.'[2] The strength of their feelings for the importance of his achievement leads them to develop a vocabulary which, or so I believe, is used

2

to express much more critical perception than is usually assumed. They appreciated Chaucer, in my opinion, for his ability in all the three areas I have just mentioned: in that of overall organization; in the wide scope of his subject matter; and in his achievement of a style sufficiently flexible and expressive for the task he had undertaken. In the final chapter of this book I have tried to show the meaning of the rather odd terminology in which all this is expressed.

Modern critics of Chaucer have, I think, sometimes shown a less accurate understanding of the situation, in that they have tended to concentrate on the newness and to deny the way in which the poet's Englishness links him to what has gone before. That this, too, is important, was long ago emphasized by W. P. Ker, when, in 1912, he delivered the Clark Lectures in Cambridge on the subject of 'Chaucer and the Scottish Chaucerians'. He protested against the terms of his assignment, which were that the lecturer should limit himself to 'English literature not earlier than Chaucer'. 'In dealing with the history of English literature,' he said, 'it is not possible to make a beginning in the reign of Edward III.'[3] Yet, in 1960 Charles Muscatine, in his excellent book *Chaucer and the French Tradition*,[4] can still declare: 'In the history of the literature in English, Chaucer is an anomaly. He has no significant predecessors.' And, in the next year, in the English translation of Walter F. Schirmer's book on Lydgate, we read that England 'lagged far behind other European countries in developing a vernacular ... [before Chaucer] there was no cultivated English literary language.'[5]

Muscatine ably demonstrates in detail Chaucer's debt to the tradition of French poetry deriving from the *Roman de la Rose*, both in the courtly style and in the low or mixed one which much of Jean de Meun's part of the *Roman* shares with Old French *fabliau*. No critic is likely to doubt the fact of such an influence or its importance in the evolution of Chaucer's manner of writing. But it does not tell the whole story. Chaucer could not have made his mark as the first *English* poet on the basis of any amount of reading in French.

In order to try to assess the extent of Chaucer's debt to the English tradition, it will be necessary to give some indication of the state of English poetry at the time when he began to write. We can start from two generalizations: first that there seems to have been very little change in attitudes towards poetry, and in the kinds of writing which were undertaken in the two hundred or so years before *c.* 1360;[6] secondly that, during the second half of the fourteenth century, a change took place which, certainly gaining momentum through Chaucer's work though not necessarily initiated by him, altered the whole aspect of English poetry and, at the same time, produced an entirely new attitude towards it.[7] Nevertheless, it must be pointed out that, throughout this period of change and long afterwards, older types of poetry continued to be popular, and the difference between the period before *c.* 1360 and that after it, which seems so striking to us, was possibly not so strongly felt by those who actually lived through the change.[8]

The range of English verse before the second half of the four-teenth century was very great. Poems of all sorts existed, from works of instruction, practical or moral, through romance narrative, in its many subdivisions, to the more occasional kinds of shorter poems, themselves including great variety, from mere mnemonics of useful facts to lyrics, both secular and religious, which show a high level of achievement. As far as we can see, however, there is little distinction between what we should call poetry – that is something which recognizes itself as an art and which deliberately aims at giving its audience aesthetic satisfaction – and verse – which has no pretentions beyond straightforward communication of a given subject-matter. It is true, of course, that the idea that poetry should exist in any sense as 'art for art's sake', could not have occurred to anyone in the fourteenth century – or indeed for centuries to come. Nevertheless, there is, I think, a palpable difference between poetry in English before *c.* 1360 and afterwards. While Chaucer and some of his contemporaries seem to aim at an audience which would be interested in the actual technique of poetry and would be capable of reacting as connoisseurs to details of workmanship, the aim of earlier writers seems to have been an appeal to the audience based almost entirely on subject-matter; and the art with which they get this across is largely concealed. This is by no means to suggest that Chaucer and his contemporaries were not also valued, and even primarily valued, for their subject-matter; it is, rather, that for them, and for their audience, 'poetry' itself becomes an important concept and can be recognized as a desirable part of the matter to be given expression, by rendering it in a more meaningful and important way.

For details of the full range of works in English before 1360 the reader should consult Wells's great *Manual of Writings in Middle English*,[9] which classifies and lists everything known to have survived.

Much, indeed, must have been lost; but, on the other hand, we need also to remember that not everything that we now know would have been available to Chaucer. Much would depend on what manuscripts came his way, and, possibly, on what he heard performed. His knowledge, for example, of the earlier lyric might well come from hearing it sung, rather than from access to any manuscript collection. He might have listened to minstrel performances of the more popular romances – although it is likely that by his day this kind of public recital had become an unsophisticated and perhaps old-fashioned form of entertainment.[10] It is notable that his identifiable references to earlier English romances in *Sir Thopas* are mainly to those found in one MS collection which he may actually have read.[11] On the other hand, the Host's reaction to *Sir Thopas* would gain added point if the parody also had reference to a style of performance which might have been, to the sophisticated ears of Chaucer and his London audience, a noisy and inartistic one.[12] There is no doubt that Chaucer was familiar with English plays through performances. His reference to the style of acting and to its staging (on a high scaffold) in the *Miller's Tale* (*CT* I, 3383–4) makes this clear.

Chaucer, however, was not a dramatic poet, and there is no sign that the style and technique of the plays affected him in any identifiable way. He *was* a narrative poet, and there is every sign that the earlier English romances played an important part in the development of his narrative style and also influenced his approach to narrative structure. This last influence will be discussed later: here it will be enough to note the kind of impression that the more detailed aspects of the technique of English romances must have made on Chaucer. *Sir Thopas* shows the debit side of the account and reflects his amusement at the occasional ineptitude of earlier writers; but we must not therefore assume that there was no credit column and that Chaucer did not appreciate and utilize seriously the undoubted craftsmanship of many of these poems.

Their importance for such a poet as Chaucer is well summed up by Rosemond Tuve, writing of Spenser's debt to medieval chivalric romance – what she says is equally true of Chaucer:[13]

> A major influence of this body of stories upon Spenser was that they taught him their flair for ordinary realism in its simplest sense: for situations drawn from daily life, natural rather than contrived or stilted conversation, unadorned reportage. . . .

The imaginatively marvellous, the elaborate, the 'other-world', were, in fact, the last things to be found in these romances; and, in keeping with this kind of content, their style was, typically, plain and unambitious, well suited to clear, matter-of-fact narration.[14] Miss Tuve wrote of French as well as English romances, and it is, indeed, difficult to distinguish clearly between the two. Most of the earlier Middle English romances were directly translated or adapted from French, and their style was, to a great extent, modelled on that of their sources. It is a fascinating exercise to try to detect and describe the peculiarly English tone of their versions; but, in practice, it is extraordinarily difficult to be precise in defining the difference. In fact, we shall probably do best to regard romance writers, in both French and English, in this period as using a kind of common narrative *koinê*. When Chaucer, too, uses this, the problem is the same: we can only with difficulty decide whether he is basing his style on his knowledge of French writing, of English or – which is more probably the case – of both. What we can, I think, say with some certainty is that it would be difficult to see how he could slip so easily into this common style in his own language if it were all to be done for the first time. However valuable for the development of his own suppleness the translations from the *Roman* (for example) were, he must also have been conscious of the sound of innumerable English lines in the same literary dialect. Nor must we ever forget that we have positive evidence of his actual close study of a number of them. Comparison of a few passages in the *koinê* will make the matter clearer.

Sir Degaré, one of the romances of the Auchinleck MS, and therefore one that Chaucer is likely to have read, provides a good example of unemphatic, continuous narrative in which the patterning of the verse is never allowed to impede the flow:[15]

> Here chaumberleyn she clepede hire to,
> And other dammaiseles two,
> And seide that hii moste alighte
> To don here nedes and hire righte;
> Thai light adoune alle thre,
> Tweie damaiseles and ssche,
> And longe while ther abiden,
> Til al the folk was forth iriden.
> Thai wolden up and after wolde,
> And couthen nowt here right way holde.

> The wode was rough and thikke, iwis,
> And thai token the wai amys.
> Thai moste south, and riden west
> Into the thikke of the forest,
> Into a launde hii ben icome,
> And habbeth right wel undernome
> That thai were amis igon.
> Thai light adoune euerichon
> And cleped and criede al ifere,
> Ac no man mighte hem ihere.

The essential stages in the narrative are steadily enumerated, and each is accompanied by just so much detail as is needed to make the actions of the characters fully intelligible. The forest, for example, is not rough and thick for any emotive cause, as a place of menace or mystery, but simply to provide the reason for the ladies' losing their way.

The same easy movement and the same clear, unemphatic enumeration of essential details is found in the *Book of the Duchess*:

> Whan we came to the forest syde,
> Every man dide ryght anoon
> As to huntynge fil to doon.
> The mayster-hunte anoon, fot-hot,
> With a gret horn blew thre mot
> At the uncouplynge of hys houndes.
> Withynne a while the hert yfounde ys,
> Yhalowed and rechased faste
> Longe tyme; and so at the laste
> This hert rused, and staal away
> Fro alle the houndes a privy way.
> The houndes had overshote hym alle,
> And were on a defaute yfalle.
>
> (372–84)

Sir Orfeo, a romance Chaucer certainly knew, provides another example:[16]

> This ich quen, Dame Heurodis
> Tok to maidens of priis,
> And went in an vndrentide
> To play bi an orchard-side,

> To se the floures sprede and spring,
> And to here the foules sing.
> Thai sett hem doun al thre
> Vnder a fair ympe-tre,
> And wel sone this fair quene
> Fel on slepe opon the grene,
> The maidens durst hir nought awake,
> Bot lete hir ligge and rest take.

These two passages illustrate the straightforward maintenance of a simple thread of narrative, with a little essential description. Another romance, which Chaucer may have known, shows a slightly different, but equally fluent, use of the style. This is the *Seven Sages of Rome*. The narrative in the following extract is more complex, since it deals with the interactions of three figures – child, dog and snake:[17]

> A nedder was norist in the wall,
> And herd the noys of riding all;
> He loked out to se that wonder
> And saw the childe stand him vnder.
> Vnto the erth he went onane;
> The childe he hopid to haue slane.
> The grehund wanders thareobout
> And sese how the nedder crepis out;
> And sone than gan he him asail,
> And toke him ful tite bi the tayl;
> And sone the nedder bate him sare,
> That he durst hald him na mare.
> Out of his mowth when he was gane,
> Vnto the credel he crepis onane;
> He fanded fast the childe to styng;
> The grehund ogayn to him gan flyng;
> And sone he hentes [him] by the bak
> And al obout his eres gan shak.
> Bitwix the nedder and the grehownd,
> The credil welterd on the grownd
> Vp-so-down, with thaire fyghting,
> So that the childe lay grouelyng.
>
> (815–36)

This writer has rather more difficulty with rhyme-words than the others we have quoted. He tends to bring in tags a little mechanically in the rhyming position. In this passage he twice resorts to 'onane' (anon) to complete his rhyme. But, in general, the movement of his verse adapts itself well to the complicated activities he is describing.

It would be easy to multiply examples of this plain and easy verse style in romance narrative. One more, from *Ywain and Gawain*, which is not one of the romances we can prove Chaucer read, but which he might have known, will be enough to show how widespread it was:[18]

> This knight that hight Colgrevance,
> Tald his felows of a chance
> And of a stowre he had in bene;
> And al his tale herd the Quene;
> The chamber-dore sho has unshet,
> And down omang tham scho hir set;
> Sodainli sho sat downright,
> Or ani of tham of hir had sight –
> Bot Colgrevance rase vp in hy . . .

Taken as a whole these poems are unlike anything Chaucer ever wrote. Yet their manner of writing can be found in many of his works. In the *Book of the Duchess*, for example, he uses the four-stress couplet in a way which is very similar to that of the author of *Ywain and Gawain*:

> So when I saw I might not slepe
> Til now late, this other night,
> Upon my bed I sat upright
> And bad oon reche me a book,
> A romaunce, and he it me tok
> To rede, and drive the night away,
> For me thoughte it beter play
> Then play either at ches or tables.
> And in this bok were written fables
> That clerkes had in olde tyme,
> And other poets, put in rime,

> To rede, and for to be in minde,
> While men loved the lawe of kinde.
> This bok ne spak but of such thinges,
> Of quenes lives and of kinges,
> And many other thinges smale.
>
> (44–59)

Or:

> With that me thoghte that this kyng
> Gan homwardes for to ryde
> Unto a place, was there besyde,
> Which was from us but a lyte.
> A long castel with walles white,
> Be seynt Johan! on a ryche hil,
> As me mette; but thus hyt fil . . .
>
> (1314–20)

Chaucer is, of course, largely adapting French sources in the *Book of the Duchess*, and it is therefore pertinent to ask whether we can be sure that passages like those just quoted are based on an English, rather than a French, version of the narrative *koinê*. In the last resort, perhaps the question is not entirely relevant. Chaucer is producing something which, as a totality, is new, but in whose parts at times one voice, at times another, predominates, as a momentarily distinct element in a whole which is compounded from many different models. Nevertheless, it seems to me that we can to some extent distinguish the English from the French tone of voice in the *Book of the Duchess*. A passage, for example, like the following, seems to me much nearer to the style of the *Roman de la Rose* than to anything that could be found in an English romance:

> And I dar seyn, and swere hyt wel –
> That Trouthe hymself, over al and al
> Had chose hys maner principal
> In hir, that was his restyng place.
> Therto she hadde the moste grace,
> To have stedefast perseveraunce,
> And esy atempre governaunce,
> That ever I knew or wyste yit,
> So pure suffraunt was hir wyt.
>
> (1002–10)

This is very much in the manner of the Chaucerian translation of the *Roman*. The difference, it seems to me, between the style of this passage and the other two just quoted from the *Book of the Duchess* is slight but definable. It lies mainly in the fact that the first two share with the English romances a tendency to treat the whole line both rhythmically and syntactically as a more rigid unit, but to tolerate, within the unit, more minor irregularity than was possible with French syllabic verse. The effect is thus not necessarily more monotonous – there is, for example, especially in Chaucer's adaptations, a fairly free treatment of the mid-pause – but it results in a narrative flow divided into smaller units. The English writers, in fact, tend to tolerate more abrupt transitions and more irregular metrical patterns than were usual in their French models, and which certainly contrast sharply with the even, quiet progress of the verse in the *Roman de la Rose*. The result is an informality which sometimes verges on inconsequence, and it is this, I believe, that Chaucer is able to exploit in the *Book of the Duchess* as part of his depiction of the simple Dreamer, who is not expecting anything very serious to happen and to whom the meaning of his experience only gradually unfolds. This kind of effect is also, I think, important in the *House of Fame* where the exploitation of a specifically narrative style – or styles – is, I believe, an important part of the poem's technique.[19]

But the main contribution of the earlier English narrative style is, obviously, to the formation of the kind of neutral, un-emphatic language which is so necessary to the poet who sets out to tell tales in verse. It is this kind of language that keeps his story moving, enables him to get from point to point, to provide transition passages and to fill in necessary background. It is, thus, not only in the *Book of the Duchess* and the *House of Fame*, both in the favourite romance couplet of four stresses, that we find this kind of language. We can see it in use in many of Chaucer's works where a plain, but flexible and efficient type of style is needed. For example, although the line is the longer one of five stresses, we can hear the same downright, clear narrator's tone in the *Wife of Bath's Tale* as the scene is set for the main development:

> And so bifel it that this kyng Arthour
> Hadde in his hous a lusty bacheler,
> That on a day cam ridynge fro ryver;

> And happed that, allone as he was born,
> He saugh a mayde walkynge hym biforn,
> Of which mayde anon, maugree hir heed,
> By verray force, he rafte hire maydenhed.
>
> (*CT* III, 882–8)

How far this somewhat perfunctory treatment of the conduct of a knight 'in th'olde dayes of the Kyng Arthour' is a part of the complicated ironies of the whole elucidation of the character of the Wife of Bath, and of the wider themes with which she is associated, is a subject for later discussion.[20] However subtle the use Chaucer makes of stylistic variation, the fact remains that in these lines he is using what we have called the common narrative *koiné*. The same style is used for the description of the fairy dance – a motif which comes into the story and leaves it again with the same inconsequence as the rape:

> And in his wey it happed hym to ryde,
> In al this care, under a forest syde,
> Wher as he saugh upon a daunce go
> Of ladyes four and twenty, and yet mo;
> Toward the whiche daunce he drow ful yerne,
> In hope that som wysdom sholde he lerne.
> But certeinly, er he cam fully there,
> Vanysshed was this daunce, he nyste where.
>
> (*CT* III, 989–96)

This description is, indeed, based on an earlier romance, *Sir Orfeo* (297 ff.). In both the model and the copy the unusual sense of something more in keeping with our idea of the 'romantic' derives from the use of the plain, direct style, which here works as significant understatement. In the *Wife of Bath's Tale*, too, we have to note the peculiar balance between the Wife's momentary indulgence in romanticism and her essential practicality – the fairy ladies vanish to leave an ugly old woman behind. Such a being is not only more easily to be met with in real life, but, as we come to realize later on in the tale, reflects the ageing Dame Alisoun's own predicament. Her youth and beauty have gone the way of the fairy dance. There is no doubt that Chaucer is deliberate in manipulating the variations in his style so as to bring out the complexity of the subject matter, as well as to serve the immediate needs of the narrative.

The *Wife of Bath's Tale* is, on the surface at least, a romance. We find, however, the same use of the narrative *koinê* in the comic tales, where it blends well with a lower style in the work as a whole. For example, two of the characters of comedy are thus gathered up and placed where the story has been leading them:

> Doun of the laddre stalketh Nicholay,
> And Alisoun ful softe adoun she spedde;
> Withouten wordes mo they goon to bedde,
> Ther as the carpenter is wont to lye.
> Ther was the revel and the melodye;
> And thus lith Alison and Nicholas,
> In bisynesse of myrthe and of solas,
> Til that the belle of laudes gan to rynge,
> And freres in the chauncel gonne synge.
>
> (*CT* I, 3648–56)

Here, as in nearly all Chaucer's comic writing, there is a precision in the choice and placing of words which is by no means a necessary part of the *koinê* – the inversion and the choice of verb in the first line, for example, suggests Nicholas's tumbling haste, whereas Alisoun is neater and more expert in deceit: she moves both quietly and quickly: 'ful softe adoun she spedde'.

The aim and result of their activities is tersely indicated in one blunt line: 'Withouten wordes mo they gon to bedde'. This may seem particularly well suited to the style of *fabliau*, and where Chaucer uses the same formula in a more courtly setting it has been hailed as a peculiarly characteristic touch of realistic humour.[21] This is in the *Complaint of Mars*, 73, where the elaborate manœuvres of the astrological lovers find a simple conclusion: 'Ther is no more, but unto bed thei go.' In fact, Chaucer could have met this particular formula in a romance setting where it describes the union of a fairy mistress and a human lover in a manner which is very characteristic of the romance way with marvels:[22]

> Whan they had sowped and the day was gon,
> They wente to bedde, and that anoon,
> Launfal and sche in fere.

In *Sir Launfal* this is merely part of the writer's plain way with his story. Chaucer certainly recognizes and exploits the inherent incongruity – but he did not invent it.

Instances of Chaucer's use of the *koiné* in the comic tales could be endlessly multiplied. For example, from the *Pardoner's Tale*:

> Thise riotoures thre of whiche I telle,
> Longe erst er prime rong of any belle,
> Were set hem in a taverne for to drynke,
> And as they sat, they herde a belle clynke,
> Biforn a cors, was carried to his grave.
>
> (*CT* VI, 661–5)

or from the *Canon's Yeoman's Tale*:

> This preest hym took a marc, and that as swithe,
> And this chanoun hym thanked ofte sithe,
> And took his leve, and wente forth his weye,
> And at the thridde day broghte his moneye,
> And to the preest he took his gold agayn,
> Wherof this preest was wonder glad and fayn.
>
> (*CT* VIII, 1030–5)

In these and many other instances we find a style which is completely adapted to the purpose of straightforward, direct narration and is as suitable to Chaucer's conception of *fabliau* as to the particular kind of unromantic romance favoured in the Middle Ages.

'Natural, rather than contrived or stilted conversation', is another of the features of medieval romance singled out by Rosemond Tuve as of importance to Spenser. It was, I think, even more important to Chaucer. His total handling of dialogue, even in his early work, is of course far in advance of anything to be found before him in English. Nevertheless, although it is not often possible to identify the direct influence of earlier writers and although he draws on more than one tradition, it is true to say that some of the characteristics which are usually singled out as most original – and as most 'Chaucerian' – in his dialogue are in fact those of earlier romances in English. To appreciate the range and flexibility of dialogue in these romances it would be necessary to read at least all those we know that Chaucer read, but a few characteristic examples will give an idea of it.

The *Seven Sages of Rome* provides many examples of dialogue made lively and natural-sounding by a free treatment of the line and couplet and by simple, direct diction:

> The lady sais sone, 'Wha es thare?'
> 'I am a knyght that wald me warm,
> And wend my way withowten harm.'
> The lady said, 'By Him me boght,
> Herin, sir, ne cumes thou noght!'
> 'Lat me cum in, dame, I the pray.'
> The lady said ful sadly, 'Nay.'
> 'A dame,' he said, 'me es ful kalde;
> A litel while harm me I walde.'
> 'Sir,' sho said, 'be Him me boght,
> In this close ne cumes thou noght!'
> 'A dame,' he said, 'par charite,
> Thare sal na man wit bot we.'
>   (2898–910)

The same kind of directness is to be found in *Floris and Blancheflour*:[23]

> 'Thou gabbest me,' he seyde thoo;
> 'Thy gabbyng doth me muche woe!
> Tel me where my leman be!'
> Al wepyng seide thenne shee,
> 'Sir,' shee seide, 'deede.' 'Deed!' seide he.
> 'Sir,' sche seide, 'forsothe, yee.'
> 'Allas, when deid that swete wyght?'
> 'Sir, withynne this fourtenyght.
> The erth was leide hur aboute,
> And deed she was for thy loue.'

Chaucer uses a very similar technique in the finale of the *Book of the Duchess*:

> 'Sir,' quod I, 'where is she now?'
> 'Now?' quod he, and stynte anoon
> Therwith he wax as ded as stoon,

> And seyde, 'Allas, that I was bore!
> That was the los that here-before
> I tolde the that I hadde lorn.
> Bethenke how I seyde here-beforn,
> "Thou wost ful lytel what thow menest;
> I have lost more than thow wenest" –
> God wot, allas! ryght that was she!'
> 'Allas, sir, how? what may that be?'
> 'She ys ded!' 'Nay!' 'Yis, be my trouthe!'
> 'Is that youre los? Be God, hyt ys routhe!'
> (1298–310)

The style of this passage is very like that of an earlier exchange which Muscatine singles out as setting a stylistic problem within the poem:

> 'Why so?' quod he, 'hyt ys nat soo.
> Thou wost ful lytel what thou menest;
> I have lost more than thow wenest.'
> 'Loo, [sey] how that may be?' quod y;
> 'Good sir, telle me al hooly
> In what wyse, how, why, and wherfore
> That ye have thus youre blysse lore.'
> 'Blythely,' quod he; 'com sytte adoun!
> I telle the upon a condicioun
> That thou shalt hooly, with al thy wyt,
> Doo thyn entent to herkene hit,'
> 'Yis syr.' 'Swere thy trouthe therto.'
> 'Gladly.' 'Do thanne holde hereto!'
> 'I shal ryght blythely, so God me save,
> Hooly, with al the wit I have,
> Here yow, as wel as I kan.'
> 'A Goddes half!' quod he and began . . .
> (742–58)

Of this Muscatine says: 'passages like these create the one difficulty of interpretation. Set in a dream, beside the conventionally rhetorical utterances of the Man in Black, their air of realism is surprising and awkward.' And he concludes: 'The style of the *Book of the Duchess*, then, shows two concurrent movements in the light of French tradition: one towards a functional use of courtly convention, the other towards a realism that suggests comic disenchantment.'[24] As we have seen, however, it is precisely this realism in dialogue which is characteristic of established narrative convention in romances in both French and English. Chaucer is merely using the *koinê*. Whether he is conscious of a particular model, we cannot determine: we can only note that his handling of the dialogue is very like that of English poems which he could have read or heard and that the ease with which he uses the style does not suggest that he is a pioneer.

The same blend of more formal utterance, especially in soliloquy, with terse, realistic dialogue can be found in another English romance which Chaucer certainly knew. This is *Guy of Warwick*, one of the best loved and most influential of the medieval romances.[25] This frequently uses the kind of colloquial interchange we have been considering:

> His ost seyd, 'sir, wite ye nought
> Of this turnament that is bithought?'
> 'No', seyd Gij, 'bi mine wite,
> Y no herd ther-of neuer yete.'
> His ost him answerd snelle,
> 'Of that turnament y schal you telle . . .'
> (797–802)

We may be reminded of the exchange in the *House of Fame*:

> And seyde, 'Frend, what is thy name?
> Artow come hider to han fame?'
> 'Nay, for sothe, frend,' quod y;
> 'I cam noght hyder, graunt mercy,
> For no such cause, by my hed!' . . .
> 'But what doost thou here than?' quod he.
> Quod y, 'That wyl y tellen the . . .'
> (1871–84)

Or again, in *Guy*, there is the little scene, with its laconic comments, in which the physicians gather round Guy on his sickbed:

> The leches ben to him y-go . . .
> Than seyd that on, 'a feuer it is.'
> 'Ya,' quod Gij, 'a lither, y-wis!'
> (505, 523–4)

Troilus makes a similarly wry comment on the obvious when he says to Pandarus:

> 'Frend, though I stylle lye,
> I am nat deef.'
>
> (I, 752–3)

After the physicians have left him, Guy soliloquizes in more patterned and formal language, very like that used by the Black Knight in his lamentations:

> 'God,' quod Gij, 'what schal y do?
> Hou long schal y liuen in wo?
> That y no might ded be,
> When y no may hir with eyghen se,
> That hath al mine hert and thought,
> And y no misgilt hir neuer nought,
> Bot on that ich [h]ir loue wel,
> And euer more loue schel!'
>
> (527–34)

Guy of Warwick is not alone in this combination of realism and rhetoric. *Sir Orfeo*, a romance from which, as we have seen, Chaucer actually quotes, shows the same mixture. There are the snatches of blunt, realistic speech:

> 'Lord,' quath he, 'trowe ful wel,
> Y nam bot a pouer menstrel;
> And, sir, it is the maner of ous
> To seche mani a lordes hous;
> Thei we nought welcom no be,
> Yete we mot proferi forth our gle.'
>
> (429–34)

> 'Nay,' quath the king, 'that nought nere!
> A sori couple of you it were,
> For thou art lene, rowe and blac,
> And sche is louesum, with-outen lac:
> A lothlich thing it were, forthi,
> To sen hir in thi compayni!'
>
> (457–62)

Yet Orfeo laments with all the formality of Guy or the Black Knight – and in very similar terms:

> 'Allas!' quath he, 'now me is wo!
> Whi nil deth now me slo?
> Allas, wreche, that y no might
> Dye now after this sight!
> Allas! to long last mi liif
> When y no dar nought with mi wiif,
> No hye to me, o word speke.
> Allas! whi nil min hert breke?'
>
> (331–8)

There is no conflict between comic realism and formal rhetoric in *Sir Orfeo*, but only the normal, flexible style of works of this kind.

It would be difficult to say whether the uninhibited outcries of the low characters in the churls' tales are wholly derived from the model of the *fabliau*-style or whether they are influenced by such outbursts within the frame of romance as that of Darius in *Kyng Alisaunder*:

> 'Ey, felaw! theof! thow schalt abygge!'
>
> (4199)

or that of Floripe in the *Sultan of Babylon* when she pushes Maragounde into the sea:

> 'Go there,' she saide, 'the devel the spede!'
>
> (1579)

The *Sultan o Babylon*, indeed, is particularly free in its language. At line 2223 it uses a colloquial turn of phrase which Chaucer echoes, with a difference. The *Sultan of Babylon* makes a character exclaim:

> 'A, stronge hore, God gife the sorowe!'

That this is a genuine colloquialism is proved by its appearance in the Paston Letters, where Margaret Paston, in trouble with her neighbours, reported to her husband, 'And thanne Wymondham called my moder and me strong hores'.[26] Chaucer makes the phrase the pattern for January's outcry when he finally sees May's guilt:

'Out! help; allas! harrow!' he gan to crye,
'O stronge lady stoore, what dostow?'
(*CT* IV, 2366-7)

The word 'stoore', rhyming with 'hoore', ensures that the reader
mentally supplies the noun that fits the sense of the adjective
'stronge', to which, of course, 'lady' is quite inappropriate. The
derangement of epithets bears witness to January's somewhat
pathetic unwillingness to admit to the evidence of his suddenly
sighted eyes. The point, however, is not that the cruder and more
realistic phrase would be inappropriate to the sophisticated and
even courtly setting of the story of May's intrigues, but that the
gentler one fixes the reader's attention, precisely because it is not
expected within a style which normally made free use of abusive
language. Colloquial and vigorous remarks of this kind are, in fact,
just as typical of the language of romance as they are of *fabliau*.
Female characters, especially, are often outspoken in romances –
it is, as a rule, only the male whose courtship involves 'talkyng
noble', in the phrase of the *Gawain*-poet. This distinction, common to
both French and English romance, is reproduced by Chaucer in
the difference between Troilus's use of 'lover's terms' and Criseyde's
blunter, though always gentle, style. In the *House of Fame* the 'noble
queen', Fame, goes much further and scolds like a fishwife. Yet, if we
look back at the earlier romances we can see that it is Criseyde's
comparative gentleness that is the innovation. In *Guy of Warwick*,
for example, the heroine, Felice, thus receives the first intimation
of Guy's love for her:

'Artow this Gij, so mot thou go,
The steward sone Suward,
Ich wene thou art a fole musard!
When thou of loue me hast bisaught,
Al to fole-hardy thou art y-taught!
Wele thou holdest me for a fole;
Thou art y-taught to a lither scole!'
(378-84)

The variety of the style in the *Knight's Tale*, with its elaborate
set-pieces of description, its excursions into a high poetic style and
its downright, colloquial comments on the action has usually been
noticed by critics. Sometimes, indeed, the variation, as in the case

of the *Book of the Duchess*, is seen as an anomaly which affects the interpretation of the work as a whole. Thus, one critic sees it as symptomatic of two, in the last resort unreconciled, voices in the poem, 'one pressing home the "derknesse" of the story, the other anxious to evade responsibility for it'.[27] Detailed discussion of the many problems of the *Knight's Tale* must be left until later, but we can note here that the bluntness with which Theseus intervenes in and comments on the action would not seem any derogation of his royalty to an audience familiar with earlier romance. The following passage, for example, could be paralleled, as far as its general tone and content are concerned, in numerous romances:

> And at a stert he was bitwix hem two,
> And pulled out a swerd and cride, 'Hoo!
> Namoore, up peyne of lesynge of youre heed!
> By myghty Mars, he shal anon be deed
> That smyteth any strook that I may seen.'
>
> (*CT* I, 1705–9)

We could compare the passage from *Kyng Alisaunder* in which the king thus accuses an enemy:[28]

> 'Thow,' he saide, 'traytour,
> Yusturday thow come in aunture,
> Yarmed so on of myne . . .
> Thou schalt beo honged and todrawe,
> And beo tobrent al to nought,
> For thou soche traytory wroughtest.'

Theseus is not quite so abusive, but all his speeches strike a similarly plain, blunt note. He addresses the mourning ladies who halt his triumphal progress in these terms:

> 'What folk been ye, that at myn homcomynge
> Perturben so my feste with criynge?'
> Quod Theseus. 'Have ye so greet envye
> Of myn honour, that thus compleyne and crye?
> Or who hath yow mysboden or offended?
> And telleth me if it may ben amended,
> And why that ye been clothed thus in blak.'
>
> (*CT* I, 905–11)

Chaucer is here following his source closely, and yet the effect is very unlike the Italian. In the *Teseida*, Teseo addresses the ladies in a long unbroken period, which, inevitably, has a less peremptory effect than Theseus's sharp, repeated questions:[29]

> 'Chi son costor ch' a'nostri lieti eventi
> co' crini sparti, battendosi il petto,
> di squalor piene in atri vestimenti,
> tutte piangendo, some se 'n dispetto
> avesson la mia gloria, a l'altre genti,
> si com' io vegge, cagion di diletto?'

This is largely descriptive, with the emphasis on what Teseo sees before him and its pathetic aspect. Chaucer places his emphasis on Theseus's expression of his feelings in reaction to what he sees; the more leisurely, near-elegiac tone is therefore lost, and a much more naturalistic passage results.

It is not only in dialogue that we meet with 'ordinary realism in its simplest sense' in the romances. They are full of simple, vivid descriptive detail of a kind more often associated with the *fabliau*.[30] In *Sir Orfeo*, for example, the steward knocks over the table in the excitement of the recognition scene:

> Ouer and ouer the bord he threwe,
> And fel adoun to his fet . . .
> (578–9)

In *Ipomedan* the detail of a slight blush adds to our knowledge of a character:

> A llyttell wax he rede, for shame;
> Ful welle that coloure hym became.
> (364–5)

Chaucer uses the same device, though with a different significance, in the *Shipman's Tale* (*CT* VII, 111) – 'And of his owene thought he wax al reed' (cf. *Troilus*, V, 925). In *Sir Launfal* (232–3) the kirtles of the two maidens are not only of 'Inde-sandel', an exotic touch, but also 'Ilased smalle, jolyf and well' – words which really enable us to visualize them and which Chaucer might have used of Alisoun.

In *Sir Degaré* the hero comes to an enchanted castle, but its most important feature is quite 'unromantic': it is a good fire, from which he draws a sensible conclusion:

> 'Par fai,' he saide, 'ich am al sure,
> He that bette that ilke fure
> Wil comen hom ayein tonight,'
>
> (763–5)

and, sitting down in front of it, he warms himself thoroughly:

> And he warmed him wel eche wais.
>
> (768)

Examples could easily be multiplied, but these will be enough to show that the kind of apt use of concrete detail we sometimes think of as typically Chaucerian is a feature of the earlier romances which he certainly knew and probably enjoyed.

We cannot ignore the influence of earlier narrative techniques, in English as well as in French, on Chaucer's poetry. Yet it would be equally wrong to understate the difference between his achievement and that of his predecessors. This is the other half of the paradox of the poet who is both essentially 'English' and essentially 'new'. In the next chapter we must explore other ways in which Chaucer develops the plain, conversational style: ways which have little connection with the earlier romance style and which involve the use of quite different and new material. Another important difference, I have suggested, lies in the attitudes to poetry before and after 1360 of both poets and audiences. This subject, too, is more fully discussed in chapter 2. Here it is enough to note that we are dealing with a new idea of the importance of poetry. This is something which manifested itself elsewhere in Europe, and which Chaucer would have found in its most impressive form in Italy. It was already reflected in Dante's writings, from which Chaucer would gain the idea of a new importance and seriousness in vernacular poetry. He may have met Petrarch; although we have no positive evidence that he did, his Italian journeys took him to the right place. At any rate, he testifies enthusiastically to the importance of Petrarch's poetry in the sounding line in which he praises him as one who 'Enlumyned at Ytaille of poetrie' (*CT* IV, 33), and his use of Boccaccio is a sufficient testimonial. He almost certainly read Boccaccio's chapters on poetry in his *de Genealogia Deorum Gentilium*, in which he would find such statements as 'poetry, like other studies, is derived from God', and that it 'is a sort of fervid and exquisite invention, with fervid expression in speech or writing of that which the mind has invented. . . . This fervour of poetry is sublime in its effect.'[31] It was, perhaps, only in Italy that the sublimity of poetry was so much emphasized, but in France, too, its status was good. Poets like Froissart, Machaut and Deschamps, whom Chaucer admired and imitated, had a good standing and an appreciative and sophisticated audience. Moreover, France valued its great poem, as Italy valued hers. It is notable that a little later on, in the early fifteenth century, when Christine de Pisan initiated an attack on the *Roman de la Rose*, even Gerson while denouncing the content, praises it as a great French poem.[32] Such a claim would be inconceivable for any of the narrative poetry in English which precedes Chaucer, but we feel no surprise when he ends his *Troilus* with the hope that it will rank with the great poetry of the past, or causes his pilgrims to comment appreciatively on the general quality and achievement of the *Knight's Tale* by calling it a 'noble story'. Moreover, the frequent references to style and technique, whether they are framed as disclaimers made by particular characters, or as general comments, show an ever-present consciousness of the demands of the poet's art and also, it is obvious, a conviction that the subject is of interest to the audience. The same type of reference is to be found in Gower's *Confessio Amantis*, but although it would be unwise to assume that earlier writers had no knowledge of the more formal aspects of the technique of writing summed up by the term 'rhetoric', it is still true to say that they never comment on them and never seem to expect that they would be of interest to their audience. In the latter half of the century, on the other hand, even Langland writes about himself as a poet and ponders the question of the usefulness of his art.[33]

This new consciousness of the usefulness and dignity of the poetic calling brings with it new possibilities for the treatment within the work of the figure of the narrator. In the older romances the teller of the tale often makes direct contact with his audience. In the more popular ones, especially, he is likely to call for a prayer or a drink or both, to open or close the recital. At especially exciting moments he may pause to denounce a villain or praise a hero in a way which invites the audience to participate in the emotions of the story. In one more sophisticated English poem, the *Owl and the Nightingale*, the poet brings himself on stage as a character in the action, but in a way which is, I think, significantly oblique. He begins the poem in the first person, telling us how he overheard a debate between two birds. This is, in fact, a common enough device, especially in lyric or debate, but it generally remains an opening device: the 'I' is heard of no more after the introduction of the real subject of the poem. In the *Owl and the Nightingale*, too, the first person pronoun is dropped after the opening lines, but we then have references made by the birds to a character called 'Master Nicholas of Guildford', whom they esteem and to whom they propose to submit their case. The poet takes no trouble to link the 'I' of the opening explicitly to this figure, but it is probable that they are, in fact, the same. If they are, it would seem that his aim in entering his poem *in propria persona* is a limited one: the denouement is helped by the presence of a figure to adjudicate in the debate; and, for an audience better acquainted with the facts than we are, there was no doubt amusing irony in the assertions of the birds as to his high deserts and fitness for preferment, with which the poem ends.[34] But – and this is the point – there is no suggestion that he is of any particular importance to his audience as a poet – that is, because he is able to transmit special material in a special way. Such a suggestion does, I think, arise from Chaucer's handling of the poet-narrator in more than one poem, although he certainly uses this figure in other ways as well. We can, perhaps, see the position most clearly in *Sir Thopas*, where the main joke is that Chaucer, the sophisticated and self-conscious exponent of the new art of poetry, can produce nothing better than 'drasty' rhyming of a particularly inept and old-fashioned kind.

Another source of information about the status of poets in the latter part of the fourteenth century is their appearance in manuscript illustrations of this date or a little later. The miniature from Corpus MS 61 which forms the frontispiece of this book is a good example. The poet (certainly not a portrait of Chaucer, but a typical figure) is not distinguished from his audience by his dress and is seen walking among them in the background scene, which shows the return to the castle after the reading is over. Sometimes the poet is presented as a more clerkly character – that is, as a serious and probably learned man. This is the case with the famous Hoccleve portrait of Chaucer himself and with the Ellesmere miniature which introduces *Melibee*: in both he is shown in a sober dark gown, suitable to a responsible civil servant or scholar. A frontispiece to a manuscript of Machaut's works shows a similarly sober figure (Plate I). Boccaccio tends to be treated in the same way when he appears in illustrations to his works. Indeed, in the miniature which shows him aghast at the sight of the 'hideous monster', Fortune (Vol. II, Plate II), he is presented as the typical man of learning whose philosophy enables him to withstand her wiles. All these illustrations are very far from any idea of the poet as a bohemian figure (like the earlier 'goliard' or 'wandering scholar'), and even further from the popular entertainer, the minstrel or *jongleur*, often depicted in manuscript margins or borders, and always quite clearly of a lower social status.

The Machaut miniature is interesting in another way. It shows, in allegorical form, the poet's relation to his medium and his subject-matter. The personifications *Sens* (matter, meaning: Chaucer's 'sentence'), Rhetoric and Music are being presented to the poet. Among them *Sens* is the dominant figure, both as the only masculine one and as the leader. The trio is presented by a young and beautiful woman wearing a crown. She is Nature, depicted very much in the manner of the *Parlement of Foules*; and to drive home the point, the landscape which surrounds the poet's house is a dual one, very like that of Chaucer's poem.[35] The foreground consists of a paradisial parkland, with scattered flowers, birds and a somewhat overlarge and architecturally overpowering fountain – a constant feature of the allegorical garden or park. But the road that leads into the back of the picture winds towards a real village, outside which a shepherd watches his sheep, with a windmill and duck-pond in the background. The poet's function, in fact, and the relation of art and nature is not a simple one. Nor, we may conjecture, are allegory and naturalism incompatible.

Another major source of difference between the poetry of Chaucer and his contemporaries and that of earlier writers is, as we have already said, the great extension of subject-matter – that is, the new importance of *sens*. Here the decisive factor was, no doubt, at least as far as Chaucer is concerned, his own reading. For him philosophy provided an important part of his material. In a general way, he shows awareness of the new science derived from the re-discovery of Aristotle; but he depends even more on an intimate knowledge of a few seminal books, from which he freely borrows not only topics, but whole passages. The most important of these are, undoubtedly, Boethius's *de Consolatione Philosophiae* and Macro-bius's commentary on the *Somnium Scipionis* (the sixth book of Cicero's otherwise lost *Republic*). The importance of these two books to Chaucer, and indeed to the Middle Ages in general, can hardly be overrated. Between them, they transmitted important aspects of Platonic and neo-Platonic thought; but what was perhaps even more important was that they are typical representatives of the late Roman blend of philosophical ideas, in which Platonism is combined with Stoicism in a form which was compatible with Christianity. Boethius, indeed, although it would have been natural to him to use what amounted to a philosophical *koiné* for a work of this kind, was probably a Christian when he wrote the *de Consolatione*. The Middle Ages certainly believed him to have been one. Macrobius was also generally believed to have been a Christian, an opinion which Chaucer would certainly have shared. A third late Roman writer who spoke the same philosophical language, although his interest was primarily in morals, was Seneca. He was also commonly believed to have been a Christian. Chaucer refers to him more than once, and, I shall suggest, draws on him to a large extent, for the material of his shorter poems.[36] We shall have, indeed, frequent occasion to refer to these three writers. They provided Chaucer, above all, with philosophical-moral material of a kind which, while it could be understood as thoroughly compatible with Christianity in its tone and content, must yet have seemed to be cast in a form which was quite unlike that used by the explicitly Christian theo-logians of a later period. It was thus much better suited to polite letters and lent itself to much more varied manipulation than could be the case with theological writings. It was also, by definition, as philosophy rather than theology, linked to science, since the major preoccupation of the philosopher was the explanation and descrip-tion of the universe. This fitted in with another preoccupation of Chaucer – that of purely scientific subjects: medicine, astronomy and astrology, and what we should now call physics – that is the structure of matter and the material universe. Here his thinking was, no doubt, reinforced by ideas more directly derived from the new Aristotelianism, but the immediate source, as we shall see, is most often Macrobius or Boethius, or a combination of the two.

Except in his purely religious works, Chaucer did not, like Dante, draw on Christian theology to provide subject matter for poetry. His narratives are often serious enough – sublime enough, in Boccaccio's phrase – for philosophy, but they are either set in a pagan background, as in the cases of the *Knight's Tale* and the *Troilus*, or they are so clearly secular in tone that theology would obviously be out of place. The kind of philosophizing to be found in Boethius and Macrobius, however, could be freely manipulated so as to fit in with almost any background, as later chapters will, I hope, show. Moreover, it must be remembered that Chaucer was not a pioneer in adapting material of this kind to poetry. Dante, of course, had already done so in an extremely serious setting, and so, in a work of much more varied tone, had Jean de Meun. For discussion of the ways in which these precedents affected Chaucer's work the reader must, once more, be referred to later chapters. Here it will be enough to emphasize that the influence of the *Roman de la Rose*, as well as being all-pervasive as far as Chaucer's style is concerned, is also of great importance for his choice and handling of subject matter. It is often the case that, demonstrably, he knows the material at first hand, but is still influenced by the way in which he found it incorporated into poetry in the French work. I have tried to show this, in particular, in relation to the *Parlement of Foules* and to the treatment of the marriage theme in the *Canterbury Tales*.

In addition to the late Roman philosophers, Chaucer, of course, knew at first hand the Roman poets, especially Virgil, Ovid and Statius.[37] A good deal of the matter of these poets was, in fact, already available in the Middle Ages in romance or other vernacular versions.[38] What was new was the attempt to imitate them more directly and to evolve new forms from them, rather than to adapt them to current literary genres. How far Chaucer does this and to what extent he is likely to have been influenced by Italian, pre-Renaissance interest in antiquity will be discussed later. Since he certainly knew and imitated Italian poems which had a certain Classical basis, this is a matter of some importance. The *Troilus*, of course, for all its Classical background and allusions, has no direct link with Homer's story of Troy, in which its plot does not appear and which Chaucer never read. Nevertheless, it can be argued that a new attitude to the great poet of antiquity, known only by repute, does help to account for an approach to the story which is very unlike that of the writers who built up the medieval version of the Fall of Troy.[39] The *Teseida* of Boccaccio, the basis of the *Knight's Tale*, has a more direct relation to its Classical prototype, since it does draw on the *Thebaid* of Statius – and so in its turn, does Chaucer's version. The main story, once more, is not in the Roman epic but it is hard to see how Chaucer could have produced his own peculiar blend of epic and romance without the ultimate Classical background. On the whole, it seems to me, the long Italian poems – the *Filostrato* and the *Teseida*, to say nothing of the *Divina Commedia* – are most important for the effect they must have had on Chaucer's whole conception of narrative structure and narrative potential, a conception which must also have been influenced by such long Latin poems as the *Aeneid*, *Thebaid* and the *Metamorphoses* of Ovid. This difficult and rather elusive question is discussed in Vol. II, ch. 2. As far as subject-matter is concerned, both Latin and Italian poems affect Chaucer's approach to the topic of the gods and, indeed, condition his whole idea of a Classical past and of history itself.[40]

The elucidation of a philosophical '*sens*', however, although it provides much material, is by no means the poet's only preoccupation. There can be no doubt that his audience expected that he would, at any rate in a large proportion of his work, deal with the topic of love. Chaucer's treatment of this topic has, I believe, sometimes been obscured by preconceived ideas about 'courtly love', especially by those writers who see in this a rigidly defined code of ideas. The subject is a complex one, and one which will constantly recur in the following pages. Here I would only suggest some guiding principles. First, that Chaucer certainly utilizes what must have been the fashionable and sophisticated behaviour of courtship in his day. In this he no doubt draws on life, although much that he has to say can be paralleled in the writings of French or Italian poets. Since manners, then as now, are sometimes at variance with intentions, this can be a matter for comedy or even, when the actor is too deeply self-deceived, of tragedy. This is the case with the pattern lover Troilus, whose love-story does not conform to pattern. Secondly, that Chaucer is constantly fascinated by the paradoxical nature of love, as a source of both good and evil, and that, in pursuit of the paradox, he explores its relation to Nature and to marriage and also its existence as passion pure and simple (symbolized by Venus). Thirdly, because of the peculiar nature of his main philosophical sources, he is able to relate the manifestations of love in the physical world to the forces which structure the universe as a whole; and, indeed, his tendency is always to pass from the particular events of a love story to general philosophical principles. This further means, I believe, that he has little or no tendency to relate human love to any ascending series which culminates in divine love in an exclusively spiritual sense. It is rather, and this once more arises from the nature of his seminal reading, that human love fits in as part of a universal and, of course, divinely instituted scheme of creation, extending from the realm of Nature – that is of our actual world – to the divine as the originator of the cosmos. As will be shown, this, in turn, means that for Chaucer the idea of marriage is a very much more complex and fruitful one than that of illicit love, which he understands as a more limited phenomenon.[41]

In the final chapter the reactions of the fifteenth- and early sixteenth-century writers who claimed Chaucer as their master are examined more closely. Nowadays, I believe, we are returning, though perhaps still with some hesitation, to an assessment of his achievement which is near that of the Elizabethans; that is, we are beginning to see him as, in every sense of the word, a great poet whose range extends from high comedy to a serious poetry of ideas. The attitude of the fifteenth century is crucial here. They were not separated from Chaucer by the gap which falls between his work and that of the Elizabethans – a gap now immeasurably wider. It might be, we may uneasily feel, that the Elizabethans, and even more ourselves, are reading into the medieval poet more than he could ever have meant to put into his work. This idea might find some support from what is often asserted as a fact – that his immediate followers in the fifteenth century, some of whom actually knew the poet saw nothing to praise except stylistic virtuosity. In Vol. II, ch. 6, I shall try to show that this view is not justified by the facts, but that, on the contrary, from the time of writers who could have discussed his work with him onwards, he was accepted as 'a true picture of a right poet' and as one who fulfilled Gabriel Harvey's conditions when, actually writing of Chaucer, he said: 'It is not sufficient for poets to be superficial humanists: but they must be exquisite artists and curious universal schollars.'[42]

The urbane manner

Chaucer wrote poems of the kind he disowned in the *Retractions* as 'worldly vanitees' throughout his working life, if we can judge from our scanty information about the dates of composition of 'many a song and many a leccherous lay'. His probable last work is the frivolous (but not lecherous) *Complaint to his Purse*, dated, we can assume, between the coronation of Henry IV on 30 September 1399 and Chaucer's reception of a grant from the king on 3 October of the same year.[1] The Envoys to Scogan and to Bukton, both humorous and both concerned with love and marriage (among other things), also belong to the 1390s; that to Scogan has been dated 1393 and that to Bukton, 1396.[2] The other surviving short poems, most of them less personal, are not easy to date, but it is likely that they were scattered throughout the poet's career. *The Complaint to his Lady*, for example, shows Italian influence in its use of *terza rima* and belongs, therefore, to the period after the Italian journeys. The reference in the *Retractions* and also that in the Prologue to the *Legend of Good Women* to the writing of

> many a ympne for your halydayes,
> That highten balades, roundels, virelayes,[3]

support the impression that such poems were not just youthful exercises but continued to be written and to find favour with Chaucer's audience throughout his life.

Most of these poems are quite fairly to be called 'minor' or 'occasional' – terms which by no means fit the much greater scope and weight of the two more mature love visions, the *Parlement of*

Foules and the *House of Fame*. The third and, almost certainly, the earliest love vision, the *Book of the Duchess*,[4] was in fact written for a specific occasion and is less ambitious in plan than the other two. I shall, therefore, include it here among those poems which seem to me to have been the vehicle, above all, for the development of a new manner of writing in English – a manner which can best be characterized as 'urbane'. Urbanity, it is true, is to be found everywhere in Chaucer's writing, but we can see it most clearly evolving as a new poetic technique in the group of poems which have as their *raison d'être* the need to communicate directly with a clearly defined and known audience of a well-bred and sophisticated type.[5] In some of the short poems, especially in the two addressed to his actual friends, Bukton and Scogan, this sense of communication is both direct and vivid. To devise a humorous verse-letter to a friend in terms which give the illusion of the closest intimacy, while at the same time they also allow a like-minded and like-mannered audience to share both in the intimacy and in the joke, is something entirely new in English. This new kind of communication with the audience means two things for Chaucer in these shorter poems. First, and most striking and pleasing to a modern reader, it means the development and exploitation of a naturalistic, conversational manner. This manner, which, as we shall see, was to become the basis of much of his comic writing, is by no means absent from his mature serious works. Secondly, in poems which are also *divertissements* designed for a circle that, it is evident, shares with the poet certain definite expectations and experiences in literature, it means the use of accepted literary forms and topics. Since most of these are unknown in English before Chaucer, what poet and audience have in common to begin with is a taste for continental poetry, principally in French.[6] Experimentation and innovation on this basis were, no doubt, welcomed; it is notable that, throughout his life, Chaucer makes his adaptations from Italian in a way which would be intelligible to an audience that knew only French or English poetry. It is most unlikely that anyone else in England in his day – or at least in his audience – shared his first hand knowledge of the Italian poets.[7] His attempt at *terza rima*, for example, in the *Complaint to his Lady* is only one of many experiments with metrical forms in this group of poems, all of which would be of interest to those who knew of the virtuosity of contemporary French poetry in this respect.

It is, of course, by no means easy to define the relation of poet and audience in Chaucer's day, and much must be conjecture. We can only say that much of his work would be quite unintelligible unless we can regard it as a response to literary interests and enthusiasms which, no doubt, grew and perhaps altered as a result of his writing, but which must have existed to call it forth. If, as we may suppose, the latter part of the fourteenth century saw the development of an interest in poetry in English which was comparable to that of Italians in writing in their own language or even to the attitude of the Elizabethans to the work of their own age, then we can only say that they were fortunate in finding a poet perfectly equipped to foster and develop their taste. The greatest works, the *Troilus* and the whole elaborate structure of the *Canterbury Tales*, are uncompromising: the poet has the last word, and they must be taken or left as he has formed them. But in the short, often experimental, poems we can sense poet and audience working together, so that an occasion or a personality must often have given life to a work which may seem to us less successful than those in which Chaucer comes a little nearer to the fifteenth-century conception of him as a 'master' of poetry, to be looked up to and closely imitated. This, it is true, makes of these smaller works minor poetry, in the full sense of the term; but it must have been, in part at any rate, through the existence of minor poetry of this sort that the milieu was created in which the major works could grow and flourish.

The *Envoy to Scogan* provides a good example, towards the end of Chaucer's career, of this kind of poetic sensitivity, operating in both spheres – the naturalistic-familiar and the purely literary. It opens with a magnificent set-piece of the mock-sublime, somewhat reminiscent of the Squire's overambitious and abortive openings, but also, of course, within recognizable reach of Chaucer's serious proems in, for example, the *Troilus*:

> Tobroken been the statutz hye in hevene
> That creat were eternally to dure,
> Syth that I see the bryghte goddis sevene
> Mowe wepe and wayle, and passion endure,
> As may in erthe a mortal creature.
> Allas, fro whennes may thys thing procede,
> Of which errour I deye almost for drede?

By word eterne whilom was yshape
That fro the fyfte sercle, in no manere,
Ne myghte a drope of teeres doun escape,
But now so wepith Venus in hir spere
That with hir teeres she wol drenche us here.
Allas! Scogan, this is for thyn offence;
Thow causest this diluge of pestilence.

(1–14)

We are (if we can range ourselves for a moment with Chaucer's original audience) at once lured into the comfortable position not only of appreciating our own quick awareness of the force of the conceit, but also our realization that its true significance lies in the inappropriateness of all this cosmic magnificence to Scogan's distressing tendency to 'hop alwey behinde' in 'the olde daunce', and even, it appears in the next stanza, to forswear it altogether.

It is, perhaps, to labour the obvious, but it is true that in all this there is a fundamental assumption that poet and audience share two things: first, the same literary awareness – the same capability to judge of the decorum of the passage; and, secondly, the same standard of manners – the same feeling for the distance a joke can go and remain friendly. Thus in the next two stanzas Chaucer plays with the idea that both he and his friend are grey-haired lovers – and, moreover, somewhat plump – in a way which takes the jest just far enough and no further:

And, Scogan, though his bowe be nat broken,
He wol nat with his arwes been ywroken
On the, ne me, ne noon of oure figure;
We shul of him have neyther hurt ne cure.

Now certes, frend, I dreede of thyn unhap,
Lest for thy gilt the wreche of Love procede
On alle hem that ben hoor and rounde of shap,
That ben so lykly folk in love to spede.
Than shal we for oure labour han no mede;
But wel I wot, thow wolt answere and saye:
'Lo, olde Grisel lyst to ryme and playe!'

(25–35)

The last line gives Chaucer a transition to the theme, always a favourite one with him, of his own poetry; and while the balance between jest and earnest is still a delicate one, the tone deepens a little:

> Nay, Scogan, say not so, for I m'excuse –
> God helpe me so! – in no rym, dowteles,
> Ne thynke I never of slep to wake my muse,
> That rusteth in my shethe stille in pees.
> While I was yong, I put hir forth in prees;
> But al shal passe that men prose or ryme;
> Take every man hys turn, as for his tyme.
>
> (36–42)

This is a gentle, and ambiguous reminder of human and poetic mutability. In his lament for a maker Chaucer is more outspoken, but we feel the same fundamentally serious mood behind both passages:

> Fraunceys Petrak, the lauriat poete,
> Highte this clerk, whos rethorike sweete
> Enlumyned al Ytaille of poetrie,
> As Lynyan dide of philosophie,
> Or lawe, or oother art particuler;
> But deeth, that wol nat suffre us dwellen heer,
> But as it were a twynklyng of an ye,
> Hem bothe hath slayn, and alle shul we dye.
>
> (*CT* IV, 31–8)

The envoy brings the real point of the poem: 'Mynne thy frend, there it may fructyfye!' Scogan, 'that knelest at the stremes hed / Of grace, of alle honour and worthynesse', is in a position to bring advancement to his friend. The whole elaboration, in fact, preserves the illusion of the quick shifts in subject of inconsequent talk with a friend and at the same time lets us pleasantly down from the world of high literary allusion of the opening into that of practical affairs at the end.

This is a complex example of a poem in which the poet, the friend addressed and a wider but congenial and known audience all participate. Everywhere, however, in these minor poems we become aware of the same familiar voice, inviting us to overhear and enjoy a conversation which is alive and vividly of the moment, but which also conforms to accepted standards:

> My maister Bukton, whan of Crist our kyng
> Was axed what is trouthe or sothfastnesse,
> He nat a word answerde to that axing,
> As who saith, 'No man is al trewe', I gesse.
> (Envoy to Bukton, 1–4)

> To yow, my purse, and to noon other wight
> Complayne I, for ye be my lady dere!
> I am so sory, now that ye been lyght . . .
> (Complaint to his Purse, 1–3)

> Nas never pyk walwed in galauntyne
> As I in love am walwed and ywounde,
> For which ful ofte I myself devyne
> That I am trewe Tristam the secounde.
> (To Rosemounde, 17–20)

> But what availeth such a long sermoun
> Of aventures of love, up and doun?
> I wol returne and speken of my peyne:
> The poynt is this, of my distruccioun . . .
> (Complaint of Mars, 209–12)

> Adam scriveyn, if ever it thee bifalle
> Boece or Troylus for to wryten newe,
> Under thy long lokkes thou most have the scalle,
> But after my makyng thou wryte more trewe;
> So ofte a-daye I mot thy werk renewe,
> It to correcte and eek to rubbe and scrape;
> And al is thorugh thy negligence and rape.
> (Chaucers Wordes unto Adam, his Owne Scriveyn)

This is a plain, colloquial, sometimes blunt, conversational style. It is the style which Chaucer uses for most of his characters of high rank – for example in the *Knight's Tale* and the *Troilus* except, as we have seen, on the occasions when they address ladies as suppliant lovers. This situation calls for the use of another style, which an earlier English romance – *The Lay of Havelok the Dane* – calls 'speken of luuedrurye',[8] and the author of *Sir Gawain and the Green Knight* 'talkyng noble'. How far this was a purely literary device, proper to poems about love designed for courtly circles, or how far it was actually practised, we cannot tell. In the Elizabethan period, it would appear, some elaborate literary styles were actually carried over into fashionable speech, and the same may have been true of court circles in Chaucer's day. The minor poems, at any rate, make much use of this style: the Complaints, the poem to Rosemounde and *Wommanly Noblesse* all reflect the fashion, with varying degrees of seriousness. The opening of the latter provides a good example:

> So hath myn herte caught in remembraunce
> Your beaute hoole and stidefast governaunce,
> Your vertues alle and your hie noblessse,
> That you to serve is set al my plesaunce,
> So wel me liketh your womanly contenaunce,
> Your fresshe fetures and your comlynesse,
> That whiles I live, myn herte to his maystresse
> You hath ful chose in trewe perséveraunce
> Never to chaunge, for no maner distresse.
>
> (*Wommanly Noblesse*, 1–9)

This is writing in 'thise . . . termes alle / That in swich cas thise loveres alle seche' (*Troilus*, II, 1067–8), and we may, if we choose, condemn the poem as somewhat dull and uninspired. The same, however, is true of Troilus's formal utterances as a lover here in Book II, or even face to face with his mistress, for example in Book III, 106 ff. The point of the use of the style in the *Troilus* is, of course, that it is dramatically justified. Troilus *is* one of 'thise loveres', and he only speaks in character. The same defence holds for the minor poems, though it will not give them permanency or raise their absolute value. Their justification lies in the occasion for which they were written; they exist as part of an agreeable exchange between poet and audience, which forms their context just as much as the totality of the poem forms the context for Troilus's speeches of love. As such, these poems must have succeeded and must have given pleasure; but, like all occasional poetry, their range is necessarily limited to an audience which accepts and shares in the convention. They are not, however, to be dismissed as bad 'lyrics' or failures to achieve art of a more ambitious kind. On the contrary, they perfectly fulfil a function which is primarily social, and which poetry is now no longer called on to fulfil – perhaps to its ultimate loss.

Not all the short poems were concerned with love. There was also a fashion for moral or philosophical *ballades*, which demonstrates that poet and audience, besides their interest in love and in light conversation, had intellectual interests in common.[9] This fashion is well attested in both France – where, for example, Deschamps contributed many poems in a style which probably provides the model for Chaucer's[10] – and in England – where, besides Chaucer, Gower wrote the *Cinkante Balades* (in French) and the Scottish and English Chaucerians took up the genre. Chaucer's achievement in his poems of this type – *The Former Age, Fortune, Truth, Gentilesse, Lak of Stedfastnesse* are all that survive, although similar themes are important in the *Complaint of Mars* – is to carry into this kind the same ease and familiarity in the conversational style which we have found characteristic of his less serious short poems. He uses an undogmatic way of writing, in which a philosophical point or a moral *sentence* is put forward for general consideration. No hard and fast conclusion is necessarily reached, though it may suggest itself to the experienced reader, and the total impression is of a free and equal interchange between poet and audience.

Sometimes, it is true, a more emphatic note is sounded. *Truth* achieves a metrical control in the imperative mood which is hardly to be met with again before the close of the sixteenth century in, for example, the poetry of Sir Walter Ralegh:

> Her is non hoom, her nis but wildernesse:
> Forth, pilgrim, forth! Forth, beste, out of thy stal!
> Know thy contree, look up, thank God of al;
> Hold the heye wey, and lat thy gost thee lede.
>
> (17–20)

The main theme, however, usually dealt with in a more leisurely way, is that of the consolation of philosophy, developed, inevitably, in Boethian terms, but with overtones of the familiar Senecan style and, I think, with the use of subject matter often more characteristic of Seneca than of Boethius.

Both Deschamps and Chaucer, in the short moral poems, use a

style which is unlike the rather discursive one of Boethius, but which is very reminiscent of the short, pithy, familiarly turned, and at times epigrammatic, sentences of Seneca. The resemblance might, of course, be accidental and due to the shortness of the *ballades* and the need to fit the thought to the verse line and the limits of stanza form. As far as subject matter is conerned there is, too, a considerable overlap between Boethius and Seneca. Both transmit the Stoic ideal of the philosophical good man who triumphs, by his inner victory over himself, over fortune and mutability. The *de Consolatione Philosophiae* however, is necessarily closely organized round Fortune as its main topic, while Seneca, in the short moral epistles and essays, discusses a wider range of topics – among them the advantages of poverty, the right attitude to riches, moderation and self-rule. All these are compatible with Boethius's thought, but are not always given separate or extensive treatment by him. As we shall see, while it has puzzled critics to find close parallels to *Truth* in Boethius, it is quite easy to do so in the writings of Seneca. These were equally available and popular in Chaucer's day, and there is no reason to suppose that he had not actually read an author to whom he refers more than once.

Both *Truth* and *Fortune* provide good examples of this style and these themes:

> Tempest thee noght al croked to redresse,
> In trust of hir that turneth as a bal;
> Gret reste stant in litel besinesse;
> Be war also to sporne ayeyns an al;
> Stryve not, as doth the crokke with the wal.
> Daunte thyself, that dauntest otheres dede,
> And trouthe thee shal delivere, it is no drede.
>
> (*Truth*, 8–14)

> Yit is me left the light of my resoun,
> To knowen frend fro fo in thy mirour
> So muchel hath yit thy whirling up and doun
> Ytaught me for to knowen in an hour.
> But trewely, no force of thy reddour
> To him that over himself hath the maystrye!
> My suffisaunce shal be my socour;
> But fynally, Fortune, I thee defye!
>
> (*Fortune*, 9–16)

Deschamps expresses himself in much the same way, though there are important differences. We could, for example, compare:

> Je ne requier a Dieu fors qu'il me doint
> En ce monde lui servir et loer,
> Vivre pour moy, cote entiere ou pourpoint,
> Aucun cheval pour mon labour porter,
> Et que je puisse mon estat gouverner
> Moiennement, en grace, sans envie,
> Sanz trop avoir et sanz pain demander,
> Car au joir d'ui est la plus seure vie.
>
> *(Balade* ccxl, 1–8)

This is, again, the Stoic ideal of an independent moderation, which is not, in fact, the same as the Christian one of patient poverty in the service of God.[11] Deschamps, through his opening lines, does, however, attempt to link it to the Christian service of God, and this is characteristic of his attitude in his *ballades*.[12] Chaucer, however, although some of the proverb-type sentences of *Truth* are derived from the Bible,[13] does not overtly attempt to Christianize the Stoic good man who has passed beyond the reach of Fortune. In *Fortune* as in the *Book of the Duchess*,[14] he puts forward Socrates as the supreme instance of such a man:

> O Socrates, thou stidfast champioun,
> She never mighte be thy tormentour;
> Thou never dreddest hir oppressioun,
> Ne in hir chere founde thou no savour.
> Thou knewe wel the deceit of hir colour,
> And that hir moste worshipe is to lye.
>
> (17–22)

Chaucer is probably remembering the *Roman de la Rose* (5845–50) here; but there is no reason why he should not also be aware of Seneca's repeated use of Socrates as the type of the man whose resignation is perfect and unshaken in the face of the worst that Fortune can do.[15]

The first stanza of *Truth* is particularly Senecan in its ideas:

Flee fro the prees, and dwelle with sothfastnesse,
Suffyce unto thy good, though it be smal . . .
Savour no more than thee bihove shal;
Reule wel thyself, that other folk canst rede;
And trouthe thee shal delivere, it is no drede.

(1–7)

It is not, of course, necessary to seek specific 'sources' in Seneca for these lines: it is rather that Chaucer (and, it would seem, the fashionable French poets of his day) writes from a general knowledge and recollection of his characteristic ideas. Thus, the first line of *Truth* contains the same idea as the seventh of the *Epistulae Morales*:[16]

Quid tibi vitandam praecipue existimes, quaeris? Turbam.

(Do you ask me what you should regard as especially to be avoided? I say crowds.)

The opening of the next epistle is even closer:

'Tu me', inquis, 'vitare turbam iubes secedere et conscientia esse contentum?'

('Do you bid me,' you say, 'shun the throng and withdraw from men, and be content with my own conscience?')

The next line is an imitation of the following Latin sentence:

Si res tue tibi non sufficiant, fac ut rebus tuis sufficias.

(If your goods don't accommodate you, accommodate yourself to your goods.)

Now this does not derive from Seneca, although it is entirely in keeping with his teaching, but from the *de Nugis Philosophorum* of Caecilius Balbus. The same sentence is quoted by Gower ir the *Confessio Amantis*, V, 7735 ff.; and there it is glossed in the margin as being from Seneca.[17] It may be, therefore, that Chaucer was not only using a tag thoroughly Senecan in tone, but one which he actually thought of as by Seneca. The rather similar idea of the next line is, again a common one in Seneca. Epistle xlii pursues it at length, especially in paragraph 6:

41

Hoc itaque in his, quae adfectamus, ad quae labore magno contendimus, inspicere debemus, aut nihil in illis commodi esse aut plus incommodi. Quaedam supervacua sunt, quaedam tanti non sunt.

(Therefore, with regard to the objects which we pursue and for which we strive with great effort, we should note this truth; either there is nothing desirable in them, or the undesirable is preponderant. Some objects are superfluous; others are not worth the price we pay for them.)

This epistle ends with a reference to the idea of self-rule:

Qui se habet, nihil perdidit. Sed quoto cuique habere se contingit?

(He that owns himself has lost nothing. But how few men are blessed with the ownership of self!)

Epistle viii recommends philosophy (Chaucer's 'truth') as of more value than the gifts of fortune. Epistle ii, paragraph 1, discusses 'besinesse' – another favourite subject of Seneca's:[18]

Non discurris nec locorum mutationibus inquietaris. Aegri animi ista iactatio est. Primum argumentum conpositae mentis existimo posse consistere et secum morari.

(You do not run hither and thither and distract yourself by changing your abode; for such restlessness is the sign of a disordered spirit. The primary indication, to my thinking, of a well-ordered mind, is a man's ability to remain in one place and linger in his own company.)

It would be possible to multiply examples of correspondences in thought, if not in expression, between Chaucer's moral poems and Seneca's writings. What is, I think, most interesting about these correspondences is that, for Chaucer, such ideas provided not only the basis for short epigrammatic poems in the familiar style, but also for much that he incorporates in his longer works, especially the *Troilus* and the *Knight's Tale*. Some understanding of the moral and philosophical themes pursued with such urbanity in the short poems, and of their background, is, therefore, of great importance to our understanding of the major works.

The *Complaint of Mars* combines all the interests that we have been considering in a short work which, while it cannot compare with the major works in poetic merit, is still technically accomplished. There is much fine writing about love; as we have already seen, the natural-istic, conversational style is also present, and the poem also has an important philosophical-moral content.

There is, for example, an impressive anticipation – or perhaps echo, since the date of composition is uncertain – of the *Troilus*:

> To what fyn made the God that sit so hye,
> Benethen him, love other companye,
> And streyneth folk to love, malgre her hed?
> And then her joy, for oght I can espye,
> Ne lasteth not the twynkelyng of an ye,
> And somme han never joy til they be ded.
> What meneth this? What is this mystihed?
> Wherto constreyneth he his folk so faste
> Thing to desyre, but hit shulde laste?
>
> (218–26)

This lacks the dramatic force and the personal intensity of Troilus's cry 'If love be good, from whennes cometh my woo?' (I, 402); and it has none of the bitterness and epigrammatic sting of Palamoun's:

> 'What governance is in this prescience,
> That giltelees tormenteth innocence?'
>
> (*CT* I, 1313–14)

What it has got, however, is, precisely, urbanity. Chaucer philo-sophizes without professionalism or dogmatism. He speaks (thinly disguised by the person of Mars) to his audience quietly and easily. A conversational 'and then', not a strictly logical connective, introduces a new stage in the argument. Frequent questions – 'what does it mean?', 'What is it?' – are posed but left unanswered (although the answer is not difficult for those who know their Boethius and Seneca), so that poet and reader remain on equal terms. The personal note required by the story is finally introduced without emphasis. The pathos is there, but it makes no unmannerly demands: 'So fareth hyt by lovers and by me' (263).

The whole poem combines the fashionable subject of love, given the fashionable treatment, with more serious but, no doubt, equally fashionable interests. It is in fact, not merely an astrologizing of the Gods, but a celestial love story worked out in terms of the actual – or at least possible – movements of the heavenly bodies.[19] Chaucer makes continual use of astrological-astronomical material throughout his works, and it must be assumed that, as well as being of interest to the poet, the topic was also acceptable to his audience. The *Complaint of Mars* would seem to make use of a current interest in much the same way that the later *Hermet's Tale*[20] made use of the then current literary interest in alchemy. A passage like this, indeed, can only be read for the amusement of fitting it to an actual astronomical situation:

> Thus be they knyt, and regnen as in hevene
> Be lokyng moost; til hyt fil, on a tyde,
> That by her bothe assent was set a stevene,
> That Mars shal entre, as fast as he may glyde,
> Into hir nexte paleys, and ther abyde,
> Walkynge hys cours, til she had him atake,
> And he preide her to haste her for his sake.
>
> (50–6)

The machinery of the Classical gods, though no doubt of great interest in itself to contemporary readers, is seldom used merely for decoration or poetic effect in the Middle Ages or Renaissance, but usually to convey scientific or philosophical information.

The *Complaint of Mars* is not a great poem – the very fact that its speakers seem only thin disguises for the poet himself no doubt tells against it. But it is an urbane poem and one in which, even if Chaucer's genius is manifestly not at full stretch, he is yet at ease with his audience. It is often said that Chaucer shows little lyrical ability. As Robinson puts it, in his introductory remarks on the short poems: 'In so far as lyrical poetry is an intensely individual expression of thought or feeling it would seem not to have been natural to Chaucer's temperament.' The same. however, might be said of all Chaucer's contemporaries and predecessors. Apart from odd snatches of song, generally only surviving as refrains, there is no medieval English lyric in this sense. To expect Chaucer's short poems to fill the gap is to miss their point. They exist as a witness to a poetic activity which was, above all, social. Some are directed at known persons, although they are to be shared by a wider circle. Others, like the *Complaint of Mars*, are not occasional in this sense, but are designed to give pleasure through the satisfaction of well-known and clearly defined tastes and interests. To say of the Squire 'He koude songes make and wel endite' is to state a social accomplishment and a reason for popularity in a certain circle. From Chaucer, as a professed poet, something more ambitious was obviously expected, in the form of longer and more elaborate *divertissements*. There is no reason to believe that these were not aimed at the same circle which accepted and enjoyed the greater and more independent works; but, like Lydgate after him, Chaucer continued throughout his life to satisfy the more intimate taste for the smaller things.

The *Book of the Duchess*, among the minor poems, impresses me as Chaucer's longest and most successful essay in pure urbanity. This is a judgement, however, with which by no means all critics would agree. For Muscatine, as we have seen, there is discordance in the range and variation of the style; and for some readers the subject matter and its handling also seem discrepant.[21] I have suggested that much of the variation in style can be accounted for by Chaucer's use of a common narrative idiom. The problem of subject matter, and the wider issues of its treatment in the *Book of the Duchess*, cannot be understood without considering the nature and aims of the poem as a whole. It is a love vision and owes much to French handling of the genre. But it is also, it seems to me, a poem in which Chaucer does two important things. In the first place he develops and sustains the scope of the easy, civil, conversational method within a pleasantly literary, but not too dramatic form: this method we found to be characteristic of the minor poems. In the second place, something else evolves, which was of the greatest importance to Chaucer as a narrative poet and which was to be eagerly imitated:[22] this characteristic, necessarily absent from the small-scale poems, was the ability to give a vivid impression, not only of the persons of the narrative themselves, but also of their relations to each other within the wider setting of the society of which they form a part. The reader, in fact, is able to experience the sensitive and yet controlled contact between human beings, arising out of the personalities before us and their immediate situation, but conditioned by and fitted to the special demands and special manners of the world to which they belong. This is what is new and striking in the *Book of the Duchess*, in its precise and realistic handling of the encounter between the Dreamer and the Man in Black. It is an encounter – provided, of course, that we accept the traditional interpretation of the poem – between two persons of predetermined, known standing and relationship. The Dreamer, the reflection of Chaucer the poet and civil servant, is an ordinary person – a 'wyght' (530) – while the Man in Black, called a 'knight' and addressed at all times with great respect and caution by the Dreamer, is the image of a great and powerful prince, well able either to harm or advance the real Chaucer. We know from the facts of Chaucer's life that he had every opportunity of meeting John of Gaunt in person. We cannot tell whether he actually formed a definite relationship with him, either of friendship or patronage, but the fact remains that, through his position as a young man in the household of the Countess of Ulster, Chaucer became a part of the kind of society to which John of Gaunt belonged and was trained to appreciate and participate in the nuances of its manners and characteristic behaviour.[23] The basic situation of the poem, then, is a meeting between two people of fundamentally different origins and social status, who are yet bound together through the fact that each has his appointed place in a social scheme which had plenty of room for both. This provides for a constant tension between the areas of experience in which they meet as equals and those in which established convention decrees that they do not – and this results in a subtle interplay of respect and caution, combined with a surprising degree of directness when they find themselves on common ground.

Chaucer's greatest achievement in this field of complicated social relationships is undoubtedly the way in which in the *Troilus*, largely through the medium of the figure of Pandarus, he builds up a picture of the world of Troy as a close social unit, which does more to condition the development of the love story than the stars ever did. It is also, of course, one of the many reasons why the comic tales are more than mere hilarious anecdotes – although the churl's world is necessarily more limited in extent, and less subtle in its reactions and interactions, it is still densely structured. Even in minor episodes this kind of perceptiveness is often of great structural importance. In the *Squire's Tale*, for example, it is the familiarity with which

members of the crowd treat each other which anchors the im-
probabilities of the story in a more sober world – and also, on
another level, helps to cast something of a gently ironic light over
both the fairy tale and the youthful exuberance of the Squire:

> 'Myn herte,' quod oon, 'is everemoore in drede; . . .'
> Another rowned to his felawe lowe,
> And seyde, 'He lyeth, for it is rather lyk
> An apparence ymaad by som magyk . . .'
>   Another answerde, and seyde it myghte wel be
> Naturelly, by composiciouns
> Of anglis and of slye reflexiouns . . .
>
>   (*CT* V, 212–30)

Or, again, in the *House of Fame*, towards the end, the Dreamer's
momentary contact with a very ordinary person, obviously of
his own rank, with whom he has a civil but commonplace exchange,
plays an important part in a denouement which very thoroughly
completes the progression from the world of the great poets of
the past, represented by the summary of the *Aeneid*, to that of
'shipmen and pilgrimes, / With scrippes bret-ful of lesinges'.[24]

> With that y gan aboute wende,
> For oon that stood ryght at my bak,
> Me thoughte, goodly to me spak,
> And seyde, 'Frend, what is thy name?
> Artow come hider to han fame?'
> 'Nay, for sothe, frend,' quod y . . .
>   (1868–73)

The conversation continues on the same easy terms up to line
1915 and does much to emphasize that the poem has now left
Jove's eagle – a bird of more arbitrary habits of speech, standing
in a less natural relation to the Dreamer – behind.

This kind of perception, so familiar to us from much later developments in narrative art, particularly in the novel, is almost entirely
lacking in earlier English narrative poetry, in spite of its undoubted
realism. It is not, of course, absent from contemporary French
literature, but I do not think that it would be easy to parallel in any
French love vision either the structural function of the relationship

between the Dreamer and the Man in Black or the complexity
with which it is described.[25] Some idea of the difference can perhaps
be given by a glance at the passage from Machaut's *Jugement dou
Roy de Behaingne*[26] on which, it is generally agreed, Chaucer based
his account of the meeting of the Dreamer and the Man in Black
and, indeed, the whole opening of the dream in the *Book of the Duchess*.
In Machaut's poem the matter is somewhat differently organized,
since the poet-dreamer does not play a part in the dialogue which
takes place between a solitary and sorrowful lady and a knight 'de
moult trés noble arroy'. The situation is thus, from the start, a more
expected and conventional one than that of Chaucer's poem:
the relation between knight and lady explains itself to the experienced
reader without the need of much elaboration on the poet's part.
Nor is the lady such a strikingly tragic figure as the Man in Black.
Her solitude is mitigated by a 'chiennet' and a 'pucelette', and there
are none of the severe symptoms of bodily weakness, described in
uncompromisingly medical terms, from which Chaucer's mourner
suffers:

Mais tout einsi, com je me delitoie
En son trés dous chanter que j'escoutoie,
Je vi venir par une estroite voie,
       Pleinne d'erbette,
Une dame pensant, toute seulette
Fors d'un chiennet et d'une pucelette;
Mais bein sambloit sa maniere simplette
       Pleinne d'anoy.
Et d'autre part, un petit loing de moy,
Uns chevaliers de moult trés noble arroy
Tout le chemin venoit encontre soy
       Sans compaingnie;
Si me pensay qu'amis yert et amie,
Lors me boutay par dedens la feuillie
Si embrunchiez qu'il ne me virent mie.
       Mais quant amis,
En qui Nature assez de biens a mis,
Fu aprochiez de la dame de pris
Com gracieus, sages et bien apris
       La salua.

Et la dame que pensée argua,
Sans riens respondre a li, le trespassa.
Et cils tantost arriere rappassa,
            Et se la prist
Par le giron, et doucement li dist:
'Trés douce dame, avez vous en despit
Le mien salut?' Et quant elle le vit,
            Se respondi
En souspirant, que plus n'i attendi:
'Certes, sire, pas ne vous entendi
Pour mon penser qui le me deffendi;
            Mais se j'ay fait
Riens ou il et villenie ou meffait,
Veuilliez le moy pardonner, s'il vous plait.'
Li chevaliers, sans faire plus de plait,
            Dist doucement:
'Dame, il n'affiert ci nul pardonnement,
Car il n'y a meffait ne mautalent:
Mais je vous pri que vostre pensement
            Me veuilliez dire.'
Et la dame parfondement souspire
Et dist: 'Pour Dieu, laissiez m'en pais, biau sire;
Car mestier n'ay que me faciez plus d'ire
            Ne de contraire
Que j'en recoy.' Et cils se prist a traire
Plus près de li, pour sa pensée attraire,
Et li a dit: 'Trés douce debonnaire,
            Triste vous voy.
Mais je vous jur et promet par ma foy,
S'a moy volez descouvrir vostre anoy,
Que je feray tout le pooir de moy
            De l'adrecier.'
Et la dame l'en prist a merciër,
Est dist: 'Sire, nuls ne m'en puet aidier . . .'

                               (41–94)

and so the dialogue continues until she is persuaded to relate her grief.

Neither party to this dialogue can really be accused of 'making it quaint'; and the possibility of 'making it tough' is of course entirely excluded by the nature of the pair.[27] The degree of tension in Chaucer's dialogue, where we are kept aware of the difference in status between the speakers, one of whom is a great enough man to be approached with a blend of daring and caution as well as with courtesy by the Dreamer, is therefore neither aimed at nor achieved in Machaut's. It is of interest here to compare another passage, in the *Dit dou Vergier*,[28] where Machaut's Dreamer does approach one of the figures of the Dream, who turns out to be the God of Love, with a similar blend of feelings. His misgivings are allayed, in much the same way as Chaucer's Dreamer's, by the courtesy of the reply he gets:

> Mais cils qui sëoit au deseure
> Seur l'arbre entreprist le parler
> Et encommença a parler,
> Et me rendi si doucement
> Mon salu, que le hardement
> Qui estoit en moy tous perdus
> Me fu par son parler rendus.
> (212–18)

Chaucer's Dreamer says very much the same:

> Loo! how goodly spak thys knyght,
> As hit had be another wyght;
> He made hyt nouther towgh ne queynte.
> And I saw that, and gan me aqueynte
> With hym, and fond hym so tretable,
> Ryght wonder skylful and resonable,
> As me thoghte, for al hys bale.
>
> (529–35)

The difference, it seems to me, is that, for Chaucer, the passage serves a structural purpose – it is a definite part of the evolution of the dialogue, which in turn is the vehicle of much of the significant content of the poem. For Machaut, it is part of the description of the gracious God of Love. Dialogue, it turns out, is not important in the *Dit* as a whole, which largely consists of indefatigable self-descriptive speeches on the part of the deity. Lastly the relation of the god and his worshipper is self-evident; and, again, of little structural importance in the poem. It is, too, not a relation which has any 'real' meaning – that is, it does not, like that of the Dreamer and the Man in Black, reflect any of the complexities of the natural world.

Again, the variety of style and diction, which Chaucer can use to express a more complicated situation, is hardly possible to the French poet. In the *Jugement*, the lady must be addressed with uniform gentleness by a knight 'de moult trés noble arroy'. We may perhaps detect a slight sharpness in her 'laissiez m'en pais', but this is not a note that is at all sustained.

Chaucer, therefore, makes a very free adaptation of his French model and is bound by it neither in the overall plan of the situation nor in style. In fact, we could say that while smoothness and uniformity of treatment is characteristic of the French passage, Chaucer, on the other hand, makes a point of contrasts. The figure of the fainting Man in Black is an abrupt invasion of the idyllic landscape; the appearance of a beautiful lady, however sad, with a little dog and a little maid to accompany her, even before she meets a knight fully equipped to take charge of the situation, is not really disturbing. It is not, of course, the case that Machaut never disturbs. There is much in the *Jugement dou Roy de Navarre*, for example, which is extremely disturbing – but this is, overall, a poem of a different sort, with its own consistency.

The love vision, in fact, as the French poets handle it, is not designed to carry a great weight either of meaning or of feeling. The *Roman de la Rose* continuation contains a great variety of material, much of it serious; and Gower successfully imitates this variety in the *Confessio Amantis*, a poem built on as large a scale as the *Roman*. Chaucer, on the contrary, keeps the graceful, manageable proportions of the love vision as he found it in the work of Machaut or Froissart. In the Prologue to the *Legend of Good Women*, especially, he gives us a perfect example of the advantages of a restricted content coupled with graceful treatment. Increasingly, however, as we shall see in the case of the *Parlement of Foules* and the *House of Fame*, he extends the range of the content and the variety of feeling and meaning to be expressed, with the result that it is a curious and unexpected fact of literary history that Chaucer actually used the essentially stylized form of the love vision to develop characteristics which are more typical of naturalism. This was not what the form as a whole, traditionally and even in Chaucer's own hands, was aimed at. It does not, for example, depend on the development of naturalistic, consecutive narrative order: the choice of the dream as a framework for what little story there is allows of a good deal of arbitrary scene-shifting. The main theme is usually a simple statement or situation, not a development involving naturalistically conceived characters in a continuous action. The slight story of the *Book of the Duchess* comes nearer to our idea of the naturalistic treatment of characters in action than do most of the love visions, but in the *Parlement* and the *House of Fame*, as the weight of content increases, so Chaucer actually decreases the realism of his handling of the narrative as a whole, although he increases it greatly in the treatment of incidents and details. This, however, is to anticipate.

The *Book of the Duchess*, indeed, is linked to actuality in so far as it is an elegy; it mourns the death of a real person and offers consolation to her husband, who, only slightly disguised, is brought within the frame of the poem as one of the protagonists. It has, thus, much in common with the shorter poems we have been considering – the poet writes of and to someone known to him, with whom he stands in a definite relationship; but he writes in such a way that a wider circle can share their communication. The choice of the love vision for the form of his poem actually aids such communication; it is a form in which a courtly circle can be assumed to take pleasure; it is known as a suitable vehicle for fine and serious, though not exalted or disproportionately intense, writing; it traditionally uses dreams and disguises and thus lends itself to the humane distancing of grief which is a necessary part of the consolation, as well as of conversational good manners. As we have seen, Chaucer brings to the French form an additional intimacy and variety of style which, particularly in the dialogue, gives him the chance of developing the relationship of the protagonists with great subtlety and flexibility.

Chaucer begins the poem, as he does his other two love visions, with an introductory section in which he writes of himself, his sleep, and his dreams. He addresses his audience familiarly and abruptly, very much in the manner of the short poems and, in this case, in close imitation of the opening lines of Froissart's *Paradys d'Amour*:[29]

> I have gret wonder, be this lyght,
> How that I lyve, for day ne nyght
> I may nat slepe wel nygh noght;
> I have so many an ydel thoght,

> Purely for defaute of slep,
> That, by my trouthe, I take no kep
> Of nothing, how hyt cometh or gooth . . .
>
> (1–7)

He continues for some fifty lines in this vein, in a passage dominated by the constantly repeated word 'sleep',[30] and by words denoting sorrow and sickness – 'sorowe', 'sorwful', 'melancolye', 'drede', 'hevynesse', 'sicknesse'. But, as a kind of counterpoint to these ominous words, counteracting any tragic effect they might have, the whole passage maintains an easy, conversational tone, avoiding both outright humour and an exclusive concentration on personal emotion, which, in the context would be unmannerly and overserious.

> For there is phisicien but oon
> That may me hele; but that is don.
> Passe we over untill eft;
> That wil not be mot nede be left;
> Our first mater is good to kepe.
>
> (39–43)

Chaucer, in fact, holds his audience's attention for the description of his uneasy, sorrowful state as the very opposite to the Ancient Mariner – his art ensures that they will not escape him, but he deals pleasantly with his troubles and suggests that they belong to a world in which consolation is not impossible – where a 'spirit of quycknesse' and of 'lustyhede' (24–5), though extinguished for the moment, may be rekindled, and where there are physicians capable of healing if they will.

This opening is important because, through its style and content, it sets the tone of the poem as a whole and shows us what Chaucer is about. He writes of grief which exists and which is pitiful and serious, but which is only one aspect of the world. It is, too, grief softened by recollection and told to others – it is not the urgent and personal outcry of immediate suffering, which he gives us in the *Troilus* and in the *Knight's Tale*. It is, in fact, grief brought down to a sympathetic and intimate conversational level, which allows for a modulation not, it seems to me, to the purely comic (which could not fail to be discordant) but to a tone of pleasant apology to a friend – the good manners which ensure that the communication is not permitted to become too painful.

The introduction leads into the story of Ceix and Alcyone, since it is related in the book which Chaucer finally takes up to while away his sleeplessness. This is a sad story of the death of kings, and of an inconsolable wife who is unable to live with her sorrow. The actual story is plainly and soberly told; and Chaucer suppresses the ending, which he must have known from Ovid, in which the parted lovers are reunited as sea-birds. Death is final, as Ceix tells Alcyone:

> 'For, certes, swete, I nam but ded;
> Ye shul me never on lyve yse . . .
> To lytel while oure blysse lasteth!'
>
> (204–11)

As part of the consolation, the story merely makes the point that bereavement is not a unique experience, but is shared with all mankind, and even with the great kings of the past. Emotionally it preserves and deepens the sorrowful tone of the opening and gives a more objective and uncomplicated, though still distanced and muted presentation of grief:

> Anon her herte began to erme;
> And for that her thoughte evermo
> It was not wele [he dwelte] so,
> She longed so after the king
> That, certes, it were a pitous thing
> To telle her hertely sorowful lif
> That she had, this noble wif,
> For him she loved alderbest.
>
> (80–7)

Alcyone's feelings rise in a gentle crescendo from an uneasiness comparable to the narrator's in the opening section, to outright sorrow; and even this is presented to the reader in the most tolerable terms – it is the feeling of a 'noble wif' and arises from her true and loyal love for her husband. In fact, as in the opening, the positive aspects of life are tactfully brought forward and juxtaposed to its more sorrowful ones – 'To lytel while oure blysse lasteth'; but we may expect some bliss.

The simple narrative of the Queen's loss and her sorrow and death is extended by a long passage describing the intervention of the gods: briefly, Juno, in answer to Alcyone's prayer for information concerning her husband's fate, sends a messenger to the Cave of Sleep to obtain a dream, through which Alcyone may learn the truth. Chaucer maintains the easy, conversational, and at times colloquial tone throughout this passage. Juno commands her messenger in familiar terms:[31]

> 'Go bet,' quod Juno, 'to Morpheus, –
> Thou knowest hym wel, the god of slep,
> Now understond wel, and take kep!
> Sey thus on my half, . . .'
>
> (136–9)

The arrival of the messenger, and his difficulty in awakening the God of Sleep, takes the same technique to the verge of outright comedy:

> This messager com fleynge faste
> And cried, 'O, ho! awake anoon!'
> Hit was for noght; there herde hym non.
> 'Awake!' quod he, 'whoo ys lyth there?'
> And blew his horn ryght in here eere,
> And cried 'Awaketh!' wonder hyë.
> This god of slep with hys oon yë
> Cast up, axed, 'Who clepeth ther?'
> 'Hyt am I,' quod this messager . . .
>
> (178–86)

It may be that in this passage Chaucer misjudged his effect, and that he allowed the complex and subtle attitude to his subject matter, which he has maintained so far with success, to harden into mere poking fun. On the other hand, our comprehension of his colloquialisms may be at fault. To take one certain case: 'Hyt am I', which may seem, to an age used to the telephone, a peculiarly pointless and maddening response was, to judge from Chaucer's use of it elsewhere, common form in polite but familiar conversation in his day.[32] Nevertheless the tone of the whole description is a light one, and it contrasts sharply, in its enjoyment in the elaboration of improbable detail, with the bare references to the King's corpse:

> Seys body the kyng,
> That lyeth ful pale and nothyng rody;
> (142–3)

and:

> Took up the dreynte body sone
> And bar hyt forth to Alcione.
> (195–6)

There is no decoration or elaboration over the core of the story, but Chaucer does allow himself, and his audience, a little light relief when it comes to the marvels of the land of sleep. And he continues to elaborate on the theme of sleep in much the same way in the next section, in which, much struck by the account of 'the goddes of slepyng' (230) which he has just read, he determines to profit by the example of Queen Alcyone, whose vows brought her sleep, and to promise:

> I wil yive hym the alderbeste
> Yifte that ever he abod hys lyve.
> And here on warde, ryght now, as blyve,
> Yif he wol make me slepe a lyte,
> Of down of pure dowves white
> I wil yive hym a fether-bed,
> Rayed with gold, and ryght wel cled
> In fyn blak satyn doutremer,
> And many a pilowe, and every ber
> Of cloth of Reynes, to slepe softe.
> (246–55)

No sooner are the words spoken than sleep comes to him and with it:

> so ynly swete a sweven,
> So wonderful, that never yit
> Y trowe, no man had the wyt
> To konne wel my sweven rede.
> (276–9)

A pattern begins to emerge. The sadness of the story of Ceix and Alcyone has been set aside, and Chaucer concentrates on another part of the tale – on the healing powers of sleep. Like Alcyone's, however, his sleep is to be visited by a dream of sorrow. But we are not to think of the sorrow as entirely bitter or unalloyed. The dream will be 'ynly swete' and will have a deeper meaning than one might at first imagine. In fact, this whole section maintains the impression of a sorrow, seen and pondered over from a little distance, which is also part of a wider scheme, and, which in the long run, does admit of consolation.

The dream itself is set in all the brightness of a May morning, with sunshine and birdsong. Its first scene, after the Dreamer has left his bed, is a hunt through a green and flowery woodland. It is, the Dreamer is told, the Emperor Octovyen who is pursuing the hart. The hunt, however is unsuccessful:

> and so, at the laste
> This hert rused, and staal away
> Fro alle the houndes a privy way.
> The houndes had overshote hym alle,
> And were on a defaute yfalle.
> Therwyth the hunte wonder faste
> Blew a forloyn at the laste.
>
> (380–6)

It seems quite likely that in describing this loss of the 'hert' (hart) Chaucer intends a punning preparation for the loss he is about to describe which concerns the 'herte' (heart). The chase as a figure of the pursuit of love is, after all, a commonplace.[33] Certainly the lack of success of the hunt helps to maintain, even within the beauty of the dream, the feeling of uneasiness which dominated the opening. It also, since it is not, after all, an irremediable loss, helps to keep grief at a distance. The Dreamer wanders on through the wood and it is only at line 445 that he finally meets the main personage of the poem, the Man in Black.

In his dealings with the Man in Black, the Dreamer has been accused by some critics of clumsiness and lack of tact.[34] As it seems to me that the effect is the very reverse of this, and that it is here that Chaucer's urbane manner, in the sense in which I have been using the term, is most fully developed, it will be necessary to look carefully at this section of the poem. In the first place, the Dreamer has been accused of obtuseness and failure to comprehend the sorrow before him. Now, Chaucer devotes a long passage to making it clear that his Dreamer does in fact know, first, how great the sorrow is, and secondly, exactly what has caused it. In the course of his description of the Man in Black, the Dreamer comments:

> Hit was gret wonder that Nature
> Myght suffre any creature
> To have such sorwe, and be not ded.
> (467–9)

And he also overhears the mourner's 'compleynte', which has no ambiguity about it:

> 'I have of sorwe so gret won
> That joye gete I never non,
> Now that I see my lady bryght,
> Which I have loved with al my myght,
> Is fro me ded and ys agoon.
>   Allas, deth, what ayleth the,
> That thou noldest have taken me,
> Whan thou toke my lady swete,
> That was so fair, so fresh, so fre,
> So good, that men may wel se
> Of al goodnesse she had no mete!'
> (475–86)

The Man in Black is reduced to a state of considerable physiological danger:

> Hys sorwful hert gan faste faynte,
> And his spirites wexen dede;
> The blood was fled for pure drede
> Doun to hys herte to mak hym warm –
> For wel hyt feled the herte had harm –
> To wite eke why hit was adrad
> By kynde, and for to make hyt glad;
> (488–94)

It is at this dangerous moment, while nature is struggling to reassert control over the mourner's bodily mechanisms,[35] that the Dreamer intervenes.

The stages by which contact is established are carefully described. At first the Man in Black is not even aware of the Dreamer's presence – his preoccupation and bodily weakness 'Made hym that he herde me noght' (510). Then, as he does become conscious that he is being spoken too, the attitudes and good manners of both characters are delicately but clearly depicted:

> But at the last, to sayn ryght soth,
> He was war of me, how y stood
> Before hym, and did of myn hood,
> And had ygret hym as I best koude,
> Debonayrly, and nothyng lowde.
> He sayde, 'I prey the, be not wroth.
> I herde the not, to seyn the soth,
> Ne I sawgh the not, syr, trewely.'
> 'A, goode sir, no fors,' quod y,
> 'I am ryght sory yif I have ought
> Destroubled yow out of your thought.
> Foryive me, yif I have mystake.'
> 'Yis, th'amendes is lyght to make,'
> Quod he, 'for ther lyeth noo therto;
> There ys nothyng myssayd nor do.'
>   Loo! how goodly spak thys knyght,
> As hit had be another wyght;
> He made hyt nouther towgh ne queynte.
>
>   (514–31)

Chaucer delightedly points out to his reader the excellence of the Man in Black's manners – and gives us plenty of material to form an equally favourable impression of his own. There is, however, a little more to the exchange than merely formal good manners. The Man in Black is neither 'tough' – brusque or snubbing – nor 'quaint' – that is he does not indulge in over-elaborate politeness. His is a sincere and plain courtesy which fits the Dreamer's sincerity of sympathy.

Finding one who is obviously a great man so 'tretable' (533), the

Dreamer looks for a conversational opening which will take him deeper into the matter:

> Anoon ryght I gan fynde a tale
> To hym, to loke wher I myght ought
> Have more knowynge of hys thought.
> (536–8)

His remark about the hunt (539 f.) gives him the opportunity he wants, and he cautiously and courteously puts forward his proffer of help:

> 'But, sir, oo thyng wol ye here?
> Me thynketh in gret sorowe I yow see.
> But certes, sire, yif that yee
> Wolde ought discure me youre woo,
> I wolde, as wys God helpe me soo,
> Amende hyt, yif I kan or may.
> Ye mowe preve hyt be assay;
> For, by my trouthe, to make yow hool,
> I wol do al my power hool.
> And telleth me of your sorwes smerte;
> Paraunter hyt may ese youre herte,
> That semeth ful sek under your syde.'
> (546–57)

The Dreamer, in fact, offers himself in the therapeutic rôle of sympathetic confidant, and the rest of the poem is a long process by which the Man in Black is at last brought to speak of his sorrow in plain terms. The poem, indeed, does not offer any easy solution to grief – to suggest one would be to insult the mourner's sense of genuine and serious loss. But the promises of healing and renewal in the opening sections are not unfulfilled. We see the mourner progress from a hopeless, solitary and uncontrolled grief which threatens him even with physical dissolution and which is contrary to nature's plan, to a stage at which he can clearly define his loss both to himself and to another person, and so stand back a little from it – a process which necessarily renders emotion more tolerable. Moreover, through his dealings with the Dreamer, he is brought back within the framework of social reference. At the end of the poem his solitary ramble in the wood is over.[36] He returns, just before the Dreamer awakens, homewards to a nearby castle; and, we feel, life is thereby taken up again.

The Dreamer's 'obtuse' comments can thus be seen as gently but firmly forcing the mourner to the full confession which will ease his sick heart. The Man in Black at first takes refuge in the figure of the game of chess with Fortune in which he loses his Queen. The Dreamer argues that a man should not regard the blows of Fortune and that, in any case:

> 'ther is no man alyve her
> Wolde for a fers make this woo!'
> (740–1)

Here Chaucer touches on the theme of the consolation of philosophy, as it is developed, for example, in *Fortune* and *Truth*, and puts before the mourner the example of Socrates:

> 'Remembre yow of Socrates,
> For he ne counted nat thre strees
> Of noght that Fortune koude doo.'
> (717–19)

But here, as in the opening section, where the consolation to be derived from the existence of a natural cycle of change and renewal is only hinted at, the subject is not developed at length; and Chaucer passes on to an elegant and learned list of examples of murder and suicide for grief (725 ff.). As in the passage, derived from Ovid, on the God of Sleep, he offers the attractions, and perhaps the dignity, of Classical poetry and story as a distraction to the mourner, rather than any reasoned argument to overcome grief.

The Dreamer's bluntness in this passage provokes the Man in Black to the admission that his sorrow has to do with a human mistress, not a mere chess piece. The effect of the momentary harshness of the Dreamer's probing is recovered in the brief exchange of courtesies which prefaces the long account of this lady, and of his courtship of her:

'Why so?' quod he, 'hyt ys nat soo.
Thou wost ful lytel what thou menest.
I have lost more than thow wenest.'
'Loo, [sey] how that may be?' quod y;
'Good sir, telle me al hooly
In what wyse, how, why, and wherfore
That ye have thus youre blysse lore.'
'Blythely,' quod he; 'com sytte adoun!
I telle the upon a condicioun
That thou shalt hooly, with al thy wyt,
Doo thyn entent to herkene hit.'
'Yis, syr.' 'Swere thy trouthe therto.'
'Gladly.' 'Do thanne holde herto!'
'I shal ryght blythely, so God me save,
Hooly, with al the wit I have,
Here yow, as wel as I kan.'
'A Goddes half!' quod he, and began.

(742–58)

His narrative continues uninterrupted for some three hundred lines, but the conversational interlude just quoted is long enough, and vivid enough, to keep the two speakers fresh in our minds.

This speech uses, in the main, the style and language of fashionable love poetry as we have seen it in the short poems and in the *Troilus*. The opening provides a good example of this manner:

'Dredeles, I have ever yit
Be tributarye and yiven rente
To Love, hooly with good entente,
And throgh plesaunce become his thral
With good wille, body, hert, and al.
Al this I putte in his servage,
As to my lord, and dide homage;
And ful devoutly I prayed hym to,
He shulde besette myn herte so
That hyt plesance to hym were,
And worship to my lady dere.'

(764–74)

Differences in style in the *Book of the Duchess* have already been discussed. We can now see that these more exalted flights are still carefully integrated into the context of the poem as a whole. This, I think, is achieved in two main ways. The paragraph openings are framed so that the reader is reminded that he is listening to a narrative within a narrative – that is to an account which the Mourner is giving to the Dreamer – for example:

> 'And thilke tyme I ferde ryght so . . .' (785)
> 'Hit happed that I cam on a day . . .' (805)
> 'I sawgh hyr daunce so comlily . . .' (848)

Another type of paragraph opening which also keeps the fact of the conversation before us is the exclamatory one – it is as if the speaker breaks off and starts again with a direct appeal to his hearer:

> 'But which a visage had she thertoo!' (895)
> 'And which a goodly, softe speche . . .' (919)

Again, the use of the formula 'to speak of' has much the same effect:

> 'To speke of godnesse, trewly she . . .' (985)
> 'And trewly, for to speke of trouthe . . .' (999)

Or there is the reminder of the circumstances of the speech:

> 'But wherfore that y telle my tale?' (1034)
> 'But wherfore that I telle thee . . .' (1088)

The paragraph endings are also used to remind us of the situation of speaker and hearer:

> 'And I wol telle sone why soo.' (816)
> 'I wil anoon ryght telle thee why.' (847)

Within the paragraphs, too, the style is not uniformly elevated. There is much that is simple and direct:

'I durste swere, thogh the pope hit songe,
That ther was never yet throgh hir tonge
Man ne woman gretly harmed.'
(929–31)

'Hyt was my swete, ryght as hirselve . . .'
(832)

'Hyt folowed wel she koude good.
She used gladly to do wel.'
(1012–13)

The Man in Black, too, uses exclamations and asseverations – 'I dar swere wel' (924, *cf.* 929, 962, 971, etc.) – and references to his own situation in the past – 'as I have now memoyre' (945); 'I was ryght yong, soth to say' (1090) – all of which combine to give an easy, even colloquial, flow to his speech and to bring it down to the general stylistic level of the poem, in spite of his use of many of the terms of 'thise loveres alle.' 'This', C. S. Lewis said, roundly, 'is the old bad manner'.[37] I would see it rather as a serious, and by no means unsuccessful, attempt to solve a problem of modulation in a poem whose occasion, and whose intimate contact with a particular audience, requires the treatment of material of different kinds in different ways.

The Man in Black dwells on the beauties and virtues of his mistress and the happiness of time past until the Dreamer once more gives him a push towards the easing of the heart which is the object of the confessional (the figure is used in lines 1112–14, where the Dreamer speaks of 'schryfte wythoute repentaunce'). Once again, he speaks with some bluntness:

'Now, goode syre,' quod I thoo,
'Ye han wel told me herebefore,
Hyt ys no nede to reherse it more
How ye sawe hir first, and where.
But wolde ye tel me the manere
To hire which was your firste speche,
Therof I wolde yow beseche;
And how she knewe first your thoght,
Whether ye loved hir or noght.
And telleth me eke what ye have lore,
I herde yow telle herebefore.'
(1126–36)

The Man in Black still winces away from the clear statement of his loss:

> 'Yee!' seyde he, 'thow nost what thow menest;
> I have lost more than thou wenest.'
>
> (1137–8)

and he continues the history of his successful courtship, ending with a description of an ideal union:

> 'Oure hertes wern so evene a payre,
> That never nas that oon contrayre
> To that other, for no woo.
> For sothe, ylyche they suffred thoo
> Oo blysse and eke oo sorwe bothe;
> Yliche they were bothe glad and wrothe;
> Al was us oon, withoute were.
> And thus we lyved ful many a yere
> So wel, I kan nat telle how.'
>
> (1289–97)

The Dreamer now puts the pertinent question, from which there is no ultimate escape:

> 'Sir,' quod I, 'where is she now?'
> (1298)

Even now the Man in Black hesitates for a moment:

> 'Now?' quod he, and stynte anoon.
> Therwith he wax as ded as stoon,
> And seyde, 'Allas that I was bore!
> That was the los that here-before
> I tolde the that I hadde lorn.
> Bethenke how I seyde here-beforn,
> "Thow wost ful lytel what thow menest;
> I have lost more than thow wenest" –
> God wot, allas! ryght that was she!'
>
> (1299–307)

The Dreamer's final question is more an exclamation of sympathetic grief than an enquiry, and it brings, at last, the plain admission which resolves all the tension that has been building up and sends both the 'hert-hunting' and the poem quietly into its final phase:

> 'Allas, sir, how? what may that be?'
> 'She ys ded!' 'Nay!' 'Yis, be my trouthe!'
> 'Is that youre los? Be God, hyt ys routhe!'
> And with that word ryght anoon
> They gan to strake forth; al was doon,
> For that tyme, the hert-hunting.
>
> (1308–13)

The figure of the hunt has shifted its meaning from the dream-Emperor's unsuccessful pursuit of the hart, through the lover's conquest of his lady's heart, to illuminate the real aim of the poem – the restoration to some ease and health of the mourner's sick heart.

The *Book of the Duchess* does not offer any profound solution, either philosophical or religious, to the problem of mortality. Christian consolation, as a matter of fact, is not proposed; and the consolation of philosophy remains a minor theme. What it does provide is an offering from one human being to another, within the strict framework of agreed manners and of an accepted social scale, of sympathetic understanding of an unhappy situation. It also provides a means of return to human contacts, and to life which continues as nature intends it to do, in spite of loss, for one whom the intensity of grief has temporarily cut off. The emphasis on social forms and on the comparative rank of the two speakers is thus by no means inappropriate to the theme of the poem as a whole – and it also arises naturally from the fact that, like most of the shorter poems we have been considering, this work is actually written to meet an existing situation and is addressed to a known person, who stands in an established relation to the poet. Chaucer has made of his poetry a vehicle perfectly adapted to the expression of all these nuances; and, even if parts of the praise of the lady read a little mechanically, the poem lives for its accurate delineation of the relationship within which the two main figures stand, both to each other and to the society which is glimpsed in the background as giving form and meaning to their encounter.

3

New themes in the love vision

The philosophical ideas which were an important part of the material of Chaucer's poetry throughout most of his working life, not only in the short poems, but also in some of his most ambitious works, played, as we have seen, only a peripheral part in the *Book of the Duchess*. In the *Parlement of Foules*, however, this philosophical material is brought into the foreground and is fully deployed in both sections of the poem, in the introductory one based on the *Somnium Scipionis*, and in the vision itself.[1] Yet, there is a great deal more to the *Parlement* than philosophical exposition. In spite of Chaucer's emphasis, at the beginning and end, on his dependence on books and his lack of personal experience – 'al be that I knowe nat Love in dede' (8) – his philosophy of Love and Nature is certainly put to some kind of practical test when it meets the varied reactions of the living birds. His disclaimers, in fact, although they reflect a poem which is weighted on the side of theory against practice, also give ironical point to an ending which decides nothing and in which the voice of the pragmatical duck is challenged, but by no means silenced. The theme of experience *versus* authority, which is so often important for Chaucer, is a major one in this poem.

The *Parlement of Foules*, according to its opening stanzas, is a poem about love as it is experienced in life, as well as described in books:

> The lyf so short, the craft so long to lerne,
> Th'assay so hard, so sharp the conquerynge,
> The dredful joye, alwey that slit so yerne,

> Al this mene I by Love, that my felynge
> Astonyeth with his wonderful werkynge
> So sore, iwis, that whan I on hym thynke,
> Nat wot I wel wher that I flete or synke.
>
> (1–7)

So far life, 'preue', experience. The next stanza turns to 'authority', books:

> For al be that I knowe nat Love in dede,
> Ne wot how that he quiteth folk here hyre,
> Yit happeth me ful ofte in bokes reede
> Of his myrakles and his crewel yre.
> There rede I wel he wol be lord and syre;
> I dar nat seyn, his strokes been so sore,
> But 'God save swich a lord – I can na moore!'
>
> (8–14)

The poet's attitude is one of awe and fascination. We are prepared for a discussion of love seen as a great natural phenomenon, with all the complexity and relentless force of Nature. We are also prepared for something ambiguous and contradictory – the *dredful joye*. It is true that phrases of this kind are a conventional part of the description of profane love – for some poets, no more than a rhetorical trick. Nevertheless, as we shall see, in this poem the contradictory nature of love is something more than a neat turn of phrase. It is one of the main themes. It is, indeed, one of the great themes, always raising questions to be searchingly explored, but never finally answered, which recurs again and again in Chaucer's poetry. It is the question posed by Mars:

> To what fyn made the God that sit so hye,
> Benethen him, love other companye,
> And streyneth folk to love, malgre her hed?
>
> (*Complaint of Mars*, 218–20)

and also by Troilus:

> If love be good, fro whennes cometh my wo?
>
> (I, 407)

Here, in the *Parlement*, the tone is lighter. The poet speaks as an observer, in much the same way as Theseus, who also looks at love with some sympathy, but from the outside:

> 'The God of Love, a *benedicite*!
> How myghty and how greet a lord is he!
> Ayeyns his myght ther gayneth non obstacles.'
>
> (*CT* I, 1785–7)

Through the half-humorous picture of the bewildered reader, helpless in the face of so much complexity, we find ourselves once more in the urbane, undictatorial world of the minor poems. We are not dealing with a poet who professes to offer infallible instruction, whether his reader likes it or not. We are, once again, invited to share the experience and form our own judgement of its meaning, of a poet who quickly modulates from the crisp rhetorical arrangement of his first stanza to the more conversational and diffuse tone of the second, ending in pure colloquialism – 'But "God save swich a lord" – I can na moore!'

The book to which Chaucer now turns for information about the subject is not, to our way of thinking, about love at all; it is, in fact, an encyclopedic volume, a mixture of science and metaphysics, with a strong bias towards cosmology. This is 'Tullyus of the Drem of Scipioun', that is, the sixth book of Cicero's otherwise lost *Republic*, with the famous commentary of Macrobius. It was through this commentary that so much of the peculiar late Latin blend of Platonic and Stoic philosophical material was transmitted to the Middle Ages, together with much which we should call (as does Chaucer) scientific, rather than philosophical in the strict sense. It is, paradoxical as it may seem to the modern reader, precisely because of this blend of science and metaphysics that Chaucer is able to link the book to the poet's proper subject of love.[2] He gives us his reasons. First, 'out of olde bokes' (presumably including this one) 'Cometh al this newe science that men lere'[3] (24–5); and secondly:

> Chapitres sevene it hadde, of hevene and helle
> And erthe, and soules that therinne dwelle.
>
> (32–3)

It is, thus, a book which deals with descriptive cosmology (or, as we should say, provides a model of the universe) and also with the rewards and punishment of human conduct after death. Given that this is its subject matter, how is it possible to say, with Chaucer, 'al this mene I by Love'? The answer is that Macrobius, drawing heavily on the *Timaeus* and on neoplatonic elaborations of its doctrines, describes a system in which a concept of love plays a leading rôle. Furthermore, an important theme of the *Somnium Scipionis* is that of the 'common profit', as the principal aim and justification of human endeavour. As we shall see, even in Cicero's treatment of the idea, it has a link with love; and to a poet familiar with the *Roman de la Rose* as Jean de Meun concluded it, the implications can become even more precise. We could, in fact, see in the *Parlement* a brilliant rehandling of the treatment of Venus and Nature, as we find it at the conclusion of the *Roman de la Rose*, in which an effective variation on the theme is achieved, partly by a bold reorganization of the material so as to lay it out in a quite different pattern, partly by juxtaposing it to the philosophical ideas of Macrobius and Boethius. Chaucer allows these ideas to remain clear-cut by separating them from the main body of the poem; Jean de Meun inserted them as digressions into the speeches of the personifications. In fact, Chaucer attacks the weak point of the love vision: he gives independent existence and life to the matter of its interminable speeches.

The *Somnium Scipionis*, as we have said, is full of descriptive cosmology. But it is also a work with a strong moral bias. It is concerned with the whole duty of man while on earth and, since human existence is not bounded by earth – 'Know thyself first immortal' – with the rewards and punishments which come to man after death. It is this aspect of the book which is brought out in Chaucer's brief summary in lines 36–84. The key phrase, used in lines 47 and 75, is 'commune profyt': those who make this the object of their lives will be rewarded by entry after death into a 'blysful place' in heaven. Those who sin, on the other hand, will be condemned to 'whirle aboute th'erthe alwey in peyne.' The sinners, however, are not merely those who neglect the common profit – Cicero's life of service to the state, as Chaucer must have realized – but those who indulge in lust – 'likerous folk'. By the 'law' that they break (78), Chaucer almost certainly means the law of nature: they indulge their passions unnaturally, or even merely unproductively.[4] They are the victims, in the phrase which he uses of Troilus, and also of Tarquin and the would-be ravisher of Constance, of 'the blinde lust'.[5] This too, is well within the spirit, if not the letter, of Cicero. The reason why Cicero opposes service to the state to self-indulgent passion is that he is thinking in terms of the Stoic good man, whose goodness consists, precisely, in the conquest of all passion.

In giving his good man the reward of stellification in return for his services to the community, Cicero is pursuing a definite line of argument, which is not taken up by Macrobius. This, as we can see from other passages in his writings, relates to the explanation of the gods as originally men, who benefited their fellows and were rewarded with divine status.[6] Macrobius does not comment on this aspect of the idea, but leaves the rewards and punishments of mankind as a loosely attached excursus within the frame of his cosmological survey, where they are juxtaposed to, but not actually incorporated in, the account of the platonic creation, originating in love and sustained by harmony.[7] Chaucer takes over these ideas for his vision of Venus and Nature, but with a difference. The common profit is now linked more directly to love; and, in keeping with the *Roman de la Rose*, it is associated with Nature's task of replenishing the earth and so maintaining the divine order of created beings.

The idea that the creation is brought about by divine love flowing outward from the godhead and that divine perfection necessarily implies the full realization of every possible variety of created being, in unbroken continuity from the highest and most perfect, which are nearest to God, to the lowest and least, which are furthest from him, is certainly present in Macrobius, in a passage like the following one:

Secundum haec ergo cum ex summo Deo mens, ex mente anima sit; anima vero et condat, et vita compleat omnia, qui sequuntur, cunctaque hic unus fulgor illuminet, et in universis appareat, ut in multis speculis per ordinem positis vultus unus, cumque omnia continuis successionibus se sequantur, degenerantia per ordinem ad imum meandi, invenietur praescius intuenti a summo Deo usque ad ultimam rerum faecem una se mutuis vinculis religans, et nusquam interrupta connexio.

(Accordingly, since Mind emanates from the Supreme God and Soul from Mind, and Mind, indeed, forms and suffuses all

71

below with life, and since this is the one splendour lighting
up everything and visible in all, like a countenance reflected
in many mirrors arranged in a row, and since all follow on in
continuous succession, degenerating step by step in their
downward course, the close observer will find that, from the
Supreme God even to the bottommost dregs of the universe there
is one tie, binding at every link, and never broken.)

> (*Somnium* I, xiv; Stahl trans.)

Chaucer never elaborates this idea in precisely this form, but it
is implied in his treatment of a cosmic love descending through all
creation in the *Troilus*, in the proem to Book III and in the *Knight's
Tale*.[8] In the *Parlement*, we have only the suggestion of the 'principle
of plenitude' (to use Lovejoy's phrase) in the description of Nature's
abundantly thronging creatures and in the emphasis on the fulfilment of the command of Genesis to go forth and replenish the earth.
Nature, as a personification of the creative energy, takes the place
of love – or rather expresses that aspect of it which is most closely
linked to the preservation of the species. Chaucer, indeed, gives
us her full significance in a single, economical stanza, which represents a long section of Macrobius's book. Her power, like that of
Venus Cytheria in other contexts,[9] is a cosmic one, which, under
God, whose 'vicaire' she is, extends over the whole created world
of matter.[10] This is, of course, not to depreciate her function of
presiding over the marriages of the lesser creatures, but only to
bring the perpetuation of the individual species into the total,
all-embracing scheme.

> Nature, the vicaire of the almyghty Lord,
> That hot, cold, hevy, lyght, moyst and dreye
> Hath knyt by evene noumbres of acord,
> In esy voys began to speke and seye,
> 'Foules, tak hede of my sentence, I preye,
> And for youre ese, in fortheryng of youre nede,
> As faste as I may speke, I wol me speede.'
>
> (379–85)

The first three lines condense Macrobius; the last four somewhat
modify the augustness of a being on whom the whole fabric of the

world depends, and for these Chaucer draws on another and different tradition.

From Macrobius, to take the first part of the stanza first, Chaucer takes the idea of a creative energy which holds together the opposing elements; and thus continues the theme of the dual nature of love, consisting in both conflict and its resolution, with which the poem began. Macrobius writes of the chain, or bond, of the elements in the following terms:

Deus mundanae molis artifex conditorque mutuatus insolubili inter se vinculo elementa devinxit sicut in Timaeo Platonis assertum est.

(The Creator of the Universe bound the elements together with an unbreakable chain, as was affirmed in Plato's *Timaeus*.)

(I vi)

For Boethius, as for Theseus, the bond is love: 'Haec concordia' (the 'amor' of line 17) 'temperat aequis / Elementa modis' (*de Consolatione*, IV, m. vi, 19–20). For both, God, as Creator, acts directly, without an intermediary. In making Nature the intermediary who actually applies the chain, Chaucer follows most closely the *Roman de la Rose*:

Si gart, tant m'a Deus enouree,
La bele chaiene doree
Qui les quatre elemenz enlace
Trestouz enclins devant ma face.

(Thus I control – God has so greatly honoured me – the fair golden chain which binds the four elements, all of which bow down before my presence.)

(16785–8)

Chaucer's use of these ideas elsewhere, however, shows that, although the framework of the *Parlement*, as a vision of Venus and Nature, requires the emphasis to be placed on the latter at this point, he is well aware of their associations with love. Thus, at the end of Book III of the *Troilus* it is Love 'that of erthe and se hath governaunce', and

So wolde God that auctour is of kynde,
That with his bond Love of his vertu liste
To cerclen hertes alle and faste bynde.

(1765–7)

Here Love and Nature are brought together, and, once more, the basis of this earthly stabilization of conflicting forces is the binding of the elements:

That elementz that ben so discordable
Holden a bond perpetuely durynge.

(1753–4)

The state that Troilus hymns in this song is that tragically temporary one in which the lovers are 'in lust and in quiete' (1819), and his use of this phrase of love, in close proximity to a passage on the chain, suggests yet another source for the enrichment of Chaucer's ideas on the subject. This is the very influential *de Divisione Naturae* of John Scotus Eriugena.[11] Here a chain of Love is described, with particular emphasis on the idea of ascent and descent – an idea which is found in Macrobius, as we shall see, and which is also important in Theseus's speech in the *Knight's Tale*.[12] Eriugena writes:

Amor est connexio ac vinculum quo omnium rerum
universitas ineffabili amicitia insolubili unitate copulatur.

(Love is a bond and chain by which the totality of all things
is bound together in ineffable friendship and indissoluble unity.)

(pp. 210–11)

Of the descent from and ascent into love he says:

Idem in eisdem: 'Age nunc, et has iterum,' hoc est amoris
virtutes, 'in unum congregantes dicamus quia una quidam est
simplex virtus se ipsam movens ad unitivam quandam
temperantiam ex optimo usque existentium novissimum et ab
illo iterum consequenter per omnia usque ad optimum ex se ipsa
et per se ipsam et ad se ipsam se ipsam revolvens et in seipsam
semper eodem modo revoluta.'

74

(The same [author] says in the same [Hymns: Eriugena is
quoting from Ps. Dionysius] 'Come now, and gathering these',
that is the virtues of love, 'again into one, let us say that there
is one simple virtue which moves itself to a unitive mingling
[of all things] from the Best to the lowest of beings, and back
from that through all things in order to the Best again, spinning
itself out from itself, through itself, towards itself and ever
winding itself up again into itself in the same way.'

(pp. 212–13)

A further definition of love, according to Eriugena is,

Amor est naturalis motus omnium rerum quae in motu sunt
finis quietaque statio, ultra quam nullus creaturae progreditur
motus.

(Love is the end and quiet resting place of the natural motion
of all things that are in motion, beyond which no motion of the
creature extends.)

(pp. 210–11)

This, I think, gives Chaucer a phrase he uses in various forms,
again and again, of the realization of the bliss of love[13] – a phrase
which gains poignancy as well as intensity from the fact that he
uses it to refer, not to the ultimate return to the One, but to a moment
which is only part of the temporal progressions of the natural
world and which necessarily shares their transience.

In the *Troilus* and in the *Knight's Tale*, ideas such as these play
a major part. In the *Parlement*, however, they are only present by
implication, as part of the nexus of ideas to which the description of
Nature's power belongs. The most important aspect of love, in the
Parlement, as we have said, is its duality; and, just as it is a force
which can produce opposite results in human life, so that Venus
presides over a temple with pictures of differing import on the opposing walls, even Nature is shown presiding over a world of matter
which contains a fundamental core of conflict. This is the 'quatuor
elementorum concors discordia' of which Alanus writes in his
de Planctu Naturae, Chaucer's other main source for this part of the
poem.[14] In the case of the creatures, Nature brings together the
opposites, male and female. The elements, too, according to Macrobius are kept together in a kind of marriage, since their ordering

depends on the odd and even numbers. These too are 'male' and 'female', and the whole creation depends on their union.[15]

Chaucer follows Macrobius closely in his account of the elemental bond. He correctly names, not the elements themselves, but their attributes, since it is through these that the actual 'knitting' takes place. Macrobius describes this in two different ways, both of which Chaucer combines in his condensed account. First, because each element has two attributes, they can be linked in a kind of circular chain by the quality they have in common, i.e., the attributes hot, cold, moist, dry in Chaucer's list:[16]

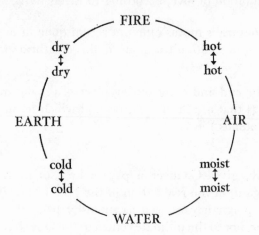

Secondly, there is another arrangement, by which the light is drawn downwards and the heavy forced upwards. This depends on the attributes of weight and lightness, the 'hevy' and 'lyght' of Chaucer's list. In this arrangement three intermediate linking factors are involved and are named 'obedience', 'harmony', and 'necessity' by Macrobius.[17]

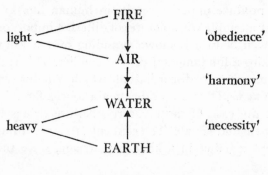

It is, I think, in this second arrangement, rather than in the first, that we have the clue to Chaucer's phrase 'by evene noumbres of accord'. These numbers are 'even' in the sense of 'exact' and are three and four.[18] As Macrobius explains, to join together four things it is necessary to have three intermediate terms. These are the numbers which make possible the realization of tangible and visible matter, as Macrobius learnt from the *Timaeus* and its neo-Platonic commentators.[19] As he reminds us, Cicero had already said of their sum, the number seven: 'qui numerus rerum omnium fere nodus est' (*Somnium* I, vi). It would thus not, I think, be possible for anyone to write of the creative stabilization of the opposing elements in terms of 'even' numbers in the sense of the opposite of odd.

The harmony which nature imposes on the elements, the building bricks of creation, is mirrored through the natural order: in his description of the surroundings of Venus's temple, the same natural landscape in which Nature later holds court, Chaucer twice indicates this. In line 191 the birds sing 'with voys of aungel in here armonye' and in lines 197–200:

> Of instruments of strenges in acord
> Herde I so pleye a ravyshyng swetnesse,
> That God, that makere is of al and lord,
> Ne herde nevere beter, as I gesse.

God, of course, hears the divine harmony of the angels and also the music of the spheres, both dependent on 'evene noumbres'.[20] Finally:

> And whan this werk al brought was to an ende,
> To every foul Nature yaf his make
> By evene acord.
>
> (666–8)

The basic harmony of creation is thus also expressed in Nature's provision for the continuance of the species.

In order to understand in more detail how these ideas are worked out in a vision of Venus and Nature, we need to look at Chaucer's other sources for this latter part of the poem and at the way in which he transforms the material he took over from them. The formative influence on the *Parlement* in this section is the device of the Complaint of Nature, as Chaucer knew it from the *de Planctu Naturae* of Alanus and from the *Roman de la Rose*. It is on this kind of material that the second half of the stanza describing Nature, which we have been discussing, is based.

Nature's complaint is that, alone among her subjects, mankind does not obey her laws. They disrupt her whole fabric by their perversity and sinfulness, instead of carrying out her purpose and helping, through an ordered and reasonable love, to keep the earth filled with good creatures. This is the central theme of Alanus's work. He does not exclude Venus, but he distinguishes between her unfallen state, in which she is an ally of Nature, and her fallen one, in which, as 'blind lust', she assists the perverse and barren loves of sinful mankind.[21] Alanus does not exclude chastity either. There is a place for her among Nature's followers, as well as for marriage: marriage, indeed, is incompatible with virginity, in the strict sense, but not with chastity.[22] In the *Roman*, Venus is drawn into Nature's orbit in a rather different way. She is, emphatically, at war with chastity, and when she is in danger of defeat in her attempt to bring to fruition the love of Amans for the Rose, Nature comes to her rescue; and through her speeches and those of her priest, Genius, Jean de Meun is able to incorporate much of the material of the Complaint of Nature – besides a great deal more.[23] Since, however, his treatment of love is a complex one, the figure of Nature is not as clearcut for him as it is for Alanus. Nature repudiates falsehood and hypocrisy, whom Love had accepted as supporters, and thus makes it clear that she will have nothing to do with the most dubious aspects of the love to which Amans is victim. Nevertheless this love is, as Jean de Meun makes clear from the beginning of his part of the *Roman*, contrary to reason and therefore, even shorn of its worst excesses, not entirely admirable. Nature, accordingly, is made to explain that though she is God's vicar on earth, and therefore, we must assume, a force for good, she has no control whatsoever over man's intelligence; she did not make that part of him to which he will owe eternal life – indeed, she says, none of her creatures are anything but mortal. It is for this reason, to keep death at bay, that she is in alliance with love.[24] It will be clear that Jean de Meun has ingeniously sidestepped the problem of reconciling the love which he satirizes in much of his work with a Nature of whom he clearly approves – as far as she goes. What Nature favours is legitimate sexuality used to perpetuate the species. But she cannot go beyond this. Reason also favours natural love as a part of the world God made, but Reason can, and does, go a good deal further. So, I think, can, and does, Chaucer. Jean de Meun's Nature and Venus together (as that poet was well aware, since such limitations were for him part of the comedy of the misguided Amans) get no further than passion, legitimate or illegitimate. At its worst this is what, as we have said, Chaucer stigmatizes as 'the blinde lust'. At its best, it is a noble thing, but only a part of the complexity of human contacts and human relationships which are included in the concept of love. This, I think, is what emerges from the debate of the birds. The common birds get immediate satisfaction for their uncomplicated impulses, and this is right and good. The more sensitive creatures have to grapple with the problems set them by their more complicated relationships with each other – and it follows that it will be even more true that human beings, with their endowment of a mind which is not the work of Nature, will not be able to solve all their problems by Nature's light, any more than they could do so by Venus's.

Chaucer shows us Venus and Nature in the same beautiful and natural setting, and thus suggests the fundamental link between them. But, within the park full of plants and creatures, Venus is to be found inside an artifact – her temple – described after the manner of the *Teseida*, its immediate surroundings peopled with personifications, not with natural creatures. Within the temple, too, love is, in the main, shown as out of step with Nature. The break with Nature is not, I believe, complete, but the emphasis falls on what is contrary to natural love – that is on jealousy and frustration:

> Withinne the temple, of sykes hoote as fyr
> I herde a swogh that gan aboute renne,
> Whiche sikes were engendered with desyr,
> That maden every auter for to brenne
> Of newe flaume, and wel espyed I thenne
> That al the cause of sorwes that they drye
> Cam of the bittere goddesse Jelosye.
>
> (246–52)

The stories depicted on the temple walls, however, are not all tragic. They are of two kinds, which occupy different positions in the building. Lines 281–7 describe the trophies won from Diana in the war with chastity:

> in dispit of Dyane the chaste,
> Ful many a bowe ibroke heng on the wal
> Of maydenes swiche as gonne here tymes waste
> In hyre servyse.

These conquests are in accord with Nature; just as, in the *Knight's Tale*, Diana's refusal to grant Emely's prayer 'not to ben a wyf and be with childe' is not regarded as tragic. Significantly, too, the maidens were wasting their time. This stanza, however, is counterbalanced by one (287–94) describing loves which were contrary to nature. The first group (except for Hercules) is of unnatural lovers, who indulged in incest.[25] The second, like Hercules, were brought to death by love instead of to fruition. The names from Dido to Troilus, are those of typical heroes and heroines of romantic tales of love. If this is contrary to nature, it is because it is unproductive. The last two names are of criminals in love – Silla, who betrayed her father to gain Minos's love and was repulsed by him in consequence, and the vestal virgin, Rhea, who broke her vows and gave birth to Romulus and Remus. Clearly, since her story is depicted on 'that other side', i.e., on the opposite wall of the temple to that which holds the spoils of Diana, Chaucer regards her in a different light to the conquered nymphs.[26] This division between the spoils of Venus's temple bears out the impression we gain from the mixture of figures, good and bad, pleasant and unpleasant, who guard its approaches:

> Tho was I war of Plesaunce anon-ryght,
> And of Aray, and Lust, and Curteysie,
> And of the Craft that can and hath the myght
> To don by force a wyght to don folye –
> Disfigurat was she, I nyl nat lye;
> And by hymself under an ok, I gesse,
> Saw I Delyt, that stod with Gentilesse.
>
> I saw Beute withouten any atyr,
> And Youthe, ful of game and jolyte;
> Foolhardynesse, Flaterye and Desyr,
> Messagerye, and Meede, and other thre, –
> Here names shul not here be told for me –
>
> (218–29)

This is a temple of human love, with all its advantages and disadvantages. There are the trophies of victories won in the war waged equally by Venus and Nature against a chastity which would deny the world the continuance of its fill of creatures. But there are also all the causes of Nature's complaint against mankind. There are the perverse and unproductive loves which only lead to suffering and death.

Chaucer has here introduced much that is unlike either Alanus or Jean de Meun – in the main, because he is using quite different visual types in the descriptions. In the case of Venus, instead of the allegory of the *Roman*, he borrows the much richer description of the temple from Boccaccio, which, in spite of its abstractions and personifications, is conceived, visually speaking, in fully naturalistic terms. In the case of Nature and her creatures, the result is much the same. Once again consistent allegory is rejected: we have neither the somewhat heated figure of Nature hammering away in her forge, from the *Roman*, nor the device of the figured robe on which all the creatures are depicted, from Alanus. Instead, we have the gracious figure in the beautiful landscape, which impressed Spenser, surrounded by the jostling, living, highly individualistic birds, who can, and do, speak for themselves. Moreover, Chaucer makes another important change when he removes the actual material of complaint from Nature's speeches to the world around her, where it is enacted, in a detailed way, in Venus's temple and, by implication, in the only partially successful love story of the noble birds. A tranquil, confident Nature is both better suited to Chaucer's purpose of avoiding too clearcut answers to the problems he poses and a more effective goddess.

The serenity and, as it were, broad daylight, of Nature is, indeed, in obvious contrast to the sighs and semi-darkness of Venus's temple – but we must remember, before we overemphasize the contrast, that Peace was Venus's doorkeeper and that, when even Nature encounters some difficulty with her more complex creatures, it is their refusal to enter into relations with Venus and her son which causes the trouble:

'I wol nat serve Venus ne Cupide,
Forsothe as yit,'

(652–3)

says the Formel Eagle. Like Emely, however, the implication is that she will submit to Nature's law after her year's respite and will turn voluntarily from the service of Diana to the service of Venus.[27] The relation, in fact, between Nature and Venus is both close and beneficial, although the perversity of the human will can make a sorry place of Venus's temple and, at the same time, invalidate Nature's plan.

Nature, as we have said, is seen in full daylight and open air:

> Tho was I war wher that ther sat a queene
> That, as of lyght the somer sonne shene
> Passeth the sterre, right so ever mesure
> She fayrer was than any creature.
>
> And in a launde, upon an hil of floures,
> Was set this noble goddesse Nature.
> Of braunches were here halles and here boures
> Iwrought after here cast and here mesure.
>
> (298–305)

But, and the fact is important, this is part of the same landscape in which Venus's temple stands – the landscape to which the Dreamer came when he first entered the gate and to which he now, again, refers:

> Whan I was come ayeyn into the place
> That I of spak, that was so sote and grene . . .
>
> (295–6)

The significance of the gate with its two inscriptions now becomes clearer. Like the opposing walls of Venus's temple, this gate has inscriptions on its opposite sides of different import,[28] again, set out in two counterbalancing stanzas, so ordered as to lend great importance to the subject matter, through the vigour and beauty of the first, and the telling image of the dry tree and gasping fish in the second:

> 'Thorgh me men gon into that blysful place
> Of hertes hele and dedly woundes cure;
> Thorgh me men gon unto the welle of grace,
> There grene and lusty May shal evere endure,
> This is the wey to al good aventure.

82

Be glad, thow redere, and thy sorwe of-caste;
Al open am I – passe in, and sped thee faste!'

'Thorgh me men gon,' than spak that other side,
'Unto the mortal strokes of the spere
Of which Disdayn and Daunger is the gyde,
Ther nevere tre shal fruyt ne leves bere.
This strem yow ledeth to the sorweful were
There as the fish in prysoun is al drye;
Th'eschewing is only the remedye!'

(134–47)

In fact, the two contradictory aspects of love are to be found in the same place and reached through the same gate. Those who pass through it will have both inscriptions to reckon with, and it is not surprising that the Dreamer is left like a piece of iron between two equal magnets (148–9). This state of conflict is further emphasized by the metaphor Africanus uses to encourage him. Even if a man does not take an active part, he likes 'at the wrastlyng for to be' (165). We therefore arrive at a picture in which Venus, unaided by Nature, lends herself to all the perversities and self-inflicted torments of which humanity is capable, but in which she still remains an essential part of Nature's plan for the perpetuation of the species. Both Venus and Nature are thus, in their different ways, involved in the irreducible core of conflict which underlies the material fabric of the universe; while at the same time, both are also the personifications of the energies which force strife into harmony. By replacing the moral-political theme of Cicero's book (with which, indeed, Macrobius does not have much to do) by a 'common profit' which concerns the maintenance of creation through the continuity of the species, Chaucer has been able to bring ideas which Jean de Meun often leaves as openly digressive to bear closely on his main theme of the duality of love.

Chaucer, in fact, like Nature, knits the elements of his poem in a firm bond; but, also like Nature, he does more than this – and a good deal more than Jean de Meun – and preserves their harmonious relationship to each other and the whole. Philosophizing does not mean exhaustive exposition at disproportionate length. Ideas which take up several pages of Macrobius's book are firmly but lightly sketched in a couple of lines. The reader is given the theme of common profit in the first part and he is left to work out its application to the second for himself. Nature is not left at comparative peace in the world of the elements, but is placed on her mound among a troop of birds who are noisy, rude and contentious, as well as capable of expressing the loftiest sentiments. Appropriately enough, it is the noisy, rude ones who are most easily brought to fulfil her laws, and the idealists who threaten trouble. From Nature's point of view the duck is in the right of it:

> 'Wel bourded,' quod the doke, 'by myn hat!
> That men shulde loven alwey causeles,
> Who can a resoun fynde or wit in that?
> Daunseth he murye that is myrtheles?
> Who shulde recche of that is recheles?
> Ye quek!' yit seyde the doke, ful wel and fayre,
> 'There been mo sterres, God wot, than a payre!'
> (589–95)

From the point of view of maximum fecundity, this is, indeed, spoken 'ful wel and fayre', and the retort of the gentil tercelet:

> 'Thy kynde is of so low a wrechednesse
> That what love is, thow canst nat seen ne gesse',
> (601–2)

is fraught with danger, although it also indicates the possibility of a richer experience. Mankind, in fact, for whose dilemmas the noble birds stand, is left to grapple with the problems set them by an endowment which is not wholly Nature's and which, while it places heaven or hell within their reach, makes the simple happiness of the duck difficult to achieve. It is true that the human situation is only lightly touched on in the *Parlement*. We have to wait for the *Troilus*, and for the treatment of the problems of love and marriage in all their variety in the *Canterbury Tales*, to learn how perceptively Chaucer could explore the subject and how complete was his awareness of the interest and importance of the variation which the human factor introduces into philosophical schemata.

Nature, at any rate, once more like the poet, does not dogmatize. She treats her more complex and wayward creatures sympathetically; and we are left with the impression that, although her law

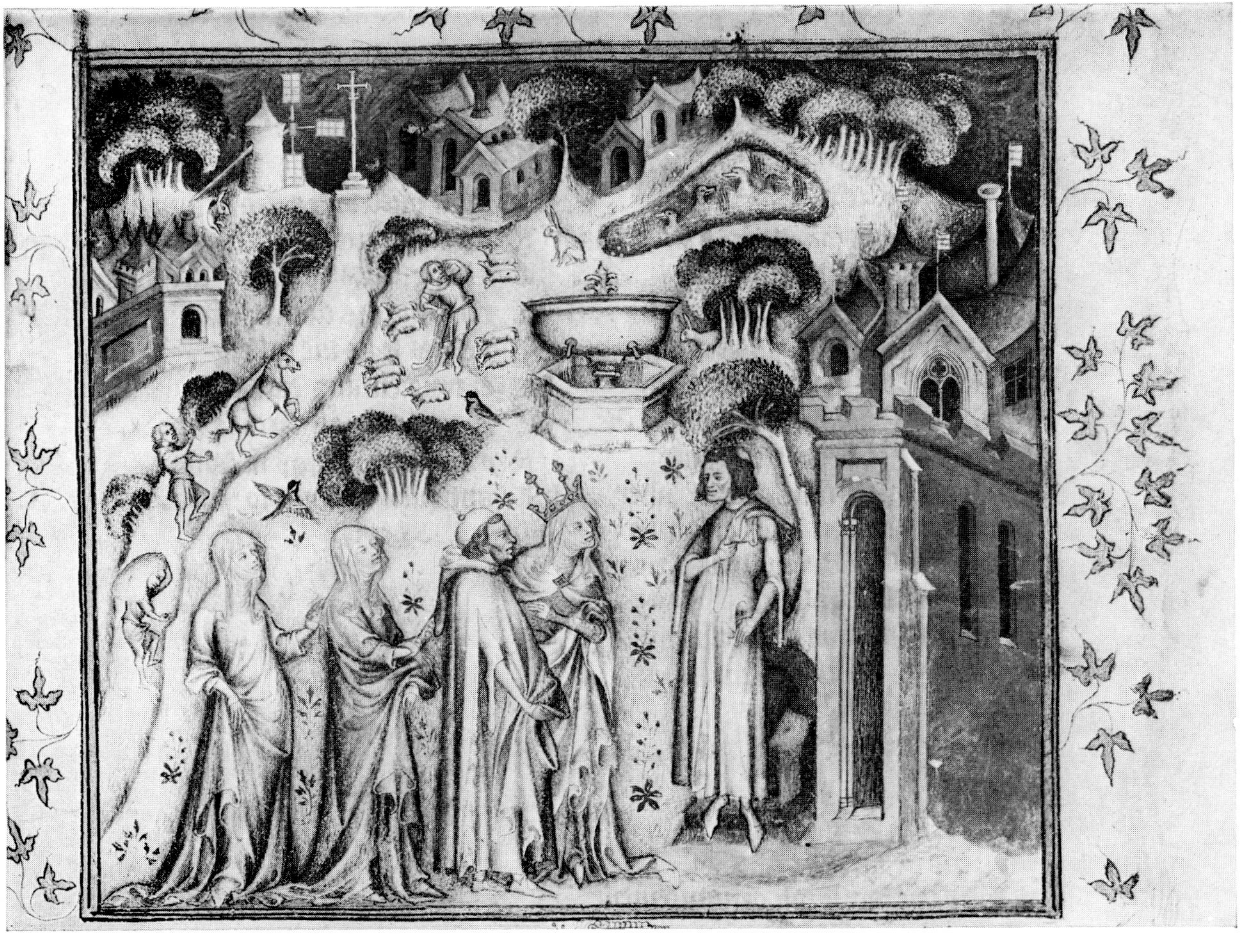

I Nature presents *Sens*, Music and Rhetoric to the Poet

II   The Gods at the Fall of Troy

of fecundity must triumph in the end, chastity properly precedes
fulfilment and is not incompatible with it. The conclusion of the
debate, however, remains a matter of impression. The poet does not
commit himself:

> I wok, and othere bokes tok me to,
> To reede upon, and yit I rede alwey.
> I hope, ywis, to rede so som day
> That I shal mete som thyng for to fare
> The bet, and thus to rede I nyl nat spare
>
> (695–9)

A clearcut solution is indeed impossible because, just at the point
when it seems about to become most abstract and definitive in its
philosophizing, with the description of Nature, the poem un-
expectedly explodes into a richness of life and movement which
make abstract theorizing irrelevant. The noise of the birds effectively
drowns any possible theoretical solution to the poet's problem, as
he posed it in his opening stanza, and it is only on reflection that we
realize how much light has been thrown on the themes, so casually
suggested in the first section, of contradictory love and common
profit.

When Africanus introduces the dreaming Chaucer into the park
which contains the temples of Venus and Nature, his purpose in
doing so is tersely expressed:

> 'I shal the shewe mater of to wryte'
>
> (168)

The matter turns out to be the application of the scientific and moral-
philosophical ideas of Macrobius and Boethius to love in its various
aspects. In the *House of Fame*, the poet's guide, now Jove's eagle, has
the same preoccupation. It proposes to extend the material available
to a poet who:

> 'hast no tydynges
> Of Loves folk yf they be glade,
> Ne of oght elles that God made.'
>
> (644–6)

This might lead us to expect an encyclopedic journeying among the wonders of creation – a popular form with which Chaucer was perfectly familiar. On the contrary, however, although the eagle does show Chaucer some natural phenomena of a marvellous kind in the course of his flight, the poet shows little interest in them:

'No fors,' quod y, 'hyt is no nede.
I leve as wel, so God me spede,
Hem that write of this matere.'
(1011–13)

Books provide all the poet needs, so far as matter of this kind is concerned, as the *Parlement* demonstrates – and indeed, as Chaucer remarks, when it comes to the observation of 'ayerissh bestes', only thought, 'wyth fetheres of Philosophye', can fly high enough to contemplate them. The destination of the flight is, in fact, a specific one – the House of the goddess Fame; and its relevance to the eagle's purpose of giving the poet material to write about is soon made obvious. The renown of the most famous of all the heroes of old, Alexander and Hercules, is upheld by the goddess herself; but, apart from these, it is the writers and poets who 'bear up' the fame of peoples and places. In fact, for Chaucer, fame means primarily the reputation assigned to persons, races, or cities by written tradition. It is, therefore, very much the affair of an ambitious working poet. What he learns from it and from the contemplation of the house of the even more capricious Rumour is, characteristically, left for the reader to decide. It is not the result of the search for specific 'tidings' which is important, but the ideas which are explored on the way.

In the *Parlement*, the different blocks of material which are juxtaposed and examined in relation, or contrast, to each other are distinguished by differences in style and technique – the texture of the poetry is not the same in the opening section, in the description of Venus's temple or in the dialogue of the birds. These differences in texture are, of course, as much a part of the exposition as the structural organization of the material. By the differences in the language used, we are made to experience the difference in viewpoint between, say, the duck and the unhappy lovers of Venus's temple in a more direct way than would otherwise be possible. In the *House of Fame*, Chaucer uses the same method, but to a quite unprecedented degree, so that not only is the surface variety very much greater than that of the *Parlement*, but it would be hard to find a poem to set beside it for sheer technical brilliance. It is as though the theme of the complexity of Fame – who is, on the one hand, responsible for all the beauty, grandeur and importance of poetry, and on the other, absurdly capricious, untruthful and ultimately based only on the even more absurd and trivial Rumour – has been woven so closely through the whole surface of the poem that there is hardly a line, and certainly not a paragraph, which does not faithfully reflect it.

To speak so decidedly about the theme of the poem, however, is perhaps to anticipate, since critics are by no means agreed about it.[29] My view will, I hope, be sufficiently supported by what follows, but first more must be said about the technical virtuosity with which the poet presents his ambiguous subject-matter. A good starting point will be the first appearance of the Eagle – a figure, like Fame herself, part majestic, part grotesque – which forms the close of Book I and the opening of Book II.

At the end of Book I, Chaucer has just finished his résumé of the *Aeneid*, a long set piece in a serious style, with the interest centering on the story of Dido's unhappy passion.[30] No contemporary reader would be likely to question the importance and interest of this material, although its relevance to the main themes of the poem only gradually emerges.[31] After this impressive interlude, one might think that the poet would be hard put to it to end the book in a sufficiently striking way. Chaucer solves this problem by using material which would form the natural opening of the next book, that is, he introduces the figure which is to be the guide to the events of the next section:

> Thoo was I war, lo! at the laste,
> That faste be the sonne, as hye
> As kenne myghte I with myn yë,
> Me thoughte I sawgh an egle sore,
> But that hit semed moche more
> Then I had any egle seyn.
> But this as sooth as deth, certeyn,
> Hyt was of gold, and shon so bryghte
> That never sawe men such a syghte,
> But yf the heven had ywonne
> Al newe of gold another sonne;
> So shone the egles fethers bryghte,
> And somwhat dounward gan hyt lyghte.
>
> (496–508)

In spite of a certain sparseness in diction and rhythm, this is a description in the grand style, and its magnificent hyperbole of the heaven's new golden sun forms a fitting end to the book, not out of keeping with the splendours of the *Aeneid*. In fact, we are already in the presence of 'the beaute and the wonder' which is never far off in the *House of Fame*, even though it is often closely jostled by the grotesque and the trivial,[32] and which wrings from a highly critical poet the heartfelt tribute:

> 'O God!' quod y, 'that made Adam,
> Moche ys thy myght and thy noblesse!'
>
> (970–1)

After the interruption of the short proem, Chaucer takes up the description in Book II where he left it, using it to open the next narrative section. But now he treats it rather differently. After the first few lines, he leaves the purely pictorial aspect alone and concentrates on conveying a complicated impression of speed in movement, as the bird of prey stoops, gathers up its victim while still in flight and soars again, without a check:

> This egle, of which I have yow told,
> That shon with fethres as of gold,
> Which that so hye gan to sore,
> I gan beholde more and more,
> To se the beaute and the wonder;
> But never was ther dynt of thonder,
> Ne that thyng that men calle fouder,
> That smot somtyme a tour to powder,
> And in his swifte comynge brende,
> That so swithe gan descende
> As this foul, when hyt beheld
> That I a-roume was in the feld;
> And with hys grymme pawes stronge,
> Withyn hys sharpe nayles longe,
> Me, fleynge, in a swap he hente,
> And with hys sours ayen up wente,
> Me caryinge in his clawes starke
> As lyghtly as I were a larke,
> How high, I can not telle yow,
> For I cam up, y nyste how.
>
> (529–48)

We are still within the bounds of the grand style here – or, at any rate of the grand style as Chaucer found it in Dante – but we are to modulate, almost at once, into something different. Chaucer, like Dante in similar circumstances, is faint and afraid:

> For so astonyed and asweved
> Was every vertu in my heved,
> What with his sours and with my drede,
> That al my felynge gan to dede;
> For-whi hit was to gret affray.
>
> (549–53)

So far, although the description does not depend slavishly on the corresponding one in Dante's *Purgatorio* (indeed, most of the best things in it are new), there is nothing in the style or mood which is inconsistent with the seriousness which Dante maintains throughout his poem. His description runs thus:

> in sogno mi parea veder sospesa
>   un' aguglia nel ciel con penne d'oro,
>   con l'ali aperte ed a calare intesa;
> ed esser mi parea là dove foro
>   abbandonati i suoi da Ganimede,
>   quando fu ratto al sommo consistoro.
> Fra me pensava: 'Forse questa fiede
>   pur qui per uso, e forse d'altro loco
>   disdegna di portarne suso in piede.'
> Poi mi parea che, poi rotata un poco,
>   terribil come folgor discendesse,
>   a me rapisse suso infino al foco.
> Ivi parea che ella e io ardesse;
>   e sì lo 'ncendio imaginato cosse,
>   che convenne che 'l sonno si rompesse.
> Non altrimenti Achille si riscosse,
>   li occhi svegliati rivolgendo in giro
>   e non sappiendo là dove si fosse,
> quando la madre da Chirone a Schiro
>   trafuggò lui dormendo in le sue braccia,

89

là onde poi li Greci il dipartiro;
che mi scoss' io, sì come dalla faccia
  mi fuggì 'l sonno, e diventa' ismorto
  come fa l' uom che, spaventato, agghiaccia.

(I seemed in a dream to see above me stoop
  An eagle of golden plumage in the sky
  With wings strecht wide out and intent to swoop.
He seemed above the very place to fly
  Where Ganymede was forced his mates to lose
  When he was snatcht up to the assembly on high.
Within me I thought: Perhaps only because
  Of habit he strikes here, and from elsewhere
  Scorneth to carry up aught in his claws.
Then, having seemed to wheel a little, sheer
  Down he came, terrible as the lightning's lash,
  And snatcht me up as far as the fiery sphere.
Then he and I, it seemed, burnt in the flash,
  And I so scorched at the imagined blaze
  That needs must sleep be broken as with a crash.
Not otherwise Achilles in amaze,
  Not knowing whither he was come, did start
  and all around him turn his wakened gaze
When Scyros-wards from Chiron, next her heart,
  His mother bore him sleeping, to alight
  There where the Greeks compelled him to depart,
Than I now started as sleep fled me quite
  And my face turned to death-pale suddenly,
  Even as a man who freezes from affright.)
                    (*Purgatorio* IX, 19–42; Binyon trans.)

Chaucer rejects the Classical similes, but what he does imitate
from Dante, with great success, is the perfect control of the movement
of the verse, in imitation of the movement of the bird in flight. The
total effect, however, without the Classical allusions, is lighter, and
the development is more rapid. We are carried along at a pace which
makes easy the transition into a kind of writing which would be
inconceivable in Dante's poem. When the eagle calls on the Dreamer
of the *House of Fame* to awake, his first dazed reaction reminds us of
Chaucer the dubiously successful lover – a person who could not

appropriately be compared to Ganymede or Achilles (as he ruefully points out in line 589):

> And, for I shulde the bet abreyde,
> Me mette, 'Awak,' to me he seyde,
> Ryght in the same vois and stevene
> That useth oon I koude nevene;
> And with that vois, soth for to seyn,
> My mynde cam to me ageyn,
> For hyt was goodly seyd to me,
> So nas hyt never wont to be.
>
> (559–66)

With these lines, we find ourselves in a familiar, everyday world, in which it comes as no surprise when the eagle, for all its miraculous beauty, speaks with a familiar voice and is preoccupied with the difficulty of testing the pulse of a wriggling burden while in full flight:

> 'Seynte Marye!
> Thou art noyous for to carye,
> And nothyng nedeth it, pardee!
> For, also wis God helpe me,
> As thou noon harm shalt have of this;
> And this caas that betyd the is,
> Is for thy lore and for thy prow; –
> Let see! darst thou yet loke now?
> Be ful assured, boldely,
> I am thy frend.' And therwith I
> Gan for to wondren in my mynde.
> 'O God,' thoughte I, 'that madest kynde,
> Shal I noon other weyes dye?
> Wher Joves wol me stellyfye
> Or what thing may this sygnifye?'
>
> (573–87)

Whatever our view of Chaucer's purpose in this transition from the sublime to the broadly comic, we cannot but admire the ease and sureness of touch with which he makes it.

Contrasts of this kind, swift passages from the grand to the trivial, the sublime to the comic, and vice versa, are such a constant feature of this poem that we must regard them as a deliberate part of the poet's method. In, for example, the formal proems and invocations (surely in themselves a sign of ambitious craftsmanship) with which the books begin, we find the same jostling together of the apparently incongruous. The proem to Book II begins humbly with an imitation of the characteristic jingle of popular English romance:

> Now herkeneth, every maner man
> That Englissh understonde kan,
> And listeneth of my drem to lere.
> For now at erste shul ye here
> So sely an avisyon,
> That Isaye, ne Scipion,
> Ne kyng Nabugodonosor,
> Pharoo, Turnus, ne Elcanor,
> Ne mette such a drem as this!

Already, with the mention of famous dreamers, the jingling line has levelled out into the normal non-committal four-stress couplet which we have seen Chaucer using to good effect in transition passages in the *Book of the Duchess*. In the second half of the Prologue, however, it changes again, and the rhythm, with its calculated shifts of the pause in the line, gains a cumulative force which is quite unlike anything that has gone before:

> Now faire blisfull, O Cipris,
> So be my favour at this tyme!
> And ye, me to endite and ryme
> Helpeth, that on Parnaso duelle,
> Be Elicon, the clere welle.
> O Thought, that wrot al that I mette,
> And in the tresorye hyt shette
> Of my brayn, now shal men se
> Yf any vertu in the be,
> To tellen al my drem aryght.
> Now kythe thyn engyn and myght.
>   (518–28)

Surely an arrogant ending for a rhymer who started so diffidently with something very like the 'rym dogerel' of *Sir Thopas*.

In the *Purgatorio*, after the description of the eagle, Dante addresses his reader and warns him that, as his matter becomes increasingly sublime, so his art must grow more exalted:

> Lettor, tu vedi ben com' io innalzo,
> la mia matera, e però con più arte
> non ti maravigliar s'io la rincalzo.
> (IX, 70–2)

It is as if Chaucer is determined to show not only the same discrimination in fitting the style to the subject matter, but also his ability to shift rapidly fron one level to another in such a way that his verse accurately mirrors each alteration in content. In the *House of Fame*, where poetry itself, according to his definition of Fame, is one of the main themes, we can see stylistic innovation – the bending, stretching, as it were elasticizing of the English poetic language – going on, if not quite for its own sake, at least as a major part of the brilliant display which is the poem's *raison d'être*. Whereas in the *Troilus*, for example, the juxtapositions and shifts of style – from the colloquialism of Pandarus to the deliberately conventionalized lover's plaints of Troilus or the grand style of the proems – all arise from the actual requirements of the story at a given point, in the *House of Fame* such changes (one or two obvious cases apart) reflect the shifting, ambiguous nature of the subject matter, which can best be handled by one who can run the whole gamut from 'drasty' rhyming to the 'rethorike sweete' of the great Italians. That this shifting style is the result of deliberate policy on the poet's part (if we were tempted to doubt it)[33] is shown by the Invocation which opens the third book, where, in a magnificent line, Apollo – 'O God of science and of lyght' – is called upon to guide the 'lytel laste bok', in spite of the fact that the 'rym ys lyght and lewed'. Here, it is true, Chaucer seems to distinguish between the form and subject-matter, since he adds:

> I do no diligence
> To shewe craft, but o sentence.
> (1099–100)

The closing lines of the invocation, however, show that we need not take this too seriously, since they refer to his total plan for form and content in this section:

And yif, divyne vertu thow
Wilt helpe me to shewe now
That in myn hed ymarked ys –
Loo, that is for to menen this,
The Hous of Fame for to descryve –
Thou shalt se me go as blyve
Unto the nexte laure y see,
And kysse yt, for hyt is thy tree.
Now entre in my brest anoon!

(1101–9)

Indeed, it is hardly likely that Chaucer would invoke the god of poetry without reference to 'art poetical', however modest his disclaimers. He could, no doubt, rely on his audience to share the joke of so noted a poet pretending to lack professional skill.

The figure of the goddess Fame is at the heart of the complexities of the poem, and in describing her rapid shifts of shape and mood Chaucer exploits to the full the stylistic variety which he has established in the earlier part. His initial description of 'this ilke noble quene' is a brilliant tour de force; in it the emphasis is on the wonder as well as the beauty of the strange figure, and also on the sheer dimension (little and great), number, or superlativeness of all her characteristics and associations:

Y saugh, perpetually ystalled,
A femynyne creature,
That never formed by Nature
Nas such another thing yseye.
For alther-first, soth for to seye,
Me thoughte that she was so lyte
That the lengthe of a cubite
Was lengere than she semed be.
But thus sone, in a whyle, she
Hir tho so wonderliche streighte
That with hir fet she erthe reighte,
And with hir hed she touched hevene,
Ther as shynen sterres sevene.
And therto eke, as to my wit,
I saugh a gretter wonder yit,

94

Upon her eyen to beholde;
But certeyn y hem never tolde.
For as feele eyen hadde she
As fetheres upon foules be,
Or weren on the bestes foure
That Goddis trone gunne honoure,
As John writ in th' Apocalips.
Hir heer, that oundy was and crips,
As burned gold hyt shoon to see;
And, soth to tellen, also she
Had also fele upstondyng eres
And tonges, as on bestes heres;
And on hir fet woxen saugh y
Partriches wynges redely.
    But, Lord! the perry and the richesse
I saugh sittyng on this godesse!
And, Lord! the hevenyssh melodye
Of songes, ful of armonye,
I herde aboute her trone ysonge,
That al the paleys-walles ronge!
So song the myghty Muse, she
That cleped ys Caliope,
And hir eighte sustren eke,
That in hir face semen meke;
And ever mo, eternally,
They songe of Fame, as thoo herd y:
'Heryed be thou and thy name,
Goddesse of Renoun or of Fame!'

(1364–1406)

I have quoted this description at length because it is not only at the
heart of the method of the poem but also of the matter. Among other
things, Chaucer uses it to make two vital points: that, for him,
Fame = Renown and does not have the Classical Latin sense of which
he must have been perfectly well aware, and, secondly, that it is the
Muses who sing eternal acclamations to Fame. The meaning of
Renown, in fact, is more closely defined as the reputation handed
down to posterity through written records and through the arts.[34]

In his further handling of the goddess, Chaucer explores the
question of the relationship of this recorded reputation to actual

fact – to the real persons and events that it purports to describe. The result, for one who has been brought up to prefer other poets to Homer because Homer was a liar, is disquieting.[35] Fame, it appears, is a sister of Fortune (1547), and equally capricious. His first encounter with her method of treating her suitors leaves the poet wondering:

> They gonne doun on kneës falle
> Before this ilke noble quene,
> And seyde, 'Graunte us, Lady shene,
> Ech of us of thy grace a bone!'
> And somme of hem she graunted sone,
> And somme she werned wel and faire,
> And some she graunted the contraire
> Of her axyng outterly.
> But thus I seye yow, trewely,
> What her cause was, y nyste.
> For of this folk ful wel y wiste,
> They hadde good fame ech deserved
> Although they were dyversly served.
>
> (1534–46)

Moreover, this 'ilke noble quene', like the eagle, which was so impressive seen at a distance and which spoke with such a familiar voice close to, proves capable of as colloquial a turn of speech as any low-life character in the *Canterbury Tales*. In fact, she scolds like a fishwife:

> 'Fy on yow,' quod she, 'everychon!
> Ye masty swyn, ye ydel wrechches!
> Ful of roten, slowe techches!
> What? False theves! wher ye wolde
> Be famous good, and nothing nolde
> Deserve why, ne never ye roughte?
> Men rather yow to hangen oughte!
> For ye be lyke the sweynte cat
> That wolde have fissh: but wostow what?
> He wolde nothing wete his clowes.
> Yvel thrift come to your jowes,
> And eke to myn, if I hit graunte,
> Or do yow favour, yow to avaunte!'
>
> (1776–88)

It is easy enough to follow the tracks of Chaucer's reading through
the learned fluency of his initial description of Fame. It is not so easy
to detect his models in a passage like the one just quoted. There is,
however, a curious resemblance in the choppy rhythm and the
energetic relish in vituperation between Fame's diatribe and the
style of an earlier English romance – the *Lay of Havelok the Dane*:[36]

> Bernard stirt up, þat was ful big . . .
> Lep to þe dore, so he wore wode,
> And seyde, 'Hwat are ye, þat are theroute,
> þat þus biginnen forto stroute?
> Go henne swiþe, fule þeues,
> For bi þe Louerd þat man on leues,
> Shol ich casten þe dore open,
> Sum of you shal ich drepen,
> And þe oþre shal ich kesten
> In feteres, and ful faste festen!'
> 'Hwat haue ye seid?' quoth a ladde,
> 'Wenestu þat we ben adradde?
> We sholen at þis dore gonge,
> Maugre þin, carl, or ouht longe.'
>
> (*Havelok*, 1774–89)

Comparisons between the vigorous, thrusting style of parts of the
House of Fame and *Havelok* could be multiplied; but, even if Chaucer
did not know its energetic rhythms and vocabulary, and its somewhat
unusual ability to sustain an effect through a long passage, he would
have found in earlier English romances plenty of short passages, lines
and turns of phrase, to serve as a basis and to give the general sound
and ring of Fame's tirades. To give one brief example, the pattern of
the opening of her speech is found in these vigorous lines of *Kyng
Alisaunder*:

> 'Fitz a puteyne!' he seide, 'lecchoure!
> Thou schalt sterue so a tretour!'
>
> (B, 3912–13)

This matter is, perhaps, worth a moment's pause, because Chaucer's
avowed preoccupation with the technique of poetry is so great in the
House of Fame – and, as we shall see, he by no means excludes the

humbler vernacular practitioners from her presence. We have already seen his exploitation of the familiar commonplace of the English romance jingle in the proem to Book II. It is at any rate worth conjecturing (as we have already done in chapter 1) that he may have deliberately drawn on such technical achievements as his English predecessors could offer him, and that an important part of his preoccupation in this poem may have been how, from the 'grant translateur', to become, with equal greatness, the poet of 'every maner man / That Englissh understonde kan'. In the development of such a poet, a moment must certainly come when the fact has to be faced that for all the help afforded by the sophisticated poets of France and Italy, his particular medium is, for better or worse, his own language, with its own traditions and its own genius. In Chaucer's case, since the earlier English tradition was not one of exalted writing, but rather of a plain, vigorous style, the question would be how far its achievements could be incorporated in a wider stylistic range which also utilized the more varied achievements of the modern French and Italian poets, as well as that of the Classical ones. In the *House of Fame*, Chaucer seems to be still at the experimental stage. It is not so much a question of producing a homogeneous blend of different styles and techniques, but rather of exploiting first one and then another as it is appropriate to the subject-matter. The result may, at times, seem harsh, and the transitions abrupt, but in the case of Fame herself, it is fitting that the shifty, delusive goddess, so zestfully compounded out of a string of learned literary allusions, should, with equal zest, speak with such an unmistakably English accent.

The pinnacles of Fame's house are set with 'habitacles', each containing figures:

> Of alle maner of mynstralles,
> And gestiours, that tellen tales
> Both of wepinge and of game,
> Of al that longeth unto Fame.
> (1197–200)

The idea of recorded Fame, in fact, is stretched to cover poetry of all kinds. The same inclusiveness is shown when the musicians are described. The list starts with Orpheus, but we soon hear of the 'smale harpers with her glëes', who:

> Sate under hem in dyvers seës,
> And gunne on hem upward to gape,
> And countrefete hem as an ape,
> Or as craft countrefeteth kynde.
>
> (1210–13)

Nevertheless, these 'small' practitioners are just as much a part of the external adornment of Fame's House as the great ones, and the same is true of the musicians:

> Tho saugh I stonden hem behynde,
> Afer fro hem, al be hemselve,
> Many thousand tymes twelve,
> That maden lowde mynstralcies
> In cornemuse and shalemyes,
> And many other maner pipe,
> That craftely begunne to pipe,
> Bothe in doucet and in rede,
> That ben at festes with the brede;
> And many flowte and liltyng horn,
> And pipes made of grene corn,
> As han thise lytel herde-gromes,
> That kepen bestis in the bromes.
>
> (1214–26)

It is, no doubt, largely because they caught Spenser's eye that these last lines seem to us representative of a manner that is peculiarly English. But there is also no doubt that they reproduce a lilt that is to be found in earlier English romances which use the four-stress couplet and which like to interpose a lyrical movement in the more straightforward narrative progression. *Kyng Alisaunder*,[37] for example, has:

> Mery is the blast of the styuoure;
> Mery is the touchyng of the harpoure.
> Swete is the smellyng of the floure;
> Swete it is in maydens boure.
> Appel swete bereth fair coloure;
> Of trewe loue is swete amoure.
>
> (B, 2567–72)

Another romance which Chaucer certainly knew, and from which he elsewhere borrows,[38] has:

> Kniȝtes and leuedis com daunceing
> In queynt atire, gisely
> Queynt pas and softly;
> Tabours and trunpes ȝede hem bi,
> And al maner menstraci.
>
> (*Sir Orfeo*, 298–302)

With this lyrical insertion in the *House of Fame*, in the manner of romances such as these, Chaucer, it seems to me, is at once utilizing something he found as a part of an earlier poetic style and laying a foundation for much that was to come.

Chaucer, it is clear, thought of the 'little' poets and musicians as operating in and with the vernacular – not only, of course, in English. Apart from 'the Bret Glascurion', there are 'Pipers of the Duche tonge' (1234), and the minstrels of Spain. Even inside the House, although the positions of dignity on the pillars are given to the great authors of the past who wrote in Greek or Latin,[39] still:

> The halle was al ful, ywys,
> Of hem that writen olde gestes,
> As ben on treës rokes nestes.
>
> (1514–16)

All this emphasizes the connection of Fame with poetry; and, just as Fame herself gives no guarantee of the ultimate truth or importance of the event she helps to preserve in memory, so the poets are of all sorts and sizes. The trivial is not excluded either from the matter or the makers.

The *House of Fame* thus has a great deal to say which bears directly on the subject of poetry and art poetical. It remains to ask how far, and in what forms, this theme is consistently developed through the poem. If we look at the ground-plan of the work, we can, I think, see that, for all the surface elaboration, it is designed to set out one main theme in a fairly straightforward way. Chaucer, as a matter of fact, with the kind of economy of effort which is not rare in poets, uses the same basic plan for much the same basic purpose in all three of his love visions, although this is a little obscured by the very striking differences between them in other respects. All three have four parts: (1) an introduction concerned with sleep; (2) a retold tale; (3) a first location and a first experience of the Dreamer; (4) a second location and a second experience.[40] To recapitulate briefly, the *Book of the Duchess* has an introduction lamenting Chaucer's inability to sleep; a retold tale, of Ceix and Alcyone, linked to the introduction, since it suggests a solution to the problem of sleeplessness – and to what follows, since it illustrates and highlights the problem of mortality and grief; a first location in which the Dreamer experiences an encounter with the Emperor Octovyen's unsuccessful hunting party, in a woodland described in terms of the *Roman de la Rose*. This part is linked, as a tactful and graceful conceit, to the last, the second location and experience, in which, deeper in the wood, the Dreamer encounters the Man in Black, and the real purpose of the poem is brought into the foreground. The *Book of the Duchess* thus shows a continuous development of its theme, although the links are of a tenuous kind. In the *Parlement*, they are much stronger; from the introduction on sleep, to the Dream, which forms a continuation to the retold tale of Africanus, and on to the twofold vision of Venus and Nature, which with all its contrasts, explores a single subject. The *House of Fame* repeats the introduction on sleep and dreams, but moves the retold tale, that of the *Aeneid*, into the dream itself and makes it a part of an extra location, the Temple of Venus. The two locations and experiences of the story proper follow in due order, though with much additional material in the form of the space-flight and the Eagle's informative discourses. These locations and experiences are, of course, the House of Fame itself, and the Dreamer's vision there, which gives him insight into the nature of Fame, and the House of Rumour, where he learns what rumour is like and where, if the poem had been finished, he might perhaps have learnt something more.

In the first part of the *House of Fame*, Chaucer brings into the foreground and develops at length one of the typical trophies of Venus's temple, which, in the *Parlement*, are only briefly mentioned as part of the general decoration of the place. In the *Parlement*, the main part of the description is the set piece depicting Venus herself. In the *House of Fame*, however, Venus is described almost cursorily, the repeated 'hers' suggesting no more than a brief reminder of attributes that every reader will readily call to mind (rather typically with Chaucer, the comb in her hand is not, in fact, an obvious one):

> Hyt was of Venus redely,
> The temple; for in portreyture,
> I sawgh anoon-ryght hir figure
> Naked fletynge in a see.
> And also on hir hed, pardee,
> Hir rose garlond whit and red,
> And hir comb to kembe hyr hed,
> Hir dowves, and daun Cupido
> Hir blynde sone, and Vulcano,
> That in his face was ful broun.
>
> (130–9)

In contrast to this, the story engraved on the tablet of brass – or possibly the series of wall paintings which accompany the inscription[41] – occupies lines 143–467. When the tale is told Chaucer leaves the temple, after only the briefest of recapitulations on the general excellence of its decoration:

> 'A, Lord!' thoughte I, 'that madest us,
> Yet sawgh I never such noblesse
> Of ymages, ne such richesse,
> As I saugh graven in this chirche.'
>
> (470–3)

Venus's temple, in fact, is here only of interest and importance as the setting for Virgil's poem.[42]

What, in fact, are the links between Venus and Virgil? One of the most obvious is, of course, that Venus is an important character in the *Aeneid* and the mother of its hero. Further, as Chaucer retells it, the *Aeneid* has all the ingredients which he himself seems to find essential to the poetry of love: a mixture of high policy and human passion, a machinery of the gods which can be brought to bear illuminatingly on human conduct;[43] and, of course, the tragic ending to a love story presided over by Venus alone, without Nature's cooperation. These, already touched on in the *Parlement*, are the stuff of which the *Troilus* and the *Knight's Tale* are made.

Chaucer retells the whole story, from the opening lines, which he translates and quotes, to its conclusion. But he gives more space to Dido and her abandonment by Aeneas than to any other part. This seems to justify the Eagle's reproach 'thou hast no tydynges / Of Loves folk yf they be glade'. It is not, however, the love story that is elaborated or commented on in the rest of the *House of Fame*. On the contrary, what makes this particular story appropriate to Chaucer's purpose and links it to the next two books is the special situation in which both the main figures are placed. Both are exposed to unpleasant gossip. Dido has lost her reputation, both for lack of virtue and because she is shamefully abandoned by her lover:

> 'O, wel-awey that I was born!
> For thorgh yow is my name lorn,
> And alle myn actes red and songe
> Over al thys lond, on every tonge.
> O wikke Fame! For ther nys
> Nothing so swift, lo, as she is!
> O, soth ys, every thing ys wyst,
> Though hit be kevered with the myst.
> Eke, though I myghte duren ever,
> That I have don, rekever I never,
> That I ne shal be seyd, allas,
> Yshamed be thourgh Eneas,
> And that I shal thus juged be . . .'
>
> (345–57)

Aeneas, too, will need to be 'excused' if his reputation is to survive unharmed, an office which Virgil performs for him:

> But to excusen Eneas
> Fullyche of al his grete trespas,
> The book seyth . . .
>
> (427–9)

Chaucer has dealt with his recapitulation of Virgil's story in a subtle way, so as to bring out his own theme. Just as, at the beginning, the inscription on the tablet of brass seems to dissolve and give way to a series of paintings, so, from about line 293 onwards, 'But let us speke of Eneas . . .', the graven images fade from view and the story is directly presented, with the characters moving and speaking. In this part, we are shown the actual events, which Virgil, and other upholders of Fame, are to hand down to posterity, together with their own particular colouring of the matter, and their own excuses for the conduct of their hero:

> Whoso to knowe hit hath purpos,
> Rede Virgile in Eneydos,
> Or the Epistle of Ovyde.
>
> (377–9)

The end of the story is told, rather hurriedly, in terms of what 'the book us tellis'. The result is, that out of a kind of frame of two-dimensional pictorial scenes, that part of the story which concerns love, and which also places the protagonists in a peculiarly equivocal position as regards their future repute, stands out in life and movement as the actual basis on which the great poets worked.

This, then, is what Chaucer finds in the Temple of Venus. He does not, as he does in the *Parlement*, see a living, breathing goddess, attended by Priapus as well as by Cupid. He finds a painting and a poem in which Venus is implicated in more ways than one. More-over, it is the poem, not the goddess to which he gives most space, and his treatment of it is not calculated to bring out its relation to Venus and her worship, but to raise questions like that of the poet's relation to his subject-matter and to the basis of the story in history.

After expressing his appreciation of the 'noblesse' of what he has seen (470–2), Chaucer emerges in an uninhabited desert. This waste-land suggests some degree of frustration or dissatisfaction with what he has just experienced.[44] His praise of the temple is for its art, and the characteristic feature of the desert is that there is in it:

> No maner creature
> That ys yformed be Nature.
>
> (489–90)

His second burst of enthusiastic praise for what he sees in the poem is for nature's creatures, not for art, and it is to their contemplation that the Eagle, plunging down into the desert, with all the brilliance of a new sun, brings him. His words then pick up and echo his praise of the temple, but with a difference:[45]

> 'O God!' quod y, 'that made Adam,
> Moche ys thy myght and thy noblesse!'
>
> (970–1)

Fame's house is certainly elaborately and richly ornamented, but she herself, however strange and unique, is one of Nature's creatures:

> A femynyne creature,
> That never formed by Nature
> Nas such another thing yseye.
> (1365-7)

The negatives pile up, but this must mean that Fame, although unlike any of Nature's other creations, was made by her. The word 'creature' could hardly be used of anything except Nature's handiwork. There is, thus, a pattern in the way in which events follow one another. The Dreamer finds only art, and no creature of any kind, in Venus's temple. In the desert, a natural place, he finds neither art nor life; then, under the guidance of the Eagle he reaches a place which, while it displays great elaboration of art in the construction and adornment of Fame's house, is teeming with creatures.

The Eagle, certainly, seems to suggest that Chaucer ought to pay more attention to experience of the actual world around him, the work of Nature, than to what he learns from books or artifacts like the richly decorated temple:

> 'Wherfore, as I seyde, ywys,
> Jupiter considereth this,
> And also, beau sir, other thynges;
> That is, that thou hast no tydynges
> Of Loves folk yf they be glade,
> Ne of noght elles that God made;
> And noght oonly fro fer contree
> That ther no tydynge cometh to thee,
> But of thy verray neyghebores,
> That duellen almost at thy dores,
> Thou herist neyther that ne this.'
> (641-51)

How exactly are we to take all this? Not, it is obvious, too naïvely, or we should find ourselves giving literal credence to the Eagle's aspersions on Chaucer's wit and morals. It is, of course, tempting to see the Eagle's criticism that too much time is being spent on books and too little on 'thy verray neyghebores' as a call for what we should think of as 'realism' in art and the exploitation of the familiar and the everyday – especially since we know (as Chaucer, at this time, presumably did not) what the poet was to make of such material in some of the *Canterbury Tales*. This would be to understand the Eagle's advice as a piece of purely literary criticism, rather like that of the great novelist to the beginner in Henry James's short story *The Lesson of the Master*:

> 'You must do England – there's such a lot of it.'
> 'Do you mean that I must write about it? . . .'
> 'Of course you must, and tremendously well, do you mind?
> That takes off a little of my esteem for this thing of yours –
> that it goes on abroad. Hang "abroad"! Stay at home and do
> things here – do subjects that we can measure.'

Although the Eagle does seem to favour the idea that Chaucer should 'do subjects that we can measure', he would obviously not be at home in this dialogue. What he does seem to be urging, if we can judge from his later summary of what Chaucer is to learn in Fame's house (672 ff.), is, merely, inclusiveness – the exploitation of the fact that life has greater variety than art, a fact which has already been indicated by the glimpse given in Book I of the actions and persons that lie behind the official 'excusing' versions of the great poets.[46] On the other hand, the Eagle's summary of the variety to be put at the poet's disposal is an undignified rigmarole, in which comedy and tragedy are not differentiated and in which one thing follows another like the disorderly crowd in the House of Rumour, when they 'troden fast on others heles, / And stampen, as men doon aftir eles' (2153–4):

> 'For truste wel that thou shalt here,
> When we be come there I seye,
> Mo wonder thynges, dar I leye
> And of Loves folk moo tydynges,
> Both sothe sawes and lesinges;
> And moo loves newe begonne,
> And longe yserved loves wonne,
> And moo loves casuelly
> That ben betyd, no man wot why,
> But as a blynd man stert an hare.'
>
> (672–81)

The variety is there, but life would seem to need the shaping hand of art. We have moved from the static, finished, 'official version' of the *Aeneid* to something so jumbled and confused as to have no significance. These, surely, are the two poles around which the *House of Fame* is organized: the finished work of art, which has its own beauty but is of doubtful validity in relation to actual fact, and the facts themselves, which, 'casuel' in their very nature, are made even more confused as they slip into the past and can only be known through Rumour and Fame. Certainly, the conclusion that renown is of little absolute value is unavoidable; but Fame's suppliants are not, as a matter of fact, asking for precisely this. The distinction is perhaps a nice one, but, as Chaucer phrases their requests, they ask for a certain version of their actions to be the accepted one, rather than for praise (or dispraise) *per se*. This is clear, for example, in the case of the wicked men who want to be known as wicked: ironically enough they want Fame's version to correspond to the truth:

> 'Wherefore we praye yow, a-rowe,
> That oure fame such be knowe
> In alle thing ryght as hit ys.'
>
> (1835–7)

Fame's activities, in fact, are, in the last analysis, only the putting out of versions – the summation of the work of the rookery of writers who people her house. It is only reasonable, therefore, that Chaucer should conclude that he has learnt nothing from her that he did not know already and that, as far as his own art is concerned, he will have nothing to do with her:

> 'I wot myself best how y stonde;
> For what I drye, or what I thynke,
> I wil myselven al hyt drynke,
> Certeyn, for the more part,
> As fer forth as I kan myn art.'
>
> (1878–82)

This is ostensibly an answer to the question 'Artow come hider to han fame?' (1872), and Chaucer does answer this in terms of personal reputation, in lines 1876–7:

> 'Sufficeth me, as I were ded,
> That no wight have my name in honde.'

In lines 1878–82, however, the meaning of the Fame he does not want seems to shift; and, although he speaks in terms that are almost riddling, the sense of 'drinking' his own experience and thought in accordance with his own knowledge of his art is, surely, that he will assume full responsibility for his own handling of the matter of his poetry and for the relation the finished product will bear to its originating material, without concerning himself overmuch with Fame in the sense of those traditions preserved by her rookery of writers, or even by her more dignified upholders on their pillars. 'Thinking' here is likely to mean the special mental activity of the poet, as 'thought' does in the proem to Book II, or, in the paraphrase of the proem to the third book, 'That in myn hed ymarked ys'.

With this manifesto on his art, the poet sets off for the House of Rumour and one more attempt to learn the tidings he was promised. What he finds here is the raw material of Fame: the even more haphazard basis of her haphazard judgements, since whatever is spoken here:

> Thus out at holes gunne wringe
> Every tydynge streght to Fame,
> And she gan yeven ech hys name,
> After hir disposicioun,
> And yaf hem eke duracioun,
> Somme to wexe and wane sone,
> As doth the faire white mone,
> And let hem goon. Ther myghte y seen
> Wynged wondres faste fleen,
> Twenty thousand in a route,
> As Eolus hem blew aboute.
>
> (2110–20)

We have travelled a long way from the splendid monument of the *Aeneid*, and yet not without Virgil's own authority for doing so. In the passage on *Fama* in Book IV, which Chaucer uses as the basis for his own portrait of Fame, Virgil describes the spread of rumours about the lovers, which finally reach King Iarbas.[47] It is reasonable enough to pass from Virgil's actual poem to the permanency of

Fame, and its uncertain and impermanent basis, and so on to the even more fleeting, unreliable rumours that feed Fame. Fame in this sense, of course, is not the same as Virgil's *Fama*, but once the new equation of *Fama = Laus* (Renown) is admitted, the whole progression is logical enough; and we can see why the story of Dido and Aeneas, in the setting of the *Aeneid*, forms the best possible starting point for a poem which plays at length with the implications for poets and poetry of the various senses of *Fama*.

The most wonderful thing about the House of Rumour, Chaucer tells us, is the distortion which every tale undergoes before it escapes to go on to the House of Fame:

> Thus north and south
> Wente every tydyng fro mouth to mouth,
> And that encresing ever moo,
> As fyr ys wont to quyke and goo,
> From a sparke spronge amys,
> Til al a citee brent up ys.
> And whan that was ful yspronge,
> And woxen more on every tonge
> Than ever hit was, [hit] wente anoon
> Up to a wyndowe out to goon.
>
> (2075–84)

Even then, in the struggle to get out, the thronging rumours cause more confusion by getting mixed up with each other:

> Thus saugh I fals and soth compouned
> Togeder fle for oo tydynge.
>
> (2108–9)

In spite of these apparent disadvantages, Chaucer hurries about with a satisfaction which the House of Fame did not afford him:

> I alther-fastest wente
> About, and dide al myn entente
> Me for to pleyen, and for to lere,
> And eke a tydynge for to here –
>
> (2131–4)

At this point, with the poem obviously nearing its end, the pace quickens into something like the *rym dogerel* of the Book II proem, and the style becomes a riddling one once more. Chaucer will not commit himself to a clear statement as to whether he has or has not in fact heard the tidings (although it sounds as if he has) and, still more, will give no inkling of what they might be:

> a tydynge for to here
> That I had herd of som contre
> That shal not now be told for me –
> For hit no nede is, redely;
> Folk kan synge hit bet than I;
> For al mot out, other late or rathe,
> Alle the sheves in the lathe.
>
> (2134–40)

This has every sign of a rapid retreat from his subject, leaving his readers to draw their own conclusions. It is, moreover, also a retreat from seriousness. There is no doubt, from many passages – the serious parts of the proems and the manifesto on Chaucer's own relation to Fame, for example – that the issues raised in the poem are of great importance to the poet. But it would not be in Chaucer's manner, or in keeping with that urbanity which we have seen as the key-note of so much of his work, to end the divertissement on too serious or definitive a note. Accordingly, even this riddling refusal to commit himself is interrupted by the crowd running and jostling to hear something new:

> For I saugh rennynge every wight,
> As faste as that they hadden myght;
> And everych cried 'What thing is that?'
> And somme sayde, 'I not never what.'
> And whan they were alle on an hepe,
> Tho behynde begunne up lepe,
> And clamben up on other faste,
> And up the nose and yën kaste,
> And troden fast on others heles,
> And stampen, as men doon aftir eles.
>
> (2145–54)

After this magnificent crescendo, in a style which, like Fame's scolding, seems reminiscent of the rhythms and methods of *Havelok*,[48] and which is certainly both colloquial and essentially English in tone, the poem breaks off, and the words of the 'man of gret auctorite' are lost to us. Caxton's solution, of a few lines telling how this loud voice woke the Dreamer up and ended his dream, is neat but, clearly, only a guess. Certainly, Chaucer can have had little more to say. He has fully explored the ideas of Fame and Rumour,[49] and it would be unlike him, as we have said, to end with any clearcut 'solution' to any of the problems he has raised.

To sum up: it seems to me that in the *House of Fame*, Chaucer has taken as his main theme the relation of poetry to the traditions which form its material. On one level, he writes in a jesting spirit which leads him to the *reductio ad absurdum* of rumours crying angrily, 'Lat me go first!' 'Nay, but let me!'; but on another he raises seriously many problems very relevant to the poet: the relation of art to nature, for example, and to other works of art as the objects of imitation; the question of the poet's personal responsibility to his own experience and creative powers. I think, too, that another basic theme emerges and another problem is examined. This is the problem of Chaucer's own, personal identity as a poet – his relationship to the great past, as represented by Virgil, and also his position in a line of descent which includes the little poets of the vernacular languages. The stylistic variations of the *House of Fame* certainly include, as we have seen, many imitations of more popular types of English writing, and it is perhaps not going too far to suggest that one of the underlying problems which Chaucer tries to thrash out in this strange poem is the exact relation of a poet of his day, with all France and Italy to draw on in addition to the Classical language of Virgil and Ovid, to his own roots in his own language. This, again, raises the even more important problem of the status of the vernacular poet: whether he was to remain among the little craftsmen, inhabiting an obscure and dusty rookery, or whether he could, as Chaucer hopes at the end of the *Troilus*, follow in the steps of the great past-masters. There seems little doubt of Chaucer's answer and no failure of confidence in the 'vertu', 'engyn and myght' of his poetic inspiration.

4

Troilus and Criseyde

The *House of Fame*, whenever we date it and however we understand it, forms an interlude in Chaucer's exploration of the theme of love. In the *Troilus*, with one of the stories that he found among the trophies in Venus's temple in the *Parlement of Foules*, he once more takes up the subject of love's problems and paradoxes. He does so, however, with a difference. In the *Parlement*, he writes as one who knows not 'love in dede', and the material for his discussion is largely drawn from books. What *is* presented as direct experience is still kept at a distance by the use of the birds to suggest and comment on the human problem, but not to represent it directly. In the *Troilus*, on the other hand, 'love in dede' is exactly what is put before us, in a story about human beings who make their impact on us with no veil of animal fable or allegory between. Moreover, although there is still much exploration of the theory of love, the tragedy lies, as much as anything, in the failure of theory, however complicated, to cope with the complexity of human reactions. In this respect, we could regard the *Troilus* as expanding the suggestion contained in the difficulties of the noble birds in love in the *Parlement*.[1]

It is true, of course, that all directness of impact is contained in the story itself: the poet is still cautious in claiming for himself knowledge derived from experience. But there is a difference between the total disclaimer of the *Parlement* and his cautious qualification of his own position at the beginning of the *Troilus*:

> For I, that God of Loves servantz serve,
> Ne dar to Love, for myn unliklynesse,
> Preyen for speed, al sholde I therfore sterve,
> So fer am I from his help in derknesse.
>
> (I, 15–18)

There is a claim in the paraphrase of the papal title, as well as a denial in the 'derknesse'; and we are left with an author who occupies a more ambiguous, but also a more ambitious position than was the case in the *Parlement*.

Again, it is true that, throughout the poem, Chaucer is careful to disclaim personal responsibility for his story. He refers, again and again, to his author – to what the book tells us, even to what people say – with poignant effect in his reluctant report of Criseyde's dealings with Diomede, at the end:

> Men seyn – I not – that she yaf hym hire herte.
>
> (V, 1050)

The result of the device, it seems to me, is not to build up the theme – which is certainly present in the *Parlement* and, though with a difference, in the *House of Fame* – of authority versus experience, but rather to increase our sense of the objectivity of the story-telling. This, we are told by a poet who is still, as he was in the *Parlement*, 'astonyed' by the 'wonderful werkynge' of love, is how it is all laid down as having actually happened. Like most of Chaucer's interventions as narrator, these statements have to be understood as guiding us not as to the facts of composition, but as to the way in which we are to regard the story at the moments in which its teller intervenes. The line just quoted, for example, heightens our sense of the pathos and the pity of Criseyde's failure, and does nothing else. The *Troilus* is an ambitious work, probably Chaucer's first one to be laid out on a really large scale and to show, fully absorbed into its texture and structure, the impact of the new Italian models and the new ideas concerning the scope and dignity of poetry which were, in part at least, the fruit of the Italian journeys. Yet, in spite of all the assurances that the poet is merely following his model, the most cursory comparison of the *Troilus* with *Il Filostrato* shows Chaucer working with great freedom, and with full control over his material.

The main differences between Boccaccio's *Il Filostrato* and Chaucer's *Troilus and Criseyde* have often been described[2] – only a brief summary will be needed here. In general plan and purpose the two poems are quite unlike. Boccaccio's is a poem straightforwardly concerned with love. It arises, he tells us, from the absence of his mistress, when, searching among old stories for the most suitable one to express his griefs, he finds that of Troilus. His retelling of it is aimed at provoking her pity. The setting is a courtly one. The prologue places the whole matter as arising out of discussion as to which of three things would give a lover most delight: sometimes to see his lady, sometimes to talk of her, or sometimes to think of her. This is spoken of as a formal discussion in Love's court among noble men and beautiful ladies.[3] Boccaccio says that he himself always maintained that thought gave most delight, until the actual absence of his lady convinced him of his error. His poem has two focal points: the rapid and complete satisfaction of Troilo's desires by a willing Criseida who takes torch in hand to light her lover to her bed,[4] and the complications of his grief at her absence and betrayal. She leaves Troy considerably sooner than Chaucer's Criseyde – half-way through Boccaccio's poem.

Boccaccio's treatment is not without its ironies and complexities; courtly ideals are sadly let down by his heroine, and his denial in the Prologue of an ambition so exalted as to hope to equal Troilo's success need not be taken wholly at its face value.[5] Nevertheless, in his conclusion, he merely warns lovers to choose more wisely than Troilo did when he set his heart on 'Criseida villana' (VIII, 28) – a phrase far too clearcut for Chaucer ever to use of his heroine. He makes no attempt to set the love story within any wider view of human life and achievement. His characters suit his story. Troilo is noble and brave, but is seen primarily as the amorous young man. Pandaro is young also; he is Criseida's cousin and guardian, but not a man of any greater standing or experience of life than the lovers themselves. Criseida is a young widow, easily won, and seeing no reason why she should not have a love affair like everybody else:

> 'Io non conosco in questa terra ancora
> Veruna senza amante, e la più gente,
> Com' io conosco e veggo, s'innamora.'
>
> (II, 70)

The story, in fact, belongs to a world where almost everybody is in love, and where other activities are of little importance.

Chaucer's poem lacks the introductory courtly and personal setting. He takes from the Italian poem the large scale, the comparatively taut construction, and the simple story, which, making much of a few episodes and involving a concentration on the feelings and motives of a small group of people, contrasts sharply with the episodic type of romance. Instead of the exclusively personal frame of reference, he places much more emphasis on the historical setting of Troy and the Trojan War – his descriptions of life and of places in the city are much fuller than Boccaccio's, and often, indeed, are additions of his own. Within this much more three-dimensional, solidly constructed frame he places characters of a more complex kind than Boccaccio attempted; and in his handling of them we see the full flowering of the flexible, infinitely varied style of the minor poems, and of the descriptive and narrative technique which I have characterized as urbane – the ability to present the relations between characters within a naturalistically conceived social setting. Boccaccio's characters are comparatively simple in themselves, and their relationships are also simple and hardly extend beyond the love story. Chaucer's characters are complex, and their relationships depend to a large extent on their positions within a stable social scheme existing independently of the love affair which brings them all, for a time, closer together.

This is most clearly seen in the case of Pandarus's relationship to Criseyde. He is her uncle, not her cousin; he is an older man, and one on whom she habitually relies for help in conducting the ordinary affairs and business of her life. More than this, he stands in the kind of intimate relationship to her which allows them to share the same jokes and to be affectionately amused by each other – it is, in fact, from this most disarming of contacts that Chaucer makes the whole intrigue begin. In Book II, when we first see him with Criseyde, the conversation begins with the topic of love and with a joke. Pandarus asks about the book he finds her reading:

> 'For Goddes love, what seith it? Telle it us!
> Is it of love? O, som good ye me leere!'
> 'Uncle,' quod she, 'youre maistresse is nat here.'
> With that thei gonnen laughe . . .
>
> (II, 96–9)

It is because he occupies this position that Pandarus is able to work on Criseyde so effectively, and it is this familiarity and dependence that he exploits when he invents an imaginary lawsuit to frighten her into appealing to the royal princes of Troy. His familiar, colloquial introduction of the matter and her response keep the impression of their intimacy vividly before us:

> He seide, 'O verray God, so have I ronne!
> Lo, nece myn, se ye nought how I swete?'
> (II, 1464–5)

And she answers in terms of, first, her fears, and then, their relationship:

> 'What is he more aboute, me to drecche
> And don me wrong? What shal I doon, allas . . .
> But, for the love of God, myn uncle deere,
> No fors of that, lat hym han al yfeere.
> Withouten that I have ynough for us.'
> (II, 1471–8)

But, besides her involvement with Pandarus, Criseyde remains constantly involved in and aware of the dangers of her position in Troy. She does not forget that Troilus is 'my kynges sone' (II, 708) and a powerful protector.[6] The genuineness of her love, at the time, is not called in question, but her reactions are now more complicated than the simple decision of Criseida to be like all the other people whom she sees enjoying love; Criseyde's love is presented as the product of her whole experience of her world.

All this means that she is shown as sensitive to a much wider range of contacts and influences than Criseida. Chaucer, moreover, gives her the character of timidity and anxious calculation – Criseida's review of her circumstances before she decides to take Troilo as a lover is superficial compared to Criseyde's constant references back to her general situation and to the careful reservations which make her a willing victim of Pandarus's intrigue in the end.[7] These characteristics, of course, also lead her into Diomede's arms, and in the pathetically self-revealing speech in which she answers his proposals, we can follow her mind as it anxiously twists and turns in the feverish survey of her own difficulties which we have come to expect of her character.[8]

For the presentation of these complexities Chaucer needs a different narrative pace and a different inclusion of detail than Boccaccio. He takes much longer over the courtship, since his concern is primarily with the cumulative pressure of a series of small events on Criseyde's mind. What he takes over from Boccaccio tends to be lengthened, and two long sections are added: II, 1394–III, 231, in which Pandarus plans and brings about the meeting with Troilus at the house of Deiphebus, and III, 505–1309, the whole elaborate organization of the meeting at Pandarus's own house which brings about the final union of the lovers. Both these sections involve a great deal of detail of place, time and circumstance, which necessarily slows the pace of the narrative in comparison with the brisk, uninterrupted progress of Boccaccio's lovers towards their consummation.

Most of the changes in Pandaro when he becomes Pandarus have already been indicated: Chaucer gives him age and experience; puts him in the kind of intimate relationship with the other characters in which humour plays an important part; makes him essentially practical, a great deviser of all the little details which forward an intrigue; and, moreover, although his affectionate pity for Troilus is perhaps heightened, he is also given a kind of practical cynicism, in the last resort not reconcilable with the friendship and understanding he feels for Troilus. For Pandarus, love is a game – 'the olde daunce' – and there will always be as good fish in the sea as ever came out of it. It is the tragedy of Troilus's situation that, in a way which it is never given to Pandarus to understand, he does not share this view.[9]

Superficially at least, Troilus is the least altered from Boccaccio's conception of the character, in that he remains an ideal lover; but on analysis the changes are numerous and significant. From the start he is given a kind of innocence in love which Pandarus and Criseyde, both experienced, do not share. Unlike Troilo he loves for the first time. Secondly, although his great worthiness as a soldier and as a patriot are heightened, as a lover he is unable to act to help himself; he is fearful and introspective. He tries to analyse and explain his own fate, especially in the long speech on predestination, which is an addition of Chaucer's (IV, 957 ff.). Like Criseyde, he is worked on by Pandarus, but in a different way: where she is manœuvred into position largely through mental pressure, Troilus has to be moved about until he is physically in the right position – a state of affairs taken to the point of broad comedy in the consummation scene, where Pandarus actually strips him and casts him into bed. Pandarus's influence on his mind is, as a matter of fact, practically non-existent. His words are often received with flat contradiction, or at least set aside; and at one point Chaucer tells us they are not even heard – they go in at one ear and out at the other (IV, 432–4). In creating the character of this Trojan prince who is active and successful to the point of heroism in the field – he is second only to Hector – but who shows mental activity coupled with almost total physical inertia in the pursuit of his own affairs, Chaucer makes the crisis which removes Criseyde convincing. Just as Criseyde is, as he depicts her, necessarily the victim of Diomede, so Troilus is put in a position, when her removal from Troy is proposed, in which his active forceful character as a soldier and patriot is accurately balanced by his inability to act as a lover. On the one hand, he could retain her by force. On the other, this would mean the betrayal of his country and, also, the open, active prosecution of the love affair – and this, besides being harmful to the lady's reputation, is just what he has shown himself incapable of.[10] Both Troilus and Criseyde, as Chaucer shows them to us, are neatly caught, at their moments of crisis, by the net which circumstances cast round their own ruling characteristics.

All this is to suggest that more emphasis is to be placed on character and on personal responsibility in the unfolding of the story than is sometimes assumed. It is true, as Curry long ago pointed out, that Chaucer makes great play throughout the poem with the forces which destiny, fate, the influences of the stars, exert on his characters and their circumstances. Some of this was in Boccaccio's poem; but much is added by Chaucer. To get the proportion right between such forces and personal responsibility in the poem, we need to turn from analysis of the characters to a consideration of the story as a whole. It is, after all, not likely that Chaucer altered his original in order to present different characters; it is rather that, because he had a different conception of the significance of their story and of the issues involved in the action, the persons necessarily emerge as unlike those of Boccaccio.

Chaucer describes his own work at the beginning and at the end. In the first stanza he proposes:

The double sorwe of Troilus to tellen,
That was the kyng Priamus sone of Troye,
In lovynge, how his aventures fellen
Fro wo to wele, and after out of joie.

(1–4)

In the closing section he addresses his work:

Go, litel bok, go litel myn tragedye
(1786)

and contrasts it with the 'comedy' he hopes one day to write.[11]
Precisely what Chaucer meant by 'tragedy' is indicated by a gloss to
the *de Consolatione Philosophiae* which he duly included in his translation. This defines tragedy as a poem with a certain kind of content:

What other thyng bywaylen the cryinges of tragedyes but oonly
the dedes of Fortune, that with unwar strook overturneth the
realmes of great nobleye? (*Glose. Tragedye is to seyn a dite of a
prosperite for a tyme, that endeth in wrecchidnesse*)

(II. pr. 2, 67–72)

The definitions of tragedy in the *Monk's Prologue and Tale* agree with
this and, within the tale at any rate, also link tragedy and Fortune.[12]
In the case of the *Troilus*, as Chaucer points out, a double movement
is present, since Troilus begins in happiness of a kind, before he falls a
victim to love. He then suffers misery, which gives way for a short
period to bliss, when his love is successful; and this, in turn, is followed
by the misery of his betrayal. This scheme does, in fact, give the work
its overall form. Where Boccaccio's poem is arranged in nine short
parts, Chaucer has a symmetrical arrangement of five books: two
for the first period of sorrow, one for the brief period of bliss, and two
more for the final sorrow and the tragic conclusion. If we look more
closely at the disposition of the material within this scheme, we shall
see that it is the basic concept of a doubly tragic love, which finally
destroys a great and worthy man, that shapes the characters. No
doubt the result is, as we should say, 'to bring them to life', and no
doubt Chaucer was as well aware of this as we can be. By deepening
and extending the scope and significance of Boccaccio's concept of
love he has, in fact, at the same time necessarily deepened and
extended the whole concept of characterization.

Tragedy, as we have said, implied for Chaucer a definite movement in human life – a pattern taken by the course of events; and, as
we read the *Troilus*, to say nothing of other works with similar
themes, it becomes clear that for him such patternings of events had
philosophical implications. These are often expressed through the
linking, which we have already seen, of the tragic pattern and the
Wheel of Fortune.[13]

For the reader of Boethius, or of Seneca, the phenomenon for
which the turning of Fortune's wheel is a figure is an inescapable
feature of all human and natural life.[14] The world is essentially
subject to change, and, indeed, it is only through change that it can
achieve any semblance of stability. This, however, is a stability of the
whole at the expense of the parts. Individuals, whether natural
objects or human beings, cannot expect material permanence, since
the continuity of nature depends on the completeness of the cycle of
birth, death, decay and rebirth which ensures the continuance of the
species. This cycle was, for Christian and Roman authors alike, an
expression of the beneficence of God's providence in the world below
the moon (according to Aristotle's widely followed view, which was
held, for example, by Macrobius, the moon forms the boundary
between the transitory and the intransitory). Theseus refers to this
in his speech on the First Mover and the Chain of Love.[15] It is also
in this sense that Nature in the *Parlement of Foules* presides as God's
vicaire over the pairing of the birds, that is over the continuity of the
species. She would also, although it does not happen to be a part of
the subject-matter of the poem, preside over the dissolution of the
individual fowl that make up her court.[16]

Although man on earth is ineluctably subject to change and to
changeful Fortune (and Chaucer knew from his reading of Boethius
that she is most dangerous and deceiving when she seems most
favourable, for then a reversal is sure to follow[17] – and this is the
pattern he in fact uses in the *Troilus*), it does not follow from this that
Chaucer's view was a deterministic one. In the first place, natural
change only applies below the moon, and it is possible for mankind to
mount beyond its sphere and exchange the values of time for those of
eternity; both Chaucer and Dante describe a man doing this.[18]
Secondly, his Roman authorities were as concerned as any later
Christian authors in explaining how man's freedom of will could set
him above the vagaries of Fortune. This is, in fact, what the *de
Consolatione* is about. It describes the Stoic good man who frees him-

self from Fortune by refusing to place his whole happiness in the transitory things over which she holds undisputed sway. The rewards open to such a man are the subject of the Proem of the *Parlement of Foules* – in contrast to the uncertain good of even natural love, working towards the preservation of the species.

The man who fixes his heart on a love which belongs exclusively to the sublunary world of change cannot expect permanence. There is, however, a love which is not under the government of the moon, and this love is not subject to loss or change. This is the 'celestial' love which Pandarus specifically rejects as unlikely to appeal to Criseyde:

> For this have I herd seyd of wyse lered,
> Was nevere man or womman yet bigete
> That was unapt to suffren loves hete,
> Celestial, or elles love of kynde . . .
> It sit hire naught to ben celestial
> As yet . . .
>
> (I, 976–84)

It is noteworthy that Pandarus calls both these loves 'natural'. St Bernard does the same:

> Excellit in naturae donis affectio haec amoris.
> (Of all the sentiments of nature this of love is the most excellent.)
> (*In Cantica Canticorum*, vii, 2)

and he adds 'praesertim cum ad suum recurrit principium, quod est Deus', a remark more in keeping with the attitude expressed in the epilogue than with Pandarus's. There is still another way in which love can achieve at least an affinity with permanence. This is through the marriage bond – the 'chaste love' of which Boethius writes and which Chaucer calls 'O parfit joye, lastynge everemo' in the *Knight's Tale*, where it provides an antidote to the sorrows of the earlier part of the poem.[19]

Troilus's love is no more 'celestial' than Criseyde's; and, since there is no possibility of its issue in marriage, Chaucer depicts it as an essentially and inevitably tragic love. This is not to say that he also depicts it as necessarily wrong or evil in itself. Its illicit nature, in being outside marriage, is certainly indicated; but, unlike many of his critics, Chaucer does not go out of his way to link it to Christian doctrine in the body of the work. Even in the epilogue, as we shall see, the implications are more complex than has sometimes been claimed.[20] Rather than explore the explicitly Christian moral and doctrinal implications of his love story, Chaucer prefers to present it as a most complete and perfect example of its kind, without at any point forgetting that its kind is not lasting. This means that the love of Troilus for Criseyde is subjected to a kind of double heightening which, on the one hand, makes their tragedy the most complete and impressive example which it would be possible to imagine and, on the other, makes their successful love as perfect and as noble (Chaucer is fond of applying the epithet 'worthy' to the lovers) as possible. This is very much in the medieval manner, which prefers to take an extreme as a typical case, where the modern mind believes that truth is better served by the average. It is this process of intensification which accounts for many of Chaucer's alterations.

In the first place, and much of this is already in Boccaccio, the story is presented in such a way that it would be hard to think of a love affair so circumstanced that it would be less likely to achieve permanence. The scene is set within the tragedy of the siege of Troy. It is near the end. It is already certain that Troy will fall and that the Greeks will destroy it utterly. Calkas knows this, and it is his knowledge which precipitates the denouement. Troilus is in daily danger of death and, in fact, is killed in the ordinary course of war, in a way which has nothing to do with his love. Criseyde must either be burnt to ashes with Troy or leave the city. All this is not a hopeful background.

Further than this, Troilus's love is secret and illicit. Criseyde will not consider remarriage; and, indeed, none of the three main characters takes the idea seriously. This subjects the lovers to uncertainty and delay as to their meetings, and to all the difficulty and inconvenience of a secrecy which is essential to preserve Criseyde's good name. This need for secrecy is one of the chief reasons for Troilus's failure to prevent her leaving Troy. Even the semi-permanence and open enjoyment of marriage is denied them.

Moreover, of the three main characters, two openly think of love as impermanent. Pandarus repeatedly reminds Troilus of its inevitably transitory nature; and, indeed, advises him to console himself by changing, in his turn, when Criseyde is lost to him. It is true that Chaucer apologizes for him – to suggest that sorrow is unnecessary:

> 'Syn thi desir al holly hastow had,
> So that, by right, it oughte ynough suffise, . . .'
> (IV, 395–6)

and that:

> 'This town is ful of ladys al aboute, . . .'
> (401)

is certainly uncourtly; and Chaucer assures us that:

> Thise wordes seyde he for the nones alle,
> To help his frend, lest he for sorwe deyde;
> For douteles, to don his wo to falle,
> He roughte nought what unthrift that he seyde.
> (IV, 428–31)

Troilus's reaction to the heresy does not have to be given us, since the words go in at one ear and out at the other (434). Such a speech, in fact, has no meaning in terms of Troilus's attitude to love; but, in spite of the apology, it has all too much in relation to Pandarus's and is entirely in keeping with his attitude throughout the poem, in its clearsighted, unswerving attachment to expediency and its equally clearsighted recognition of the kind of natural process he is dealing with:

> 'Swich fir, by proces, shal of kynde colde;
> For syn it is but casuel plesaunce,
> Som cas shal putte it out of remembraunce.
>
> For also seur as day comth after nyght,
> The newe love, labour, or oother wo,
> Or elles selde seynge of a wight,
> Don olde affecciouns alle over-go.'
> (IV, 418–24)

This 'casual' love is, like the natural cycles typified by day and night, bound by its very nature to suffer change. Criseyde herself, of course, sufficiently demonstrates the truth of Pandarus's statement.

Both Pandarus and Criseyde take up similar attitudes towards the end. Criseyde closes her farewell to Troilus with the words:

'But al shal passe; and thus take I my leve'.
(V, 1085)

and Pandarus comments thus on Troilus's unquenchable hope that
she may yet return:

'Ye, fare wel al the snow of ferne yere!'
(V, 1176)

The narrator's own comment towards the end of Book V drives home
the point:

Gret was the sorwe and pleynte of Troilus;
But forth hire cours Fortune ay gan to holde . . .
Swich is this world, whoso it kan byholde;
In ech estat is litel hertes reste.
(V, 1744–9)

Pandarus uses the argument of love's impermanence to persuade
Criseyde to love in the first place. This is an argument which
Boccaccio's Criseida uses on herself – but with a difference. She
simply asks, and answers, herself:

'Chi me vorrà se io invecchio mai?
Certo nessuno'.

('Who will ever desire me if I grow old?
Certainly no one')
(II, 71)

Pandarus, on the other hand, states a general law, in which Troilus
is also involved:

'Thenk ek how elde wasteth every houre
In ech of yow a partie of beautee;
And therfore, er that age the devoure,
Go love; for old, ther wol no wight of the.'
(II, 393–6)

In his inability to change and his demand for permanence from
something which, on every count, could never last, Troilus is
certainly set for tragedy.

But Troilus's love is not only presented in its nature, and through all its attendant circumstances, as a love unlikely to last for ever in happiness; it is also given the highest possible value in our eyes, so that, as we are made to feel that his highest point of fortune was indeed high, so we feel that his fall is a great one. Chaucer achieves this in a variety of ways. In the first place, he devotes considerable space to the praise of love itself. It is everything that is good, except permanent. Early in the first book he establishes the universal, inescapable power of love:

> For evere it was, and evere it shal byfalle,
> That Love is he that alle thing may bynde,
> For may no man fordon the lawe of kynde.
>
> (I, 236–8)

There is, it is true, warning here, as well as praise. The law of Nature, which, through love, ensures the continuity of the world and its multifarious species, is, as we have seen, however noble and ultimately beneficient in itself, not a law which ensures the temporal preservation of the individual. Nevertheless, Chaucer emphasizes that it can only be seen as a power for good:

> Now sith it may nat goodly ben withstonde,
> And is a thing so vertuous in kynde,
> Refuseth nat to Love for to ben bonde,
> Syn, as hymselven liste, he may yow bynde.
>
> (I, 253–6)

If there is irony here and in the coincidental meeting with Criseyde (shortly to be described) which brings Troilus into the power of this great natural force, it is an irony inherent in the life of man, seen from a limited and temporal viewpoint, and not a cheap joke of the poet against the folly of lovers.

The first stanza of Troilus's song elaborates the idea of love as a great force whose ultimate goodness is not necessarily clearly demonstrated in individual instances of its power – Chaucer, and Dante before him, both following Boethius, took the same view of Fortune:[21]

If no love is, O God, what fele I so?
And if love is, what thing and which is he?
If love be good, from whennes cometh my woo?
If it be wikke, a wonder thynketh me,
When every torment and adversite
That cometh of hym, may to me savory thinke,
For ay thurst I, the more that ich it drynke.

(I, 400-6)

At the end of Book I the effect of this power on Troilus is shown as an influence for good:

And in the town his manere tho forth ay
Soo goodly was, and gat hym so in grace,
That ecch hym loved that loked on his face.

For he bicom the frendlieste wight,
The gentilest, and ek the mooste fre,
The thriftiest and oon the beste knyght,
That in his tyme was or myghte be.

(I, 1076-82)

These ideas are taken up again in the central third book, which celebrates Troilus's happiness. First, comes the very beautiful proem in invocation of Venus:

O blisful light, of which the bemes clere
Adorneth al the thridde heven faire!

(III, 1-2)

This is, of course, based on Troilo's song in *Il Filostrato*. Both versions deal with love from the philosophical and cosmological viewpoint, as a force concerned in the creation and maintenance of the universe. In Chaucer's version:[22]

In hevene and helle, in erthe and salte see
Is felt thi myght, if that I wel descerne;
As man, brid, best, fissh, herbe, and grene tree
Thee fele in tymes with vapour eterne.
God loveth, and to love wol nought werne;
And in this world no lyves creature
Withouten love is worth, or may endure.

Ye Joves first to thilke effectes glade,
Thorugh which that thynges lyven alle and be,
Comeveden, and amorous him made
On mortal thyng . . .

(III, 8–18)

The effects of love on the individual are described in much the same
terms as were used of Troilus himself:

And as yow list, ye maken hertes digne;
Algates hem that ye wol sette a-fyre,
They dreden shame, and vices they resygne;
Ye do hem corteys be, fresshe and benigne.

(23–6)

Troilus's song – based on the *de Consolatione*, (II, m. 8) – 'Love, that
of erthe and se hath governaunce' (III, 1744 ff.) – also deals with a
cosmic and philosophically conceived love; and the book finally ends
with a further assurance of the ennobling power love exerts on
Troilus:

Benigne he was to ech in general,
For which he gat hym thank in every place.
Thus wolde Love, yheried be his grace,
That Pride, Envye, and Ire, and Avarice,
He gan to fle, and everich other vice.

(III, 1802–6)

It is obvious that these passages in Book III, the book which hymns
the consummation of Troilus's love and presents it to us, in some of
the most beautiful love poetry in the language, as of great nobility
and worth, are crucial to our understanding of the poem, and that
we must give them full weight when we come to consider Chaucer's
viewpoint in the epilogue. For the moment, however, this problem
must be set aside while we examine the whole organization of the
material of Book III. It may be, indeed, that the beauty of much of
the writing in praise and description of successful love blinds us a
little to the purpose of this section within the work as a whole. As the
first stanza of Book I makes clear – to say nothing of the epilogue –
the *Troilus* is not primarily intended to set forth and praise the joys of

love. It is a tragedy. And the brief period when the lovers are 'in lust and in quiete' (III, 1819) is a part of the tragic pattern; it is, in fact, the fatal period when Fortune is most to be feared.

Chaucer does not really leave us in any doubt of his ultimate purpose in Book III. His account of the union of the lovers is shot through with foreboding – a foreboding which, as we have seen, is actually built into his conception of love as a part of nature. It is in Book III that Pandarus makes his serious speech in justification of his own actions:

> 'For the have I bigonne a gamen pleye,
> Which that I nevere do shal eft for other,
> Although he were a thousand fold my brother.
>
> That is to seye, for the am I bicomen,
> Bitwixen game and ernest, swich a meene
> As maken wommen unto men to comen; . . .'
>
> (III, 250–5)

His argument is an uneasy one. He can only entreat Troilus to be discreet, and plead that what he has done was done for love and not for money. Nor can we claim, with C. S. Lewis, that Pandarus operates on a different plane to Troilus, in that he stands outside the charmed circle within which the lovers have their being. Troilus's response is to offer to become a procurer in his turn:

> 'I have my faire suster Polixene,
> Cassandre, Eleyne, or any of the frape,
> Be she nevere so fair or wel yshape,
> Telle me which thow wilt of everychone,
> To han for thyn, and lat me thanne allone.'
>
> (III, 409–13)

It is clear that Pandarus, with his usual ability to see, but not necessarily to comprehend, has uncovered something fundamental, and threatening, to the love story. The ugly moment should prepare us for the language of the epilogue; and, indeed, it represents a basic conflict of values which Chaucer displays, but does not resolve.

Book III also contains Criseyde's speech on false felicity, which foreshadows so many of the phrases of the epilogue:

'O God!' quod she, 'so worldly selynesse,
Which clerkes callen fals felicitee,
Imedled is with many a bitternesse!
Ful angwissous than is, God woot,' quod she,
'Condicioun of veyn prosperitee; . . .
O brotel wele of mannes joie unstable! . . .
Wherfore I wol diffyne in this matere,
That trewely, for aught I kan espie,
Ther is no verray weele in this world heere.'

(III, 813–36)

Ironically enough, this long speech is called forth by a false accusation of unfaithfulness – part of Pandarus's manœuvring. The irony, however, does not end there, and the speech makes its effect as an ominous prelude to the felicity the lovers are about to experience. We are reminded of it at the end of the book, when, in his attempt to describe their joy, Chaucer echoes Criseyde's words:

Felicite, which that thise clerkes wise
Comenden so, ne may nought here suffise;
This joie ne may nought writen be with inke!

(1691–3)

We have read the earlier speech, and we know that wise clerks write of false felicity as well as true.

In Book III, too, Pandarus speaks of Fortune in terms necessary to the development of the tragic theme, but somewhat incongruous to his moment of success, when all his scheming has at last brought about the desired result:

'For of fortunes sharpe adversitee
The worste kynde of infortune is this,
A man to han ben in prosperitee,
And it remembren, whan it passed is.
Th'art wis ynough, forthi do nat amys;
Be naught to rakel, theigh thow sitte warme;
For if thow be, certeyn, it wol the harme.

129

Thow art at ese, and hold the wel therinne;
For also seur as reed is every fir,
As gret a craft is kepe wel as wynne.
Bridle alwey wel thi speche and thi desir,
For worldly joie halt nought but by a wir.
That preveth wel it brest al day so ofte;
Forthi nede is to werken with it softe.'

(III, 1625–38)

The ostensible purpose of the speech is to exhort Troilus to secrecy and discretion; but, in its references to Fortune and to the transitory nature of worldly joy – Criseyde's false felicity – it actually goes a good deal further; and by setting forth the Stoic view of moderation and mistrust of the unreliable pleasures of the world, a view not normally held by Pandarus, it casts a coldly ominous light on the transports of the lovers. Chaucer, in his own comment on this part of the action, once more brings together the key words 'Fortune' and 'joy' (by now firmly established in our minds as transitory):

And thus Fortune a tyme ledde in joie
Criseyde, and ek this kynges sone of Troie.

(III, 1714–15)

A couplet which also suggests, aptly enough, the standard definition of tragedy.

Surrounded as it is by doubts and dangers, we are yet convinced of the value, in its kind, of the love of Troilus and Criseyde. But, more than this, Chaucer is at pains to convince us also of the personal value and excellence of the lovers. We have already seen that Troilus is conceived as one of the great heroes of Troy, second only to Hector. He is possessed of all the princely virtues, and they are even, as we have seen, increased by love. He is capable, too, of putting the commonweal before his private passion, and of refraining from the attempt to prevent Criseyde from leaving Troy when the country's good requires her exchange for Antenor. It is true that later he seems more ready to entertain the idea of keeping her by force, but his reason still holds him back in the fear that harm might come to her person and her honour if he indulged the impulse to violent action. Criseyde continually expresses her appreciation of his 'worthiness' –

which is also constantly praised by Pandarus[23] – and she esteems him, too, for his 'moral vertu':

> 'For trusteth wel, that youre estat roial,
> Ne veyn delit, nor only worthinesse
> Of yow in werre or torney marcial,
> Ne pompe, array, nobleye, or ek richesse
> Ne made me to rewe on youre destresse;
> But moral vertu, grounded upon trouthe,
> That was the cause I first hadde on yow routhe!'
>
> (IV, 1667–73)

We need not doubt either Criseyde's or Chaucer's sincerity: Chaucer uses similar terms of his hero in the epilogue:

> Swich fyn hath, lo, this Troilus for love!
> Swich fyn hath al his grete worthynesse!
> Swich fyn hath his estat real above,
> Swich fyn his lust, swich fyn hath his noblesse!
> Swych fyn hath false worldes brotelnesse!
>
> (V, 1828–32)

The point of both love story and tragedy is that they involve a man of the highest excellence.

The description of the way in which Troilus first feels love is organized, I think, so as to enhance this effect. He meets Criseyde by chance, and he succumbs to the direct stroke of the jealous God of Love. Moreover Chaucer emphasizes the naturalness of love and the inevitability that one of his age and condition should sooner or later feel it. When it is established, his love is frequently spoken of in terms of illness and, indeed, produces the physical symptoms of illness. Troilus disguises the cause of his weakness at the house of Deiphebus, but we are expressly told that he did not have to pretend as to his physical state (II, 1527 ff.). He suffers, in fact, from love at its most violent and devouring, and is left with very little ability either to help himself towards its consummation or to cure himself when he has lost Criseyde. Thus, on the one hand, seen as one of the ways in which nature operates in the world for good, love expresses itself through, and even enhances, the nobility of a noble nature; on the other, it can also be thought of as a great natural calamity – an irresistible force like flood or earthquake, which brings destruction with it. As far as Troilus is concerned, love always has this double aspect, and, as we shall presently see, this quality is established from the early part of Book I and runs consistently through the poem.

The presentation of Criseyde's character is profoundly affected by Chaucer's conception of the importance of Troilus's love. He emphasizes her corresponding worthiness, and also her sincerity – at least at the moment. But he is not as lavish in her praise as he is in Troilus's and thus leaves the way open for future cause for blame. In the first description of her, for example, only her beauty is mentioned, and even this only as an appearance: it is so great that she *seemed* 'As doth an hevenyssh perfit creature' (I, 103–4). She is praised for her popularity and good reputation in Troy (I, 130–1), that is, again, for what she *seemed* to onlookers to be. The ironic possibilities are even greater when Pandarus praises her for freedom from vice after he has corrupted her, in a speech which leaves no room for doubt that he regards his act as corruption (III, 257). The poem is not, however, so ordered at these points that we can understand these passages as clearly satirical. It is, surely, rather that they contain latent ironies and ambiguities. Criseyde is good enough, but not for the demands of Troilus's love, in the situation in which she is placed – and Chaucer's praise of her never implies that she is.

The long second book is devoted to her gradual conversion to the idea of love by a combination of the influence of Pandarus and of circumstances. It is here that Chaucer diverges most widely from Boccaccio. He gives us fair warning, when he explains that her love was not 'sodeyn':

> For I sey nought that she so sodeynly
> Yaf hym hire love, but that she gan enclyne
> To like hym first, and I have told yow whi;
> And after that, his manhod and his pyne
> Made love withinne hire herte for to myne,
> For which, by proces and by good servyse,
> He gat hire love, and in no sodeyn wyse.
>
> (II, 673–9)

The gradualness of her conversion and the difficulty and length of the process are the material of all Book II, and a great part of Book III, and this detailed treatment can only add to the impression that there is nothing light or wanton about her, and that she is, in fact, a worthy object of love for this 'Ector the secounde'. Nevertheless, with all her worth, she does, in the end, betray Troilus; and Chaucer uses Books II to III with great subtlety, not only to build her up as a sympathetic and admirable character, but also to show how her mind is open to be worked on. The conclusion is unavoidable: the woman who can be influenced once can be influenced again – and more quickly.

Only a line-by-line analysis of these parts of the poem could show just how all this is achieved. Here it will be enough to give some examples of the way in which Chaucer shows us how a combination of skilful persuasion and the force of circumstances brings about the desired results in a not unwilling subject. Pandarus's first suggestion, an oblique and cautious introduction to the theme of love, that Criseyde should set aside her widow's weeds, is received with horror:

> 'I? God forbede!' quod she, 'be ye mad?
> Is that a widewes lif, so God yow save?
> By God, ye maken me ryght soore adrad!
> Ye ben so wylde, it semeth as ye rave.
> It sate me wel bet ay in a cave
> To bidde and rede on holy seyntes lyves;
> Lat maydens gon to daunce, and yonge wyves.'
>
> (II, 113–19)

Not only is her reaction an exaggerated one (Pandarus is not really either mad or raving), but her picture of herself as a penitent saint in a cave (she has in mind the typical figure of the penitent Magdalen)[24] is hardly appropriate: as she says herself in a moment of franker self-assessment, ' "What, par dieux! I am naught religious" ' (II, 759). It is not, therefore, altogether surprising when a repetition of the suggestion is much more mildly received. Pandarus has contrived to fill her mind with curiosity concerning the news he has for her, and she has no thought for anything else:

> Quod Pandarus, 'Now is it tyme I wende.
> But yet, I say, ariseth, lat us daunce,
> And cast youre widewes habit to mischaunce!
> What list yow thus youreself to disfigure,
> Sith yow is tid thus fair an aventure?'

'A! Wel bithought! for love of God,' quod she,
'Shal I nat witen what ye meene of this?'

(220–6)

Pandarus uses the same tactics when he puts forward his more
startling suggestion that she should give her love to Troilus. This is
first received with tears and cries of dismay:

And she began to breste a-wepe anoon,
And seyde, 'Allas, for wo! Why nere I deed?
For of this world the feyth is al agoon.
Allas! what sholden straunge to me doon,
When he, that for my beste frend I wende,
Ret me to love, and sholde it me defende?'

(408–13)

and she continues in this vein for two stanzas more. By the end of the
long argument her response is much milder. When Pandarus finally
insinuates:

'Ther were nevere two so wel ymet,
Whan ye ben his al hool, as he is youre;
Ther myghty God yet graunte us see that houre!'

(586–8)

she reproves him sharply, but there are no tears, and she is easily
pacified:

'Nay, therof spak I nought, ha, ha!' quod she;
'As helpe me God, ye shenden every deel!'
'O, mercy dere nece,' anon quod he,
'What so I spak, I mente naught but wel,
By Mars, the god that helmed is of steel!
Now beth naught wroth, my blood, my nece dere.'
'Now wel,' quod she, 'foryeven be it here.'

(589–95)

Her private thoughts on the subject, as Chaucer gives them, for
example at 600 ff. and 694 ff., are expressed in sober language: she
does not make any virtuous outcry when there is no one to hear it;
she is concerned, rather, to weigh chances and contingencies:

And, Lord! so she gan in hire thought argue
In this matere of which I have yow told,
And what to doone best were, and what eschue,
That plited she ful ofte in many fold.
Now was hire herte warm, now was it cold.

(694–8)

We can see the same hidden receptiveness to an idea – the same ability to let it work on her mind even while she protests against it – in Criseyde's answer to Diomede in Book V, 956 ff., where every statement is qualified and her thoughts always seem to run ahead of her words: the Greeks are noble, but so are the Trojans (967–8); I know that you (Diomede) are expert in love, but I cannot consider such a subject, and yet I know that you are nobly born (972–80); I can have nothing to do with love (it would suit me better to live in wo and lamentation until I die), but of course I can't say what I shall do after that, and at any rate I cannot think of such things yet (983–7); perhaps much later, if things go in a way that I don't expect – if the town is won, if I see things I never thought to see – and, anyway, let me speak to you again tomorrow, but not of love (990–6); and I will at least say that you are the only Greek that I could think of in this light; and I do not say that I will love you (but then I do not say that I won't); and I can only say, in conclusion, that I mean well! (998–1004).

There is high comedy in the vagaries of Criseyde's mind, and the speech has behind it the weight of all that we have seen and learnt about her. With one final stroke, indeed, Chaucer places her reaction to Diomede within the context of her whole experience of life as he has shown it to us; he is not merely poking fun at the illogicality of the feminine mind, he is demonstrating to us what the world looks like, and indeed is, to Criseyde. She turns her thoughts towards Troy and uses a phrase which echoes one used of the lovers' time of bliss in Book III (1819), when Troilus was 'in lust and in quiete':

> 'O Troie town,
> Yet bidde I God, *in quiete and in reste*
> I may yow sen, or do myn herte breste.'

(V, 1006–8)

'But, in effect . . .', Chaucer continues, she actually stays and listens to Diomede. For Criseyde it is the security of her world, as it presents itself to her at any given moment, that matters and that turns her towards the known safety of Diomede and away from the risk of returning to Troy. Troilus saw love otherwise.

Criseyde's mind is as receptive to the pressure of circumstances as to Pandarus's suggestions. In Book II, Chaucer shows her responding, with increasing effect, to the coincidental happenings which bring the idea of love and of Troilus constantly before her. First, when he rides past her window from the battlefield:

> So fressh, so yong, so weldy semed he,
> It was an heven upon hym for to see.
> (II, 636–7)

she responds with a directness which cuts cleanly through Pandarus's manœuvring and reminds us that her love is, in its way, as spontaneous and sincere as Troilus's:

> Criseÿda gan al his chere aspien,
> And leet it so softe in hire herte synke,
> That to hireself she seyde, 'Who yaf me drynke?'
> (II, 649–51)

When Criseyde is debating with herself whether or not to accept Troilus's love (II, 771 ff.), she hears Antigone sing a Trojan love song (827 ff.), and responds at once to the suggestion contained in it. The song of the nightingale in her garden (II, 918 ff.) reinforces this effect; and finally, she is visited by a dream in which an eagle takes her heart from her breast (925 ff.); that is, the preoccupations of her own mind show her the matter under debate as already decided.[25] She is presented as readily susceptible to the pressure of all these circumstances; but she is, emphatically, not presented as forced by them into the position of acting against her inclinations or without consideration for the probable consequences. Even when Pandarus is at his busiest, in the organization of her meeting with Troilus at his house, when Chaucer the narrator has most to say about the influence on the affair of the stars and of destiny, we can, if we read carefully, see that Criseyde is very far from being the passive victim of contrivance.

Before the episode begins Chaucer makes it clear that the relationship of Troilus and Criseyde has progressed to the point which makes such a meeting likely. Troilus:

> so ful stood in his lady grace
> That twenty thousand tymes, er she lette,
> She thonked God that evere she with hym mette.
>
> (III, 472–4)

The impression is, once more, of a frank, wholehearted response on Criseyde's part, which leaves little for scheming to do; although we are assured that Pandarus left nothing undone:

> For he with gret deliberacioun
> Hadde every thyng that herto myght availle
> Forncast and put in execucioun,
> And neither left for cost ne for travaile.
> Come *if hem list*, hem sholde no thyng faille.
>
> (519–23)

The lovers must still complete his preparations by playing their voluntary part.

Now, the main part of Pandarus's preparation is simple observation of the probabilities of the weather. It is 'upon the chaungynge of the moone', and it looks like rain (549–51). Any English countryman today would agree with Pandarus that a change of moon is likely to bring change of weather, and that, if it has been dry, it will then be wet; and, if 'auctorite' is needed, Macrobius says so too. Criseyde, presumably, could have made the same prediction. In fact, she does not have to do so because, when the invitation is given, the rain has actually begun:

> she lough, and gan hire faste excuse,
> And seyde, 'It reyneth; lo, how sholde I gon?'
>
> (561–2)

Pandarus insists, as usual trading on their friendly relationship – he will never see her again if she fails him (566–8). She then asks him, in a whisper, whether Troilus would be there. He swears that he is out of town; but, Chaucer says:

Nought list myn auctour fully to declare
What that she thoughte whan he seyde so –
(575–6)

and, indeed, Pandarus is careful to prepare her mind for Troilus's presence:

'Nece, I pose that he were;
Yow thurste nevere han the more fere.'
(571–2)

Her plea for discretion in lines 582–8 shows that she is pretty certain that Troilus will, in fact, be there; if he were not, there would be no need 'For to ben war of goosish peoples speche', for an ordinary dinner-party at her uncle's ought not to give rise to gossip. Her final, resigned comment is, to say the least of it, ambiguous:

'Em, syn I most on yow triste,
Loke al be wel, and do now as yow liste.'
(587–8)

Criseyde, then, sets out, in the rain, prepared for what she is to find. The rain duly gets worse, and it is here that Chaucer invokes Fortune, destiny and the planetary aspects which are the physical causes of the weather:

But O Fortune, executrice of wyrdes,
O influences of thise hevenes hye!
Soth is, that under God ye ben oure hierdes,
Though to us bestes ben the causes wrie.
This mene I now, for she gan homward hye,
But execut was al bisyde hire leve
The goddes wil; for which she moste bleve.
(617–23)

And it is at this point that he describes not merely the changing moon – enough in itself to ensure the probability of rain – but a conjunction of planets which he may well have observed during the exceptionally rainy year of 1385, as J. D. North explains.[26] Once more the fullest possible pressure of circumstances is brought to bear on Criseyde's inclinations. Owing to the operation of forces beyond her control, she cannot *now* go home without serious inconvenience. 'Now were it tyme a lady to gon henne!' as Pandarus says. Criseyde, indeed, shares with her women 'a verray feere' of the smoky rain. She has not been presented to us as a character at all likely to resort to heroic means to protect her honour. She is no Constance or Lucrece to risk even wet feet to ensure her safety from Troilus. Indeed, as her inclination is wholly on his side, she does not even fall back on the more simple expedient of saying no, when she finds herself in the position which all the probabilities of the case have lead her and the reader to expect.

Why, then, does Chaucer insert the passage on Fortune, 'executrice of wyrdes'? It is, in the first place, part of a whole system of references to the gods and to the planetary influences which runs through the poem, especially in Troilus's various appeals and prayers. These have been collected and analysed by Curry;[27] and we must leave the consideration of their significance in the poem as a whole until we come to examine the epilogue and its relation to the themes and ideas of the main part of the *Troilus*. In the context, however, after the delicate comedy of an exchange in which both Pandarus and Criseyde have much to conceal, and in which each is manœuvring for position, it seems fair to ask whether we can take this rather elaborate intervention of the narrator wholly seriously. It is, I think, more reasonable to read it as a part of the whole serio-comic development of the scene between uncle and niece. It is not altogether safe to argue from one work to another, where the poet's total purpose may be quite different, but we can compare another solemn appeal to the ineluctable power of destiny, at a point where Chaucer has been at some pains to show the comic development as the result of the sheer folly of his character; this is in the *Nun's Priest's Tale*. Here, when the cock has got his well-earned reward (and his responsibility for his own foolishness is pointed up through the fun poked at learned arguments concerning necessity and free will in lines 3234 ff.), Chaucer exclaims: 'O destinee that mayst nat been eschewed!' (*CT* VII, 3338). It is true that the *Nun's Priest's Tale* is wholly comic,[28] while the *Troilus* is not; nevertheless, if we look closely at the context of the invocation in the *Troilus* we can, I think, see that, far from being the expression of determinism, it constitutes an ironic comment on Criseyde's conduct and situation.

In the first place, there is a distinction between *God* and *the goddes*.

Fortune and the planetary influences operate on mankind under the control of God; they cannot, therefore, be thought of as so disposed as to compel Criseyde to an act which she thinks of as wrong, against her will. Since, as Chaucer has shown us, her will is by no means in wholehearted opposition to that of Pandarus and Troilus, it is not surprising that, since she has placed herself in a position in which the operation of Fortune and the planets with regard to the weather can affect the issue – giving her her choice between being placed in an equivocal position or wetting her feet – the *goddes* will is actually carried out, i.e., she does allow her conduct to be influenced by the weather; she does stay, and she does find herself in bed with Troilus. Secondly, Chaucer uses a phrase which, if we are to judge from his use of it elsewhere, has very definite implications for him. He speaks of mankind, under the influence of Fortune and the stars, as 'us bestes'. Now, in *Truth* he speaks of the man who falls under the influence of Fortune, and all the chances and changes of this transitory world, as a 'beast', with the exhortation:

> Forth, beste, out of thy stal!
> Know thy contree, look up, thank God of al.
> (*Truth*, 18–19)

The good man is *not* to be, like a beast, at the mercy of chance, but is to use his freedom of will to undertake a pilgrimage to his true home. The same terms are used in Palamoun's falacious argument that mankind is like the helpless beasts before the power of the uncaring gods:

> 'O crueel goddes that governe
> This world with byndyng of youre word eterne,
> And writen in the table of atthamaunt
> Youre parlement and youre eterne graunt,
> What is mankynde moore unto you holde
> Than is the sheep that rouketh in the folde?
> For slayn is man right as another beest.'
> (*CT* I, 1303–9)

If we take Palamoun's argument in the context of the *Knight's Tale* as a whole, there is, I think, no doubt that his acceptance of the position of a helpless beast under the power of the gods (plural; i.e., the planetary influences) is a tacit criticism of his conduct from the narrator's viewpoint.[29] We could, perhaps, find one more indication that the invocation in the *Troilus* has an ironical function in the similarity of its somewhat grandiose style to that of the opening of the *Envoy to Scogan*: 'Tobroken been the statutz hye in hevene'. Again, the purpose of the whole poem is quite different, but we could with justification conclude that Chaucer associated a certain grandiose way of writing with a shifting off of human responsibility on to planetary machinery, with an ironical or even (in the *Nun's Priest's Tale*) frankly comic approach to his subject matter.

It is certain, at any rate, that, like the cock in the *Nun's Priest's Tale*, Criseyde is caught:

> What myghte or may the sely larke seye,
> Whan that the sperhauk hath it in his foot?
> (III, 1191–2)

and the metaphor is emphasized by being carried over into Troilus's speech:

> 'O swete, as evere mot I gon,
> Now be ye kaught, now is ther but we tweyne!
> Now yeldeth yow, for other bote is non!'
> (III, 1206–8)

But, unlike Chauntecleer, Criseyde negates this effect of the helpless victim of circumstances by honestly admitting her own responsibility and, incidentally, at the same time allowing us to put a higher value on her love:

> To that Criseyde answerde thus anon,
> 'Ne hadde I er now, my swete herte deere,
> Ben yold, ywis, I were now nought heere!'
> (III, 1209–11)

In the whole scene, with its complex ironies, Chaucer has given us something which has nothing to do with either determinism or Christian didacticism, but which belongs to the highest realm of human comedy.

It is, probably, in the case of Pandarus that we are most tempted to detect a 'character study' in the modern sense, that is, a self-contained, self-regulating entity shown as affecting the development of the story in certain ways precisely because it is a being of a certain sort. In a sense, too, this is what Chaucer achieves, since Pandarus is, in the main, naturalistically presented; but to put the emphasis in the *Troilus*, or in any medieval work, on the integrity of character rather than on the integrity of the story and of the thematic material is, surely, to get it wrong.

Considered in relation to the structure of the poem as a whole, Pandarus's function is complex. He provides a fixed point of reference for the whole action, and also for the other two main figures, who are very largely presented through his eyes and his speeches; he is used, in part, as an observer of an action in which he himself is also involved – a role Theseus plays (with a difference) in the *Knight's Tale*. He helps to develop the major themes, in that, as we have seen, much of the material concerning the natural brevity and changeability of love is contained in his speeches, so that he stands beside Troilus somewhat in the manner of a character in a morality, urging him to action likely to prove ultimately destructive but, at the same time, showing awareness both of his own place in the scheme of things and of the true consequences of the actions he recommends. So a 'Pride of Life', or a 'Riches', can utter a self-analysing speech which shows full awareness of its true nature and position in the overall moral scheme. 'Goodes', for example, is just as ready to tell Everyman of his true nature as Pandarus or Criseyde are to tell Troilus of the true nature of love: on the one hand, Goodes says:[30]

> 'Syr, and ye in the worlde haue sorowe or aduersyte
> That can I helpe you to remedy shortly.'
>
> (401–2)

on the other:

> 'I am to brytell, I may not endure.
> I wyll folowe no man one fote, be ye sure.'
>
> (425–6)

The morality character exists to give expression to the logic of circumstances, and there are moments when Pandarus and Criseyde do the same: Pandarus, for example, in the speech in which he attempts to console Troilus by explaining the very temporary nature of earthly love (IV, 380 ff.); and Criseyde in her farewell at the end of her letter to Troilus, when she seems to leave the stage with the finality of a morality personification, whose essential nature makes it necessary for it to step out of an action which has moved beyond it:

> 'And, gilteles, I woot wel, I yow leve.
> But al shal passe; and thus take I my leve.'
>
> (V, 1084–5)

So Beauty takes leave of *Everyman*:

> 'Adewe, by Saynt Johan!
> I take my tappe in my lappe, and am gon!'
>
> (800–1)

Unlike such a personification, however, Criseyde still lingers to produce the inconsistencies and hesitations of her final letter (V, 1590 ff.).

The morality personification remains inhuman and is apt to take a brutal view – so Goodes says, logically but not kindly:

> 'Mary, thou brought thy selfe in care,
> Wherof I am gladde.
> I must nedes laugh; I can not be sadde.'
>
> (454–6)

In the same way the personifications of the Vision of Fortune in *Piers Plowman* do not go out of their allegorical definition, but cheerfully fail their victim when his actions have brought their logical result.[31] Criseyde and Pandarus, however, are tender-hearted, although Criseyde's tenderness does not stretch to a subject not actually before her eyes. Pandarus's sympathy and the pain that Troilus's sufferings cause him are continually emphasized;[32] and Criseyde, with some prompting from Pandarus, and with her own safety at the back of her mind, does, in fact, show an earnest desire to 'quenchen al this sorwe' in the scene at Pandarus's house (III, 1100 ff.). But the poem is organized from the point of view of Troilus – it is *his* double tragedy. In the end, therefore, the other two main figures drop away and we are left, in the description of his death and in the epilogue, with Troilus alone. Nevertheless, Pandarus and Criseyde are not abstractions derived from him: they do not represent his vices or attributes, although they are so handled by the poet that they show us the working out of his, and only his, destiny. There is no reason for us to hear of the final fate of either Pandarus or Criseyde. Their function in the poem is over when their contribution to Troilus's story is complete. In this sense they do play a part similar to that of the morality personifications; but Troilus's destiny is shown as working itself out in the external world, naturalistically conceived, and not in an internal retrospect, as in *Everyman*, or through the externalization of an internal conflict, which is the subject of many allegories. Pandarus and Criseyde therefore have a separate existence as 'characters' of a kind that the personifications could never have.

Moreover, it is in relation to this external 'real' world, in which Troilus's experience takes place, that Pandarus plays his most important part. He is the link between the two lovers and the medium through which their union is shown as the result, not of an instantaneous and self-contained marriage of true minds, but of an interplay of forces and circumstances arising from their whole background and setting within the world of besieged Troy. This is, of course, especially clear in the way in which Pandarus brings pressure to bear on Criseyde. As we have seen, he exploits the relationship, with its peculiar intimacy, which exists between them, and also makes full use of the hopes and fears which arise from her situation: her prospects of safety in Troy in the state in which she finds herself; her fears for what other people think; her practical difficulties in managing her affairs, when he pretends that she is threatened with legal action, and so lures her to the house of Deiphebus. All the scenes which develop the social background of life in Troy depend on Pandarus's presence. The description of Criseyde's paved parlour, where she reads with her maidens, and of her house with its different rooms,[33] exists as a part of the exposition of her intimacy with him. An overwhelming passion does not require an elaborate backcloth for its representation, but the greater complexities of the kind of intimacy which exists between Criseyde and Pandarus does. So, in the course of Pandarus's busy activity, we find that we need a description of Deiphebus's house and garden, and of the details of Pandarus's own house and the entertainment offered there. It is in relation to Pandarus that we hear of ordinary day-to-day pastimes: reading, singing, dancing, story-telling, amusing talk.[34] The only social contact of Criseyde's in which he does not play a part is the occasion when she is visited by the ladies of Troy to condole with her on her departure, and we have a view of some of the people whose opinion she is always thinking of, besides an indication of the extent to which they bore her.[35] It is, in the main, through Pandarus that we hear of all the other people of Troy who impinge on the story for a moment, usually by his contrivance. Thus, Hector, Deiphebus, Helen, are brought into Criseyde's range through his devices; it is through him that we hear of 'false Poliphete', with whom Criseyde has had dealings before – 'What is he more aboute, me to drecche' (II, 1471) – and who is supported by Antenor and Eneas (II, 1474).

Troilus, too, is drawn within the circle of these people by Pandarus. It is through Pandarus's intervention that he is brought to the house of the 'brother that thow lovest best', and that he is there the subject of the sympathy in his illness of both this brother and 'the faire queene Eleyne' (II, 1571 ff.). It is in this scene, too, that we have the little sub-scene in which Deiphebus and Eleyne pore over a letter sent by Hector on behalf of someone condemned to death – a passage which is solidly convincing as to their ordinary, friendly relationship, as well as to the existence of a busy and complicated world of affairs extending beyond the confines of the love story:

> Deiphebus gan this lettre for t'onfolde
> In ernest greet; so did Eleyne the queene;
> And romyng outward, faste it gonne byholde,
> Downward a steire, into an herber greene.
> This ilke thing they redden hem bitwene,
> And largely, the mountance of an houre,
> Thei gonne on it to reden and to poure.
>
> (II, 1702–8)

In the careful presentation of the details of Pandarus's house, as they affect his contrivance for the lovers' meeting, Chaucer uses a technique reminiscent of that of the *fabliau* in its concentration on particular objects and details of the setting in their relation to the twists and turns of the plot.[36] Troilus is hidden away where he can look through 'a litel wyndow in a stewe' (III, 601). Criseyde is placed in Pandarus's 'litel closet', while her women are 'in this myddel chaumbre that ye se', and Pandarus is to sleep in 'that outer hous allone'. There is reference to the closet door, to the unpinning of the door of the 'stew' – of the 'secre trappe-dore' (759) to which Pandarus leads Troilus 'in by the lappe', so that he is, as he tells

145

Criseyde, 'thorugh a goter, by a pryve wente, / Into my chaumbre come in al this reyn' (787–8). There are references to 'this furred cloke upon thy sherte' (738), to the bed and the 'beddes syde' on which Troilus sits and from which Pandarus withdraws with 'an old romaunce' and a light (976, 989–90) – the same light which he finally takes back to the chimney (1141) – to the cushion for which he runs (964), and to the 'bare sherte' to which he strips Troilus (1099). In fact, there are probably more references to details of objects and background in this passage than anywhere else in the work. The effect is at once to emphasize the thoroughgoing nature of Pandarus's contrivance and to place the consummation of the love of Troilus and Criseyde within a setting which we feel as extending in its solidity of detail from their centre of ideal bliss back into a wider world of ordinary life – in this case that of Troy with its ominous problems.

The same technique is used, again through the medium of Pandarus, when Troilus's sorrow is also placed against the same solid background, although the detail is less striking. Troilus and Pandarus are on 'the walles of the town' (V, 1112) to see if they can see Criseyde coming. This location of the scene is carefully kept before us: Troilus says 'I wole unto the yate go. . . . I wol don hem holden up the yate' (1138–40). In his efforts to see 'fer his hed over the wal he leyde' (1145); the gates in the wall are mentioned again and a little scene is sketched:

> The warden of the yates gan to calle
> The folk which that withoute the yates were,
> And bad hem dryven in hire bestes alle,
> Or al the nyght they moste bleven there.
>
> (1177–80)

It is not only that the wall and its gates are kept before us: what Troilus sees from them is also indicated, briefly and lightly, but naturalistically, as it would in fact have been seen by anyone in such a position. Every figure seen in the distance raises his hopes until it comes near enough to be recognized:

> Tyl it was noon, they stoden for to se
> Who that ther come; and every maner wight
> That com fro fer, they seyden it was she,
> Til that thei koude knowen hym aright.
>
> (1114–17)

In the same way, an object glimpsed in the distance raises hopes, only to be recognized as it comes nearer:

> 'Have here my trouthe, I se hire! Yond she is!
> Heve up thyn eyen, man! maistow nat se!'
> Pandare answerede, 'Nay, so mote I the!
> Al wrong, by God! What saistow, man, where arte?
> That I se yond nys but a fare-carte.'
>
> (1158–62)

The same sense of perspective is observed – though, again, only lightly indicated – in Troilus's desperate survey of the ground:

> He loketh forth by hegge, by tre, by greve,
> And fer his hed over the wal he leyde.
>
> (1144–5)

Time, as well as space, is carefully marked out. Troilus sends for Pandarus at daybreak, after a sleepless night (1105 ff.). They wait until noon, when Troilus finds excuses for Criseyde: she would not come in the forenoon (1114 ff.). They dine and come again in the afternoon (1130 ff.). 'The day goth faste, and after that com eve' (1142), and more excuses are made (1147 ff.): she will come at night – 'And, deere brother, thynk not longe t'abide. / We han naught elles for to don, ywis.' (1155–6). Finally, the gates are shut, and anyone caught outside will have to stay there – 'And fer withinne the nyght, with many a teere / This Troilus gan homward for to ride' (1181–2). The details of place and the continual references to the wearing out of the long, anxious day contribute to build up the strongest impression of Troilus's feelings as he watches.

Again, in an earlier scene in Book V, when Troilus goes with Pandarus to look at Criseyde's empty house, besides his elaborate address to it as 'O paleys desolat', we have such concrete and naturalistic detail as:

> How shet was every wyndow of the place
>
> (534)

or the precision of

'And at that corner, in the yonder hous,
Herde I myn alderlevest lady deere
So wommanly, with vois melodious,
Syngen . . .'

(575–8)

Pandarus, as we have said, is not a mere static figure out of a
morality. Chaucer shows him not only manipulating the affairs of the
lovers, but reacting strongly to them. He loves Troilus whole-
heartedly and wishes him well. He shows both tact and sensibility in
his dealings with Criseyde. His business, the zeal with which he
drives his niece like a deer to Troilus's net, may at times appal us,
but we cannot deny that the total effect is of a figure for whom we
feel liking and that his charm and tact reflect a pleasant light on the
other two main figures – to have provoked such zeal and such devotion is an added worthiness. It is not Pandarus alone who has this
positive effect. The whole social world of Troy – to which, as we have
seen, Chaucer links the lovers – is conceived in terms which help to
create the conviction that we are dealing with people of the highest
excellence. Hector, the greatest of the heroes of Troy, is kind and
courteous to Criseyde; Helen is gracious and sympathetic and shows
responsibility in her attention to the demands of Hector's letter.
Deiphebus, Troilus's favourite brother, shows the same qualities.
Hospitality is always ready and good manners and consideration for
guests are unfailing in the houses of Criseyde, of Deiphebus and of
Pandarus. Unfortunately, all these people, together with Troy itself,
are at the mercy of forces which have little regard for excellence; the
bright feathers of Troy are plucked away; Hector, who was so kind to
Criseyde, is dead before the poem ends; Troilus also falls a victim to
the war as well as to love; the Trojans are to be defeated and their
town burnt. Like Troilus's love for Criseyde, the whole gracious
world of Troy is not built to last.

It remains to consider the end of the poem, the death of Troilus and
the epilogue, for the light which they throw on the themes of the
work as a whole. The thematic material, indeed – the conception of
love, the moral and philosophical content – is woven through, and is
not detachable as a coherent, separate 'message'. In fact, it would be
true to say that we have to look for structural and dramatic coherence

in the *Troilus*, not for coherence of 'doctrine'. Nevertheless, it is in the light of the finale that we can best consider the underlying assumptions and ideas.

The end of the poem has been felt by some critics to come as an anticlimax, or even as a repudiation – tacked on by Chaucer the fourteenth-century Christian, rather than by Chaucer the poet – of what has gone before. We are, I think, faced with two problems here. First, what does Chaucer really mean in this final part, and, secondly, is the result artistically and structurally justified?

To take Troilus's actual death first, Chaucer tells us that his spirit, freed from the body, goes 'ful blisfully' up to the hollow of the eighth sphere, passing the elements on its way. It is, I think, clear that by the eighth sphere he means the sphere of the moon – that is the eighth counting downwards, from the sphere of the fixed stars,[37] towards the earth. If this were not so, there would be little point in mentioning the elements rather than the successive planetary spheres through which Troilus would have to pass on his way upward. According to medieval, Aristotelian-derived cosmology, he would, in fact, in mounting to the sphere of the moon, pass the realms of the different elements, probably in the order earth–water–air–fire.[38]

From the sphere of the moon he sees, and hears, above him, the planets and the music of the spheres – the part of the universe which is not subject to change. Looking downward he sees sublunary nature – the changeful world which he is now in a position to understand and to assess at its true value. He realizes that it is as nothing compared to the 'pleyn felicite' of heaven – that is, we have a final summing up of the theme of true and false felicity, which was developed in Book III – and he at last compares the changing world of nature with the unchanging realm above and, by implication, natural with spiritual love. The result is that he laughs at those who are mourning for him, just at the moment when they should rejoice at his discovery of true values and his freedom from the wheel of change. He also explicitly condemns all the effort that goes into the pursuit of the 'blynde lust': the undirected, unreasoning desire – 'the which that may nat laste'.

After he has been vouchsafed this revelation Troilus's spirit is taken away by Mercury to its permanent home 'ther as Mercurye sorted him to dwelle' (V, 1827). The next stanza laments his end, the end of all his 'grete worthynesse' as well as of his 'lust', his desire, and includes this in 'false worldes brotelnesse':

Swich fyn hath, lo, this Troilus for love!
Swich fyn hath al his grete worthynesse!
Swich fyn hath his estat real above,
Swich fyn his lust, swich fyn hath his noblesse!
Swych fyn hath false worldes brotelnesse!
And thus bigan his lovyng of Criseyde,
As I have told, and in this wise he deyde.

(V, 1828–34)

Now, what has Chaucer actually done? He has not sent Troilus's soul to heaven, nor has he caused him to be 'stellified' any more than he was himself in the *House of Fame*. He has merely placed him for a moment at a vantage point where he can make the same admission which we have already seen the other two main characters make – that earthly love is subject to change, as are all worldly joys under the dominion of Fortune – and where, as the other two could not, he can find an alternative. When Mercury takes his spirit off to its permanent dwelling, we can only assume that Chaucer thought of him as conducting Troilus to join other pagan heroes in such afterlife as was their lot; and the exact significance of this insistence on the pagan past must presently be considered in more detail. For the moment it is enough to say that Troilus, without surrendering his status as a hero of old, pagan times, has learnt that he has been pursuing 'the blynde lust', instead of the 'pleyn felicite' of heaven, and that, in the nature of things, the joys that belong to the sublunary world cannot last. In contrast, the 'hevene above' is not subject to change. There is no reason to believe that Chaucer thinks of this as in any sense an exclusively Christian revelation. That stability is gained by freeing the soul of blind passions is as much the message of pagan philosophy as of Christianity; and pagan epic allows special treatment to the souls of certain heroes.[39]

Moreover, we cannot say that there is anything here which has not been amply prepared for in the body of the poem. There are, as has already been pointed out, significant echoes or part-echoes of earlier phrases in the closing section, especially of Book III near the beginning. But even in Book I, we already hear of the blindness of passion in the sublunary world:

O blynde world, O blynde entencioun!

(I, 211)

That this is a very deliberate guiding of the poem, from its start, along lines which are to be consistently developed right through to the epilogue, with its explicit rejection of the blindness of passion, is, I think, clear, if we pause to look closely at the relation of this early passage to the corresponding one of *Il Filostrato*.

In the early part of the first book of the *Troilus*, Chaucer follows Boccaccio closely. The proem is new, and he emphasizes the theme of the Trojan War in a stanza based on the *Aeneid* (II, 57–63), but after this he renders Boccaccio almost stanza-by-stanza until he approaches stanza xxv of Book I of *Il Filostrato*. Within, and just before, this stanza, comes a change: Chaucer introduces into his version a slight but important shift, which at once completely alters the tone of his original and prepares the way for the neat dovetailing in of a new and independent passage.

The first three lines of Boccaccio's stanza read:

> O cecità delle mondane menti,
> Come ne seguon sovente gli effetti
> Tutti contrarii a' nostri intendimenti!

(O blindness of mundane minds! How often follow effects all contrary to our intentions!)

This stanza comes immediately after Troilo's raillery against lovers and his asseveration that he will take care not to fall again into the snare. This is the 'intention' which is about to be contradicted by the course of events, and the rest of this stanza emphasizes this: before Troilo leaves the temple he is to be transfixed once more by love:

> Troil' va ora mordendo i difetti,
> E' solleciti amor dell' altre genti,
> Senza pensare in che il ciel s'affretti
> Di recar lui il quale amor trafisse
> Più ch' alcun altro, pria del tempio uscisse.

(Troilo now raileth at the weakness and anxious loves of other people without a thought of what heaven hasteneth to bring upon him, whom Love transfixed more than any other before he left the temple.)

Chaucer, of course, as part of his different conception of Troilus's character, made his love for Criseyde the first that he had ever felt. He therefore shortens the mockery of lovers that he found in Boccaccio, since it is in part concerned with Troilo's earlier experience of love, and, in the process, takes the second part of Boccaccio's stanza xxv first, placing it immediately after the conclusion of Troilus's mocking speech and rendering the general sense thus:

> At which the God of Love gan loken rowe
> Right for despit, and shop for to ben wroken.
> He kidde anon his bowe nas naught broken;
> For sodeynly he hitte hym atte fulle;
> And yet as proud a pekok kan he pulle!
> (I, 206–10)

Then, after this description of the vengeance of the God of Love, not before, Chaucer exclaims in an apostrophe based on the first three lines of Boccaccio's stanza xxv, but with significant changes of wording and meaning, and with an expansion which fills the place of the lines he has already used:

> O blynde world, O blynde entencioun!
> How often falleth al the effect contraire
> Of surquidrie, and foul presumpcioun;
> For kaught is proud, and kaught is debonaire.
> This Troilus is clomben on the staire,
> And litel weneth that he moot descenden;
> But alday faileth thing that fooles wenden.
> (I, 211–17)

This expansion leads on, through the simile of 'proude Bayard', to a completely new passage (218–66) of philosophical reflection on the subject of love.

Boccaccio's stanza contained no more than a proverbial commonplace of the type 'Man proposes, God disposes', introduced merely to point the joke at Troilo's expense, and causing no delay in the progress of the narrative, which immediately hurries on, in stanza xxvi, to Troilo's first sight of Criseida. Chaucer gives a fuller, and a different, significance to his expanded version of this casual apostrophe. This arises partly through the difference, slight as it seems at

first sight, in its position. Chaucer has arranged his material so that
the apostrophe stands at the close of a section, not as a comment
made in passing. He has already described Troilus's rebellion
against love and the punishment meted out to him by the God. This
is presented as happening at this point, 'for sodeynly he hitte hym
atte fulle', though the actual events through which the God's sentence
is carried out are still to come. These, in fact, form the next section in
Chaucer's narrative, a section which is formally introduced by a
stanza which brings the poet back after his digression, and which
also repeats the summary of Troilus's whole story which Chaucer
gave us in the first stanza of the poem:

> But for to tellen forth in special
> As of this kynges sone of which I tolde,
> And leten other thing collateral,
> Of hym thenke I my tale forth to holde,
> Bothe of his joie and of his cares colde;
> And al his werk, as touching this matere,
> For I it gan, I wol therto refere.
>
> (I, 260–6)

In between these two sections Chaucer has placed the passage of
philosophical comment which we are considering, comment which
relates to love in general and which casts its shadow over the whole
development of his story, not merely over the moment in it with
which he is concerned in Book I. In this new position, as a comment
on something completed, the words 'O blynde world, O blynde
entencioun' have a significance other than that of the Italian that
corresponds to them, and they enable the passage of general reflection
which follows to develop naturally and smoothly. The comment is,
no doubt, primarily on the immediate blindness of Troilus, who has
no foresight of the fall which his pride is about to have, and this, as
we have seen, is its whole significance in Boccaccio's poem. But as
Chaucer phrases it and as Chaucer places it, it cannot, I think, fail to
carry with it wider implications. Certainly the ideas that follow (and
which are not in *Il Filostrato*) have this wider reference.

The lines:

> This Troilus is clomben on the staire,
> And litel weneth that he moot descenden;
>
> (I, 215–16)

introduce the idea of the inevitability of the descent from good to ill fortune, which applies to all human affairs and to the whole pattern of tragedy which lies ahead. This stair is the same as that on which Troilus moves when 'his aventures fellen / Fro wo to wele, and after out of joie' (I, 3–4). From the idea of Fortune which imposes an inescapable pattern of alternate ascent and descent on human affairs, including love, Chaucer goes on to give another reason for the inevitability of the way in which Troilus's story develops. Love itself is part of the direction which Nature, by her laws, gives to all living beings. The point of the Bayard simile is that the horse that 'gynneth for to skippe / *Out of the weye*' is forced to realize:

> 'Yet am I but an hors, *and horses lawe*
> I moot endure, and with my feres drawe.'
>
> (I, 223–4)

Applied to Troilus, 'this fierse and proude knyght', the simile teaches us that:

> evere it was, and evere it shal byfalle,
> That Love is he that alle thing may bynde;
> For may no man fordon the lawe of kynde.
>
> (I, 236–8)

Further, as an ennobling power that 'causeth moost to dreden vice and shame' (252), love ought not to be resisted, even if it were possible. That it is not possible, Chaucer emphasizes even more strongly by the introduction of the idea of the relation of love to the freedom of the will:

> So ferde it by this fierse and proude knyght:
> Though he a worthy kynges sone were,
> And wende nothing hadde had swich myght
> Ayeyns his wille that shuld his herte stere,
> Yet with a look his herte wax a-fere,
> That he that now was moost in pride above,
> Wax sodeynly moost subgit unto love.
>
> (I, 225–31)

These are ideas which, as we have seen, recur in the *Troilus*, especially in Book III, for example in the proem and in Troilus's song

'Love, that of erthe and se hath governaunce' (III, 1744 ff.); and they are to be found, too, in *Il Filostrato*, notably in Troilo's song (III, stanza lxxiv ff.). But Boccaccio does not emphasize them, and only uses them to help to show the perfections of his Troilo as a lover. He certainly would not have felt them appropriate to a straight-forward narrative passage like that of Book I. That Chaucer does find them appropriate shows that even at this stage he is concerned with the first meeting of the lovers as something which sets in motion a train of events whose implications go far beyond the immediate moment, perhaps beyond the love story itself.

The moment at which Chaucer begins to shift the direction of Boccaccio's work in such a way as to make the insertion of a passage containing these ideas possible is, as has been said, the first line of the apostrophe, which, in Chaucer's hands becomes 'O blynde world, O blynde entencioun'. This is clearly in part derived from 'O cecità delle mondane menti . . . nostri intendimenti', but Chaucer has com-pressed the Italian into one line composed of two parallel phrases of nouns qualified by the adjective 'blynde'. The effect is terser and more striking: as we have seen, the position of the apostrophe has become more important, and Chaucer's line is better suited to that position. It is obvious, too, that Chaucer's phrases are much more general in meaning than were Boccaccio's. The change of adjective to noun in 'world' necessarily has this effect. 'World' here, I think, means the state or conditions of human life.[40] In the working out of these conditions an 'entencioun' can appropriately make itself felt.

It is clear from the context of Boccaccio's lines that he meant by 'intendimenti' very much what we mean to-day by 'intentions', which are not always borne out by events. To Chaucer, I think, the word 'entencioun' meant something quite different: 'the action of straining or directing the mind or intention towards something'.[41] He does, in fact, use it in this way in his translation of Boethius: 'al the entencioun of the wil of mankynde . . . hasteth to comen to blisful-nesse' (IV, pr. ii, 49–51). Chaucer, in fact, is making a comment which concerns the conditions and strivings of human life in general, not merely, as Boccaccio was, remarking in passing on the inability of minds like Troilo's to foresee the future with its ironic reversals.

It remains to ask why Chaucer should bring together the words 'blynde' and 'entencioun' in this context, and what, precisely, he meant by them. He has already, again in passages which depart from *Il Filostrato*, introduced into our minds the idea of darkness and

blindness in relation to love. In the proem he speaks of himself as
unhappily cut off from love:[42]

> So fer am I from his help in derknesse.
>
> (I, 18)

In the stanza which Chaucer substitutes for Troilo's dispraise of
women, he makes Troilus apostrophize lovers as 'O veray fooles,
nyce and blynde be ye!' (V, 202). Finally, in the epilogue, the translated soul of Troilus condemns:

> al oure werk that foloweth so
> The blynde lust, the which that may nat laste.
>
> (V, 1823–4)

Thus Chaucer relates blindness to love[43] in three ways: it is associated, in the references to Chaucer himself, with the failure to achieve
love (regarded as a desirable end); in Troilus's jesting words and in
the epilogue, with misdirected love; and in the 'blynde entencioun',
of line 211 of Book I, I believe, with the idea also of something
which mistakes or fails to achieve its proper direction.

We can now paraphrase Chaucer's apostrophe: 'O blindness
inherent in the conditions of human life! O blind striving of the
mind!' When Chaucer wrote this I think that he blended into his
rendering of Boccaccio's wording a phrase which he had used in his
translation of Boethius's *de Consolatione Philosophiae*:[44] 'What sekith
thilke blynde thoght?' It cannot, of course, be proved that he had
already used the phrase 'blynde thoght' in Book V of the *de Consolatione* when he wrote Book I of the *Troilus*, though there is nothing
against the assumption. It might, of course, be argued that a memory
of a phrase used in the *Troilus* influenced him when he came to m. iii
of Book V of the *de Consolatione*, since to assume that the wording of
this translation affected Chaucer's choice of words early in Book I of
the *Troilus* is to assume that the Boethius translation was complete,
or nearly so, almost before the *Troilus* was begun.[45] But 'blynde
entencioun' is an unusual phrase, as we have seen, not fully accounted
for by the Italian source, and its meaning is not, I think, altogether
clear until it is related to the thought of Boethius. The words 'blynde
thoght', on the other hand, would probably have come to Chaucer's
mind naturally enough as he read the Latin, and, whether the translation as we have it was complete or not, it is obvious that he
had read the Latin, and read it carefully, before he began *Troilus*.

'What sekith thilke blynde thoght?' renders 'quid caeca petit', where the antecedent is 'mens caecis obruta membris'. 'Mens' (quite suitably translated 'soul' in I.T.'s translation of 1609) would be likely to suggest 'thought' to a medieval translator. In *Piers Plowman* (B, XV, 23 ff.), where a commentary on the characters of the Dowel section is given on the basis of a passage from the *Differentiarum Liber* of Isidore of Seville listing the various faculties of the soul, Langland renders 'dum scit, Mens est' as 'for that I can and knowe, called am I *mens*' (B, XV, 25), and '*mens*' clearly corresponds to the character called Thought in the previous section.

The fifth book of the *de Consolatione* contains the discussion of God's foreknowledge and man's free will, which Chaucer utilized later on in the *Troilus* (in Troilus's speech, IV, 955 ff.). In Book V, prosa ii, the servitude of the human will had been discussed: where there is reason, the will is free,

> But the soules of men moten nedes be . . . lasse fre whan thei slyden into the bodyes; and yit lasse fre whan thei ben gadrid togidre and comprehended in erthli membres.
>
> (V, pr. ii, 26 ff.)

In prosa iii follow the arguments against free will, ending with the conclusion:

> 'it byhoveth by necessite that the lynage of mankynde . . . be departed and unjoyned from his welle, and failen of his bygynnynge (*that is to seyn, God*).
>
> (V, pr. iii, 208 ff.)

Metrum iii considers the cause of this 'unjoining' and sees it not in the reality of things, but in the nature of man:

> ther nis no discord to the verray thinges, but thei clyven alwey certein to hemself. But the thought of man, confownded and overthrowen by the derke membres of the body, ne mai nat be fyr of his derked lookynge (*that is to seyn, by the vigour of his insyghte while the soule is in the body*) knowen the thynne subtile knyttynges of thinges.
>
> (V, m. iii, 10 ff.)

But if the soul lacks knowledge of truth, how is it that it feels 'so gret love' and 'that it angwisshous desireth to knowe?' On the one hand, no one labours to learn what is known already; on the other:

> yif that he knoweth hem nat, what sekith thilke blynde thoght?
>
> (V, m. iii 28–9)

The answer is:

> But whanne the soule byholdeth and seeth the heye thought
> (*that is to seyn, God*), thanne knoweth it togidre the somme and
> the singularites (*that is to seyn, the principles and everych by hymself*).
> But now, while the soule is hidd in the cloude and in the
> derknesse of the membres of the body, it ne hath nat al foryeten
> itself, but it withholdeth the somme of thinges and lesith the
> singularites.
>
> (V, m. iii, 38 ff.)

Thus, in the closest relation to the question of free will we are given a picture of the soul as inherently filled with love and desire for something which, in its association with the body, as part of the common and unavoidable lot of human kind, it can only approach blindly, through darkness and cloud.

Boethius has, of course, much to say in the *de Consolatione* concerning the power and function of love, of which this love of the soul is a part, in the universe as a whole and in the life of mankind. For him, the love which holds the whole universe in its course is the cause of the 'attempraunce' which 'norysscheth and bryngeth forth alle thinges that brethith lif in this world; and thilke same attempraunce, ravysschynge, hideth and bynymeth and drencheth undir the laste deth, alle thinges iborn' (IV, m. vi, 34 ff.). Love, in fact, like Fortune, imposes a pattern of ascent and descent, natural death as well as natural life. He relates the love which controls the universe to individual human lives thus: 'This love halt togidres peples joyned with an holy boond, and knytteth sacrement of mariages of chaste loves' (II, m. viii, 21 ff.).

The *de Consolatione*, therefore, provides the model of a love which is an essential part of the whole frame of the universe, and which is as essential to the microcosm as it is to the macrocosm, in that it is expressed in the pattern of individual births and deaths and of individual loves. Thus, at the beginning of Book I, Troilus, in common with the rest of humanity, is subject to the necessity of submitting to love in some form; but this 'entencioun', this inherent urge of the soul, is as yet blind, and its only potentiality not directed to an end. Books II and III describe, once it is directed towards Criseyde, his ascent into successful love. The two great paeans of praise in Book III, the proem and Troilus's song, emphasize the successful, positive side of love, but, as we have seen, in their insistence on love as a universal, cosmic force they also imply the darkness of the opening of Book I and the pattern of descent after ascent imposed on earthly love according to Book I (and to Boethius) by Fortune – or even, according to the *Knight's Tale* and, again, to Boethius, by the nature of earthly love itself, which is built after the same manner as Fortune. Chaucer is not really, in fact, presenting us in these passages with a view of love so optimistic that it clashes with the implications of the opening and close of the poem.

The descent which follows Troilus's successful ascent in love begins in Book IV; and, when it is complete, Chaucer looks back to paraphrase line 211, of Book I. Troilus's soul freed now from the 'derke membres of the body' condemns:

> al oure werk that foloweth so
> The blynde lust, the which that may nat laste;
> And sholden al oure herte on heven caste.
>
> (V, 1823–5)

This passage is, of course, based on the *Teseida* of Boccaccio, and in the corresponding stanza Boccaccio also uses the word 'cechitate'; but Boccaccio's statement is very much vaguer. The corresponding lines are:[46]

> . . . la vanitate
> forte dannando dell' umane genti,
> li quai, da tenebrosa cechitate
> mattamente oscurati nelle menti,
> seguon del mondo la falsa biltate,
> lasciando il cielo.

(Strongly condemning of the vanity of the human race, which, out of dark blindness follows the false baseness of the world, abandoning heaven.)

> (*Teseida*, XI, 3)

Boccaccio's source here was probably in part the *Somnium Scipionis*,[47] which Chaucer, of course, also knew and used elsewhere, but it is possible that, in the reference to the blindness of the human race, he may also have had Boethius in mind. It is worth noting that the *de Consolatione* (IV, m. 1) also has a striking description of the flight of the soul from its earthly bonds, though in this case it refers to the living soul, winged by philosophy. There are, however, points in common between the description of Boethius and that of the *Somnium Scipionis*. Although Chaucer does not, as far as I can see, use any part of Boethius's description of the soul's flight in his account of the voyaging of Troilus's soul, it may still have forged one more link in the chain of associations which influenced him as he wrote the *Troilus*; and it is to be noted that he does refer to it in the *House of Fame*.[48]

In the third stanza of Book XI of the *Teseida*, Chaucer found once again the idea of darkness and blindness as inherent in the condition of the human race, leading them to follow 'falsa biltate' instead of setting their minds towards heaven. These ideas seem to have coalesced in his mind in the phrase 'blynde lust', which, like the 'blynde entencioun' of Book I, line 211, is at once terser and more precise in meaning than the Italian equivalent, and, we may now say, more obviously linked to the *de Consolatione* (V, m. iii). The sense of 'lust' is, I think, complex. It could still, in the fourteenth century, mean merely desire, or the pleasure at which desire was aimed, without qualification as good or bad.[49] It therefore contains the meaning of 'entencioun' as it was used in Book I, line 211. But it also, I believe, implies a change of focus and carries a more precise range of meaning. For one thing, by Chaucer's day the shift towards 'sexual desire' was already in progress with or without the qualification 'of the flesh'.[50] In the next century, Hoccleve, for example, could use it without qualification in a way which shows that this sense was then securely established – 'Thou deemest luste and love convertible' (*de Regimine Principum*, line 1563). For another thing, there are signs that the whole phrase 'the blynde lust' had special connotations for Chaucer. It is, in all probability, modelled on Dante's 'cieca cupidigia' (*Inferno*, XII, 49), the blind rage of those who sin by violence; this, in the context, like the 'blynde lust' of the *Troilus*, is related to the transitoriness of earthly life and the contrasting unchanging quality of eternity:

> O cieca cupidigia e ira folle,
>   che sì ci sproni nella vita corta,
>   e nell' etterna poi sì mal c'immolle!

(O blind lust, that with guilt and folly goes!
   That in the short life fires so with its spark
   And in the eternal plungeth to such woes.)
      (*Inferno*, XII, 49–51; Binyon trans.)

Chaucer uses the phrase elsewhere, where there can be no doubt of its implication. In the *Man of Law's Tale* it forms part of a comment on the would-be ravisher of Constance, whom she pushes overboard to his death by drowning:

O foule lust of luxurie, lo, thyn ende!
Nat oonly that thou feyntest mannes mynde,
But verraily thou wolt his body shende.
Th'ende of thy werk, or of thy lustes blynde,
Is compleynyng.
      (*CT* II, 925–9)

In the *Legend of Good Women*, the same phrase is used of Tarquin:[51]

'His blynde lust was al his coveytynge'
      (F, 1756)

In spite of the fact that Chaucer thus uses the phrase in contexts in which it implies outright condemnation, this need not be the precise nuance in the *Troilus*. Troilus, after all, is no ravisher of unwilling women. What is implied is that the passionate, irresistible impulse – the *vis amoris* of medieval Latin writers[52] – which is an unavoidable part of love, has carried him into a position in which destruction is inevitable. The reason for this lies in part in the object of his love – his misfortunes arise through 'his lovyng of Criseyde' (V, 1833) – and through the unrestrained violence with which he pursues this object. This aspect of Troilus's passion, which is crystallized in the phrase 'blynde lust' at the end, is constantly brought before us. In Book III, when the lovers are first parted, there are three references within three consecutive stanzas to the insatiable and uncontrollable nature of his desire:

So harde hym wrong of sharp desir the peyne . . .
      (1531)

. . . she, for whom desir hym brende . . .
      (1539)

Desir al newe him brende, and lust to brede
Gan more than erste.

(1546–7)

There is, perhaps, a further hint, if one is needed, that Chaucer does not intend to class Troilus with Tarquin and those who are led into criminality by their unbridled desires. This comes through an association of lust with the journey of the soul after death which he had already used in the *Parlement of Foules*. There, as we have seen, he adapted a passage concerning the fate of those who give themselves up to uncontrolled 'libido' at the end of the *Somnium Scipionis*:[53]

eorum animi, qui se corporis voluptatibus dediderunt, earumque se quasi ministros praebuerunt, impulsuque libidinum voluptatibus obedientium, deorum et hominum iura violaverunt, corporibus elapsi, circa terram ipsam volutantur; nec hunc in locum, nisi multis exagitati saeculis, revertuntur.

(the souls of those who have given themselves up to bodily pleasures and become their slaves, and who, being driven by their passions in obedience to those pleasures, have violated the laws both divine and human, when they are freed from the body, revolve round the earth and return hither only after long ages of torment.)

(II, xvii)

This becomes, with a significant addition, in the *Parlement*:

But brekers of the lawe, soth to seyne,
And likerous folk, after that they ben dede,
Shul whirle aboute th'erthe alwey in peyne,
Tyl many a world be passed, out of drede,
And than, foryeven al hir wikked dede,
Than shul they come into this blysful place,
To which to comen, God the sende his grace.

(78–84)

Chaucer has added a prayer which, with its reference to God's grace, has a distinct Christian colouring.

Now, in the description of Troilus's death and the comments on it, all this material is present, but it is, as it were, separated out. Troilus is certainly not one of those who 'maxime se a corpore abstrahet' (*Somnium*, II, xvii) or who is free from that involvement in the passions which Cicero and Macrobius constantly deplore. Nevertheless, 'His lighte goost ful blisfully is went' (1808), suggesting the final arrival at the blissful place of the *Parlement* and the swift flight (*velocius*) 'in hanc sedem et domum suam' of the *Somnium Scipionis*. The prayer of the *Parlement*, in so far as it is Christian in tone, is removed from the immediate vicinity of the description of Troilus's death and forms a part of the epilogue proper (1860 ff.), where it becomes an explicit appeal to love the Trinity.

According to Cicero it is the soul, which on earth was occupied by the 'curae de salute patriae' – what Chaucer in the *Parlement* renders as the 'commune profite' – that takes the swiftest flight to its heavenly home. It is, I think, because of this special 'worthiness' in Troilus that his soul, too, flies blissfully upward. He actually dies in the course of a war on his country's behalf, not because of love, and he is carefully introduced to us as one of his country's greatest soldiers. Moreover, as we have seen, he is shown as mindful of his country's safety and willing to put it before his own love in the matter of Criseyde's exchange for Antenor. In pagan terms, therefore (and Chaucer would presumably recognize this material as belonging to Cicero, however he regarded Macrobius), Troilus qualifies, as a true son of his country, for flight to a place of bliss rather than to the punishment which his involvement in the bodily passions might lead one to expect. In Christian terms, of course, the matter could be very differently viewed, and Chaucer is careful to separate the explicitly Christian comment, which he added without a break in the *Parlement*, and place it in the epilogue proper. In fact, he is not altogether explicit about Troilus's fate. He suggests, by the blissful flight of his soul, the death of a pagan statesman or patriot, as described by Cicero or by Lucan; and then, by introducing Mercury Psychopompus, who leads his soul to its final abode, he suggests the death of a hero of pagan epic. Troilus's fate after death is thus pointedly described in terms of antique paganism – 'of payens corsed olde rites' (1849). Chaucer thus avoids, while he actually has his hero before the reader's eye, any involvement with Christian loss or Christian damnation; yet, by sending him finally *sub umbras* to join the shades of other examples of pre-Christian worthiness, he prepares the way for a change of focus, standing back now from the old, far-off story with which we have been so closely involved, to comment, in the Christian terms appropriate to his own day, on the pity of it all.

I do not think that the explicit Christianity of the epilogue, with its deliberate use of conventional forms in the exhortation to love Christ crucified and its closing address to the Trinity, is intended so much to repudiate the values of the main part of the poem – we have seen that a pessimistic view of love is built into it from the beginning – as to mark out the story as belonging to the distant past – 'Lo here, the forme of olde clerkis speche' (1854) – and to emphasize that it has been treated in a way which we could, loosely, call 'historical'. If this is so, it tells us more about Chaucer the poet, and less about Chaucer the fourteenth-century Christian, than has sometimes been supposed.

Chaucer, it seems to me, shows a clear sense of the past here and elsewhere in his poetry. This manifests itself in two ways. In the first place, in a feeling – which we are used to associate with the Renaissance – for the value of Classical literature and in a desire to emulate it in the vernacular; that he felt this strongly in the case of the *Troilus* is shown by lines 1786–92.[54] And secondly, in an understanding – which we, again, associate with the period from the Renaissance onwards – of the past as having its own identity, as being essentially unlike the present. This shows itself in the careful reproduction in the *Troilus* – as in the *Knight's Tale* – of some at least of the typical features of pagan life and ceremonial, and also, I think, in the constant preference for the Platonic-Stoic blend of philosophical and moral thought which was typical of the late Roman authors on whom Chaucer was relying. It is true that he is likely to have believed at least some of these authors – Seneca, Boethius and perhaps Statius – to have actually been Christians. Nevertheless, such ideas are kept distinct from expressly Christian references; so much so, in the case of the *Troilus*, that the incursion of incontrovertibly Christian ways of thinking and speaking in the epilogue comes as a shock to most readers. It is hardly to be expected that Chaucer should, with all this, show a view of history which is like the modern one and regard the past as existing solely in the light of its own integrity. For him and for his age, history is progress, part of a great pattern which unfolds, according to the divinely ordained scheme, from the comparative sadness and dark-ness of the pre-Christian era to the light and hope brought by

Christianity. A poem which has a historical viewpoint, in the sense that it presents the past as past, would, in this view, hardly be complete unless it also gave some indication of the whole framework of the historical progression. Troilus is led away under the pre-Christian shades by Mercury; but 'yonge fresshe folkes', of Chaucer's own day have quite other expectations after death and will not encounter the old messenger of the gods.

It is in the stanzas in which Chaucer sets the 'corsed olde rites' against the love of Him who died on a cross, that this essentially historical contrast is most uncompromisingly expressed:

> Lo here, of payens corsed olde rites,
> Lo here, what alle hire goddes may availle;
> Lo here, thise wrecched worldes appetites;
> Lo here, the fyn and guerdoun for travaille
> Of Jove, Appollo, of Mars, of swich rascaille!
> Lo here, the forme of olde clerkis speche
> In poetrie, if ye hire bokes seche.
>
> (V, 1849–55)

Here, Chaucer is certainly reiterating what he has already repeatedly said in the main part of the poem concerning the transitory and ultimately unsatisfactory nature of such a love as Troilus's for Criseyde. But he is also concerned to comment on the whole pagan world of the love story, its aspirations and the gods who ruled it. The 'payens corsed olde rites' are not in any sense the rites of love. They belong to the worship of 'Jove, Apollo, of Mars, of swich rascaille'.

The gods have, indeed, been much involved in the love story. It is the God of Love in person who sets the whole action in train, and Troilus makes frequent resort to the temples of the gods, where he offers prayers to their unresponsive inhabitants. He has, indeed, been in the position of the unhappy lovers depicted in Venus's temple (among whom he is included by name) in the *Parlement of Foules*, whose devotion to the goddess brought them no relief. Moreover, both Troilus and Pandarus have been shown as addicted to other practices which Chaucer certainly associates with pagan worship. These are astrology and divination by dreams and auguries.

Chaucer makes so much use of such beliefs as a part of the machinery of his plots in the *Troilus* and elsewhere, that it is important to try to determine his attitude to them. A study like Curry's, for example, in *Chaucer and the Medieval Sciences* seems to me at times uncritical, in that it fails to distinguish what is said or done by an imagined character from Chaucer's own view (usually expressed as narrator) and fails to take into account the function of such references in the development of the story. Both astrology and divination, by dreams or other means, involve a crucial problem: they affect the concept of human free will, and it is in the main for this reason, and on this basis, that the revival of astrology was opposed in the west in the twelfth to thirteenth centuries.[55] The actual physical rapport of the planets with inanimate objects, or with nature apart from the human soul, was not usually questioned and, indeed, played a considerable part in medieval medical practice, as Chaucer's own account of the Physician in the Prologue to the *Canterbury Tales* (*CT* I, 414 ff.) shows – to say nothing of such medically detailed passages as the description of Arcite's illness and death in the *Knight's Tale*. In this sense, of course, the planets are seen as exerting an influence on human life. That they could rule the human mind and determine the human fate was, however, vigorously contested.[56] Chaucer's own view is quite clearly and unambiguously expressed in the *Treatise on the Astrolabe* when he discusses personal horoscopes 'as wel in alle nativites as in questions and eleccions of tymes' (II, iv, 1–3). These, he says are 'rytes of payens, in whiche my spirit hath no feith' (II, iv, 58–9). It seems certain, therefore, that Chaucer includes in the 'payens corsed olde rites', which bring the hero to destruction, the use of fortunate and unfortunate ascendents (*Astrolabe*, II, iv, 30 ff.) for determining the best time for an undertaking, especially in Books II and III.[57]

Dreams and auguries are specifically included in pagan religion in Book V, when Pandarus says:

> For prestes of the temple tellen this,
> That dremes ben the revelaciouns,
> Of goddes . . .
>
> (365–7)

although he goes on to give other explanations (367 ff.: auguries are mentioned in line 380). This is a passage which comes immediately after Troilus's speech about his own death, when he speaks of the funeral rites 'and pleyes palestral' (304), of the dedica-

tion of his shield to Pallas, and calls on Mercury to guide his soul –
as, in fact, he very shortly does. We are, indeed, in this part of the
poem, firmly held within the world of pagan custom and belief.
The very dream which gives rise to this discussion is a reminiscence
of pagan epic. Troilus dreams:

> he were allone
> In place horrible, makyng ay his mone.
> Or meten that he was amonges alle
> His enemys, and in hire hondes falle.
>
> (V, 249–52)

Similarly, Dido in the *Aeneid*:

> agit ipse furentem
> in somnis ferus Aeneas, semperque relinqui
> sola sibi, semper longam incomitata videtur
> ire viam, et Tyrios deserta quaerere terra.

> (In sleep, Aeneas himself fiercely drives her on to frenzy, and
> she seems always to be left alone, always on a weary journey,
> seeking her Tyrians in a deserted land.)

Yet Pandarus continues on a different note:

> 'Wel worthe of dremes ay thise olde wives,
> And treweliche ek augurye of thise fowles,
> For fere of which men wenen lese here lyves,
> As revenes qualm, or shrichyng of thise owles.
> To trowen on it bothe fals and foul is.
> Allas, allas, so noble a creature
> As is a man shal dreden swich ordure!'
>
> (V, 379–85)

Condemnation of dependence on omens is not necessarily an
anachronism in the mouth of Pandarus. Chaucer knew the *Thebaid*
of Statius well, and there he would find condemnation just as outspoken. For example:[58]

> unde iste per orbem
> primus venturi miseris animantibus aeger
> crevit amor? divumne feras hoc munus, an ipsi,
> gens avida et parto non umquam stare quieti,
> eruimus, quae prima dies, ubi terminus aevi,
> quid bonus ille deum genitor, quid ferrea Clotho
> cogitet? hinc fibrae et volucrum per nubila sermo
> astrorumque vices numerataque semina lunae
> Thessalicumque nefas. at non prior aureus ille
> sanguis avum scopulisque satae vel robore gentes
> mentibus in usae.

(Whence first arose among unhappy mortals throughout the
world that sickly craving for the future? Sent by heaven,
wouldst thou call it? Or is it we ourselves, a race insatiable,
never content to abide on knowledge gained, that search out
the day of our birth and the scene of our life's ending, what the
kindly Father of the gods is thinking, or iron-hearted Clotho?
Hence comes it that entrails occupy us, and the airy speech
of birds, and the moon's unnumbered seeds, and Thessalia's
horrid rites. But that earlier golden age of our forefathers,
and the races born of rock or oak were not thus minded.)

(III, 551–61)

Statius, it is clear, links divination of various kinds with the casting
of horoscopes ('seeking out the day of our birth'). Pandarus mentions
the effect which the changes of the heavens, as expressed in the
changing seasons and by the moon, have on dreams:

> 'And other seyn, as they in bokes fynde,
> That after tymes of the yer, by kynde,
> Men dreme, and that th'effect goth by the moone.'
>
> (V, 375–7)

concluding: 'But leve no drem, for it is nought to doon' (378).
It is, thus, likely that Chaucer intended to condemn the casting of
horoscopes, and unqualified belief in the determining power of
the stars, as part of the 'ordure' of line 385, just as he condemns
them as 'rytes of payens' in the *Treatise on the Astrolabe*.

It is tempting to see, in this emphasis on man's nobility as freeing
him from such beliefs, a foreshadowing of later ideas, like those of

Pico della Mirandola, that the inherent dignity of human nature, independently of any religious attitude, places man above the influence of the stars, or of any determining power. This would be, however, to miss the exact nuance of Pandarus's words, with their reference forward to the epilogue (V, 1831), where Troilus's 'noblesse' is brought to a final end. In these lines, indeed, Pandarus does, I think, go beyond the immediate context and expresses something which is not entirely compatible with its epic paganism. We have already seen that this is characteristic of Pandarus's comments on the action. It is, for example, he who introduces the idea of celestial love at a moment when, in strictly naturalistic terms, he would hardly be thinking of it, and who reintroduces the idea of the inevitability of a descent from Fortune's favours at a key point in Book III. Here, I think, Pandarus goes even further beyond the immediate context and anticipates the narrator's own final judgement on the story in the epilogue. What Pandarus, the character we have come to know, would have meant by 'noble' is perhaps uncertain. What Chaucer means can be ascertained if we look at some other passages in his works.

In the *House of Fame*, 'nobility' is the term Chaucer applies to God as the creator of the first, perfect man:

> 'O God!' quod y, 'that made Adam,
> Moche ys thy myght and thy noblesse.'
> (970–1)

In the *Second Nun's Prologue* he uses the same term with reference to the recovery of the perfection of the creation through the action of the second Adam, when he says, of the Blessed Virgin:

> Thow nobledest so ferforth oure nature,
> That no desdeyn the Makere hadde of kynde
> His Sone in blood and flessh to clothe and wynde.
> (*CT* VIII, 40–2)

These passages[59] suggest that the nobleness which ought to save mankind from the practices condemned by Pandarus, and by implication by the epilogue, is of a special kind.

In the *Second Nun's Prologue*, Chaucer is, in fact, following a passage in the *Divina Commedia*, in which Dante relates the ennobling

of man through the incarnation to his whole nature, which includes
the body:

> Tu se colei che l'umana natura
> nobilitasti sì, che'l suo fattore
> non disdegnò di farsi sua fattura.
>
> (*Paradiso*, XXXIII, 6–7)

In extending the nobility of man back to his creation, as well as
making it dependent on the effects of the incarnation, Chaucer is
in accord with the eucharistic prayer:

> Deus, qui humanae substantiae dignitatem mirabiliter condidisti,
> et mirabilius reformasti; da nobis per huius aquae et vini
> mysterium, eius divinitatis esse consortes, qui humanitatis
> nostrae fieri dignatus est particeps, Jesus Christus.

> (O God who in creating human nature didst wonderfully
> dignify it, and hast still more wonderfully renewed it; grant
> that by the mystery of this water and wine, we may be made
> partakers of his divinity who vouchsafed to become partaker
> of our humanity – Jesus Christ.)

Macrobius also wrote of the nobility of man, in a passage which
Chaucer certainly read; but for him this is restricted to the soul
and consists in the cultivation of the virtues:

> Sic enim anima virtutes ipsas conscientia nobilitatis induitur;
> quibus post corpus evecta, eo unde descenderat, reportatur;
> quia nec corpora sordescit, nec onerata eluvie, qui pure ac
> leve fonte virtutum rigatur.

> (Thus the soul through its very realization of its high estate,
> assumes the virtues by which, the body left behind, it is raised
> to the place from whence it came; for a soul which is permeated
> by the pure and subtle stuff of the virtues is not defiled or
> weighed down by the impurities of the body.)
>
> (*Somnium*, I, ix)

Chaucer, Dante and the eucharistic prayer relate the nobleness
of man to God's creation and redemption of humanity as a whole,
not to any such neo-Platonic descent of the soul into matter.[60]
Man, in fact, for the Christian writers, is noble in so far as he is
created in the image of God, and this necessarily implies the possession

of free will, which, in its turn, implies a natural bent towards the virtues. It is for this reason, as a challenge to the freedom of the will, I believe, that Pandarus (or Chaucer) condemns belief in the determining power of omens, etc., in such strong terms: 'swich ordure' in the *Troilus*; 'swich filthe' in the *Parson's Tale* (*CT* X, 608). St Thomas Aquinas expresses the same view as to the freedom of the good man from the influences of the stars – a freedom rather different to that envisaged by later thinkers like Pico della Mirandola. In his consideration of the question 'Utrum corpora caelestia sint causa humanorum actuum' (*Summa Theologica*, I, qu. cxv, iv) he quotes an old saying of 'the astrologers themselves'; 'sapiens homo dominatur astris'.[61] The reason for this is that 'nihil prohibet aliquem hominem per liberum arbitrium passionibus resistere'; so that, although the passions are 'motus sensitivi appetitus, ad quas cooperari possunt corpora caelestia', yet, since they are within human control, the celestial influence is also under control for the wise man 'inquantum scilicet dominatur suis passionibus'. On the other hand, it could also be argued that, in so far as a man places himself at the mercy of his passions (as Chaucer repeatedly assures us Troilus did), so he also places himself at the mercy of the 'cruell goddes' or the planetary powers. Chaucer's quiet comment at the end of his emphatic description of the intense and unbridled nature of Troilus's passion seems to imply some such conclusion:

> Desir al newe hym brende, and lust to brede
> Gan more than erst, *and yet took he non hede*.
>
> (III, 1546–7)

The gods, and the rites which belong to their worship, are thus condemned not only in the epilogue, but also within the main part of the poem. There is another passage, too, in Book V, which contributes to this effect. This is the stanza in which Troilus curses the gods:

> And ther his sorwes that he spared hadde
> He yaf an issue large, and 'deth!' he criede;
> And in his throwes frenetik and madde
> He corseth Jove, Appollo, and ek Cupide,
> He corseth Ceres, Bacus and Cipride,
> His burthe, hymself, his fate, and ek nature,
> And, save his lady, every creature.
>
> (V, 204–10)

This involves an alteration of Boccaccio,[62] and I think the reason for it is that Chaucer intends to range his hero away from 'swich rascaille' and so to prepare not only for the measure of bliss which he is able to give him after his death, but also for the whole conception of human destiny which is implied at the end of the poem. This passage comes within the section which we have already noticed as being particularly careful to treat Troilus as a pagan epic hero; and it is, I think, likely that Chaucer has in mind another famous hero who also reviled the gods, and who indeed was so far ranged against them that his 'virtus' was called 'iniqua'. This hero is Capaneus in the *Thebaid*,[63] and we know that he was in Chaucer's mind in this part of his poem from the fact that his death is included in the summary of the story of Thebes which is given to Troilus by Cassandra. She tells him:

> 'also how Capaneus the proude
> With thonder-dynt was slayn, that cride loude.'
> (V, 1504–5)

His cries are in defiance against the gods, and they cause so much alarm and confusion on Olympus that the lesser gods even fear that Jove's thunderbolt may not be enough to subdue him. In contrast to the enmity shown him by the gods of Olympus, his glorious shade (*insignem umbram*) is received in Elysium with universal praise:

> dum coetu Capaneus laudatur ab omni
> Ditis et insignem Stygiis fovet amnibus umbram.
> (*Thebaid*, XI, 70–1)

Instead of receiving punishment after death for his defiance of the gods, Capaneus gains a worthy place in an after-life over which the gods of Olympus appear to hold no sway. Statius's epic is overshadowed and haunted by the ancient curses of the gods, by omens and divinations of all kinds; but Chaucer could certainly have gathered from it the impression that, even in this old dark world of Theban guilt, as much the work of gods as men, which Statius takes as his theme – 'sontesque evolvere Thebas' (I, 2)[64] – a worthy hero might sometimes escape from the power of the gods after death. Nor is Capaneus the only hero in the *Thebaid* who gains glory after death. The spirit of Menoeceus, who, even more than Capaneus, dies for the commonweal, is given a celestial flight and a place among the stars. His story is told in the same tenth book in which Chaucer would have read of the death of Capaneus. He dies as a willing sacrifice for the good of Thebes, and Virtus, a goddess and the close companion of Jove, and Pietas 'clasped and bore his body lightly to the earth – for his spirit long since is at the throne of Jove and demands for itself a crown among the highest stars'.[65] It is Virtus, indeed, who is responsible for stellifying heroes, and when she comes down from heaven 'the shining stars gave way before her, and those fires that she herself had fixed in heaven' ('quosque ipsa polis adfixerat ignes', X, 637).

Chaucer, like Boccaccio before him, must have formed his idea of the status and probable fate of epic heroes very largely on the basis of the *Thebaid*; although, as we have seen, there are other sources involved in the descriptions of the flights of Arcite's and Troilus's souls. From the *Thebaid*, too, Chaucer could not fail to get the impression of a kind of double way of looking at the gods. At times they are all, including Jupiter their king, no more than a 'rascaille', quarrelling in heaven and desolating earth. But at other times the lesser gods are seen in the service of a Jove who is the creator of the stars, 'great author of the earth and of the gods',[66] and the founder of the heavenly abode: 'effusum chaos in nova semina texens' ('making the vast expanse of chaos into the new seeds of things', III, 484). This is the Jupiter who is 'auctor of nature', and the Creator 'Thorugh which that thynges lyven alle and be' of the proem to Book III.

Whether or not Chaucer, like Dante, thought of Statius as a Christian poet,[67] he thus could not fail to get the impression that in the *Thebaid* the machinery of the gods is used on two levels. On the one hand, it expresses philosophical and cosmological ideas which are not incompatible with the Christian idea of an all-powerful and benevolent creator; on the other, it corresponds to the apparently irrational forces which affect human life. The gods are constantly referred to in the *Thebaid* in company with chance, fortune, the stars.[68] Indeed, in the very passage just quoted, in which Jupiter appears unequivocally as creator, there is a reference to 'unpropitious Jove', which to a medieval reader would inevitably seem to refer to the planet.[69] At times, even, the gods seem to mean no more than the worst and most irrational of the human passions – and, as we have seen, since the passions are peculiarly liable to lay man open to the influences of the stars, this would not seem incongruous to a fourteenth-century reader. This emerges clearly near the beginning of the epic in Oedipus's prayer to the gods of Tartarus and to Tisiphone:

> 'da, Tartarei regina barathri,
> quod cupiam vidisse nefas, nec tarda sequetur
> mens iuvenum; modo digna veni, mea pignora nosces.'

('Grant me, O queen of Tartarus's abyss, that I may see the evil that I long for; nor will the minds of the youths [his sons] be slow to follow. Only come worthy of yourself; you will recognize them as my sons.') (I, 85–7)

This is an issue which is of the greatest importance for the understanding of the *Knight's Tale*, and we shall have to return to it. As far as the *Troilus* is concerned, ambiguities of this kind give the poet the possibility of treating his hero's fate in a way which, while it avoids the anachronistic imposition of Christian values, still makes it possible to link the ideas of an historical past with those of the present in such a way as to lend high seriousness to the tragedy.

Yet with all its high seriousness, and its high comedy, the *Troilus* is not primarily a philosophical poem. It does not exist to present a clearcut message or to elucidate a point of doctrine. Its unity is a poetic, and not necessarily a logical one; and within its poetic integrity there is, surely, no problem in reconciling the two high points of ecstatic lyricism, the one in Troilus's moment of blissful love, the other in the invocation to the Christian God of love in the epilogue. It is true that a consistent philosophical position underlies the work. There are no contradictions in the idea of love which it presents, either in human life or in the universe as a whole – provided always that we allow for the contradiction implicit in love itself. It remains 'a dredful joye', and Troilus's question 'If love be good, from whennes cometh my woo?' (I, 402) is, to the end, both crucial and unanswered.

The poet's method, in fact, is, fundamentally, still that of the shorter poems and of the love visions. His manner is still essentially urbane. No compulsion is brought to bear on the reader. Even in the epilogue it is a case of the arrangement of a graceful, and gracious, withdrawal of poet and audience from the closeness of their contact with a story which must now be seen as a part of the past, in spite of the vividness with which it has up to now been felt as immediately present, rather than of any sudden imposition of a new and doctrinaire approach.

Within the body of the poem, too, the philosophizing is always urbane. Troilus handles the argument on predestination as an amateur – as it were, with gentlemanly inaccuracy, and the whole passage is really more important as a manifestation of his character than as a philosophical statement. Chaucer certainly knew the solution to the dilemma, which follows in the passage of the *de Consolatione* which he is using. It seems likely that he could rely on his audience's knowing it too; at any rate, he makes no officious narrator's comment, but leaves them to press matters to their due conclusion, or not, as they please.

In the proem to the third book, there are also ambiguities and a certain philosophical holding back. The beauty and lyricism of the verse make their effect, as an introduction to the love scenes which are to follow, in a quite unambiguous way; but the ideas expressed are more complicated. For example the line:

> God loveth, and to love wol nought werne
> (III, 12)

which represents a significant alteration of Boccaccio,[70] has more than a single implication. On the one hand, within the cosmological setting of the whole passage, it means no more than that the creative love which brings nature into being is reflected in the pattern of individual loves which ensures its continuity. More precisely, it could also imply, with the *Roman de la Rose* (to say nothing of the Wife of Bath), that human sexual love is authorized as part of the divine plan for the world. Applied more precisely still to the story we are actually reading – an application which we can hardly fail to make – it means that the love of Troilus and Criseyde and its consummation are also authorized, in that they reflect a divine act of love. Once this last application is made, the question naturally arises as to whether we are dealing with the Christian creator (the passage is an invocation to Venus – which does not necessarily simplify the matter); with the pagan cosmological creator-Jove, or with a notoriously amorous King of the Gods, addressed in the next stanza in terms both of creator and lover of mortal women (the words 'amorous him made / On mortal thyng' carry out the

ambiguity). The same kind of exploitation of the ambiguities inherent
in the late pagan view of the gods is to be found, though in a much
cruder form, in a Latin poem preserved in a twelfth-century manuscript. The poet describes the love affairs of Jove and concludes:[71]

Nec qui gesserunt	peccare dii potuerunt –
Aut monstravere	nobis ea facta licere.
At si que nobis	virtus dominatur amoris,
Igne sui teli	superavit numina celi.
Quid culpare soles	quod amat nunc carnea proles?
Et mortale genus	quid ob hoc culpare solemus?

(The gods who did such things could not have sinned –
rather they have shown us that these actions are right. If any
power of love prevails in us, it is that which has conquered the
gods by its burning shaft. Why do you ever censure the fact
that now mankind also loves? Why are we wont to blame the
race of men for this?)

This poem, like the proem to Book III, is an odd mixture of cosmology and philosophy, combined with a perfectly frank invitation
to sexual intercourse:

Quandos nos vobis	pacto sociamur amoris
Hec sunt magnorum	connubia sacra deorum!

When we are united with you in love, this is the sacred
marriage rite of the great gods!

(88–9)

There is, of course, not the slightest reason to believe that Chaucer
ever read these lines, but they testify to a medieval way of using
the machinery of the Classical gods to bring about more than one
result at the same time.

Chaucer further confuses the philosophical issue towards the end
of the proem, when he paraphrases, and changes, Boccaccio's
lines. Boccaccio wrote of Venus:

Tu sola le nascose qualitadi
Delle cose conosci, onde 'l costrutto
Vi mette tal, che fai maravigliare
Chi tua potenza non sa riguardare.

176

(Thou alone knowest the hidden properties of things, out of
which thou bringest such order that thou makest marvel
whoever knoweth not how to regard thy power.)

(III, 78)

This is the cosmic power of love which rules the elements and
preserves the order of nature. Chaucer, however, after a beginning
which leads us to expect a philosophical conclusion, changes both
meaning and tone. He starts:

> Ye knowe al thilke covered qualitee
> Of thynges, which that folk on wondren so,
> Whan they kan nought construe how it may jo
>
> (III, 31–3)

but, instead of the hidden properties of the universe, we suddenly
find that we are dealing with information of a very different kind:

> . . . how it may jo
> She loveth hym, or whi he loveth here,
> As whi this fissh, and naught that comth to were.
>
> (III, 33–5)

In fact, Chaucer, at one and the same time, achieves a great lyrical
effect, suggests a serious cosmology and demonstrates the kind
of familiarity, both with his ideas and his audience, which enables
him to play with his philosophical material and to use it to underline
the fact that his work has comic as well as serious aspects. This kind
of shifting and glancing from one facet of the subject to another
without any awkward or violent transitions, seems to me a happy
instance of Chaucer's good relations with his audience, as well as
with his subject matter, and to exemplify the kind of urbanity in
the handling of philosophical argument which is to be found in the
shorter poems. It also plays an important structural part in this
much greater poem, in that, in this key position, it ensures that our
attitude to the love story remains as flexible as Chaucer's very
complex treatment of it requires.

Indeed, the love story, not doctrine, is the heart of the poem, and
Chaucer has done with it what he was never to do again – exposed
his reader directly, with only the slightest intervention on the part

of the narrator, to the full impact of the action and the actors, that is, to 'love in dede' with all its inherent, painful and irresolvable contradictions. The naturalism with which the events and characters are presented in the *Troilus* is, certainly, repeated again and again in the *Canterbury Tales*, but never again at such close quarters without the intervention of the device of the frame and of a narrator who is clearly differentiated from his narration. The narrator, certainly, is present in the *Troilus*, but present as a familiar of the reader, addressing him quietly and intimately, in a way which is a continuation of the technique of the minor poems. It is this intimacy with the reader which makes possible a subtlety of detailed treatment which would be out of place in the longer perspective of the *Canterbury Tales*. The variations in feeling, the precise indications of what is held back, as well as what is openly said, in scenes, for example, like that in which Pandarus gives and Criseyde accepts the invitation to dinner, or the consummation scene itself, in which the lovers' moment of bliss flowers brilliantly out of the equally brilliant web of intrigue and cross-purposes; these are like nothing that we know of in any medieval literature, and they were not to find any parallel for a long time. Chaucer, at any rate, never exactly reproduced the manner or the achievement of the *Troilus*.

Notes

Cross references to the present volumes are given in bold type

1 Introduction: Chaucer and the English tradition

1 See also **pp. 5 ff.** It is often assumed that, because Chaucer laughs at some features of earlier English romances in *Sir Thopas*, the form itself must have been an outmoded one. In fact, appreciation of the joke depends on a very precise identification of formulae and motifs, which presupposes an audience familiar with works of this kind.

2 See the quotations from George Ashby and an unknown writer in Caroline F. E. Spurgeon, *Five Hundred Years of Chaucer Criticism and Allusion* (Cambridge, 1925) I, pp. 54 and 49; and **II, chapter 6.**

3 R. W. Chambers, ed., *Form and Style in Poetry* (London, 1966), p. 50.

4 Charles Muscatine, *Chaucer and the French Tradition* (Berkeley and Los Angeles, 1960), p. 244.

5 Walter F. Schirmer, *John Lydgate: A Study in the Culture of the Fifteenth Century*, trans. Ann E. Keep (London, 1961), pp. 31–2.

6 Such dates are, of course, arbitrary. In 1360 Chaucer would have been about twenty and a decade was to pass before he wrote the *Book of the Duchess*, the earliest of his poems that we can date with certainty, but hardly his first. The works of his most important contemporaries – Gower, Langland and the *Pearl*-Poet – come well after this date. Going back two hundred years, we come to the approximate period of the Peterborough Chronicle continuation (extended to 1154), an accomplished piece of prose writing in a language identifiably Middle English. It is, of course, only during the next century that literary works in the vernacular become numerous.

7 It may be significant that the words 'poetry' and 'poetical' are late fourteenth century introductions – perhaps Chaucer's own. Even 'poet' is not recorded before 1300, when it first appears, applied to Homer, in the *Cursor Mundi*. See the articles on these words in the *OED*.

8 Romances, for example, long continued to be popular – in the case of *Guy of Warwick* new editions continued to be printed well into the seventeenth century. Caxton considered the older type of adaptation from a Classical text, the *Roman d'Enée*, worth re-printing in an age which was producing good translations. The alliterative style continued

in use until the early sixteenth century, in spite of Chaucer's preference for a less idiosyncratic, more universal kind of language.

9 J. Edwin Wells, *Manual of Writings in Middle English* (New Haven, Conn., 1916), with supplements. A new edition is in preparation under the general editorship of J. Burke Severs (New Haven, Conn. 1967–).

10 In *The Lay of Havelok the Dane*, 2327, 'Romanz-reading on the bok' is part of the public, and mainly outdoor, festivities to celebrate Havelok's coronation. In *Troilus and Criseyde*, a romance (of Thebes) is read privately, in a parlour, by Criseyde and her maidens. The itinerant performer would hardly be welcome in such a setting, but this does not, of course, mean that his repertory did not continue to be owned and read.

11 See Laura H. Loomis in *Sources and Analogues of Chaucer's Canterbury Tales*, W. F. Bryan and Germaine Dempster, ed. (Chicago, 1941), pp. 486 ff., and the same author's 'Chaucer and the Auchinleck MS', *Essays and Studies in Honour of Carleton Brown* (New York and London, 1940), pp. 111 ff.

12 *Sir Thopas* is a 'tail-rhyme' romance. For the view that these were the work of a distinct 'school' of poets and may therefore have had a distinctive style of performance, with or without music, see 'The English Tail-rhyme Romances', A. McI. Trounce, *Medium Aevum*, I–III, pp. 168 ff.

13 Rosemond Tuve, *Allegorical Imagery: Some Medieval Books and their Posterity* (Princeton, N. J., 1966), p. 337.

14 See Dorothy Everett, 'A Characterisation of the Middle English Romances' in Patricia Kean, ed., *Essays on Middle English Literature* (Oxford, 1955), pp. 1 ff.

15 G. Schleich, ed., *Sir Degarré* (Heidelberg, 1929), ll. 51–70. For more convenient comparison with Chaucer, I have eliminated the special letters ʒ and þ in Middle English quotations in this chapter. As far as possible, romances are quoted from the most recent and authoritative edition. When no good modern edition is available, I have, for convenience, used W. H. French and C. B. Hale, ed., *Middle English Metrical Romances* (New York, 1930). Quotations without further reference will be found there.

16 A. J. Bliss, ed., *Sir Orfeo* (Oxford, 1966, 2nd ed.), ll. 63–74. Quotations from this poem are from the Auchinleck MS.

17 For a more northerly, and also more vigorous, version see K. Brunner, ed., *Seven Sages of Rome*, EETS, 191 (1933). The *koiné* tends to be more clearly defined in the south.

18 A. B. Friedman and N. T. Harrington, ed., *Ywain and Gawain*, EETS, 254 (1964), ll. 59–67.

19 See **pp. 86 ff.**

20 See **II, pp. 152 ff.**

21 See Wolfgang Clemen, *Chaucer's Early Poetry*, trans. C. A. M. Sym (London, 1963), p. 193.

22 A. J. Bliss, ed., *Sir Launfal* (London, 1960), ll. 346–8. See further **pp. 22–3.**

23 G. H. McKnight, ed., *Floris and Blancheflour*, EETS, 14 (1901), ll. 235–44.

24 Muscatine, *French Tradition*, p. 107.

25 J. Zupitza, ed., *Guy of Warwick*, EETS, 42, 49 and 59 (1883, 1887 and 1891). Whenever possible I quote from the Auchinleck MS.

26 See 'To John Paston, 1448, 19 May', *Paston Letters*, selected and edited by Norman Davis (Oxford, 1958), vii, p. 8.

27 E. Salter, *Chaucer: The Knight's Tale and the Clerk's Tale* (London, 1962), pp. 23–4.

28 G. V. Smithers, ed., *Kyng Alisaunder*, EETS, O.S., 227 (1952 for 1947), 3942–51.

29 Aurelio Roncaglia, ed., *Teseida*, Scrittori d'Italia, 185 (1941) II, 26.

30 Muscatine points out the early presence of the mixed style in French romance, especially in Chrétien. In Chaucer's case, however, he places the main emphasis on the *fabliau* as a source of realism. Muscatine (*French Tradition*, pp. 41 ff. and ch. 3).

31 *Boccaccio on Poetry*, trans. Osgood (reprinted New York, 1956), pp. 37, 39.

32 'In loquêntia gallica non habet similem.' On the debate see A. Piaget, 'Chronologie des Epîtres sur le *Roman de la Rose*', *Études romanes dédiées à Gaston Paris* (Paris, 1891), pp. 113 ff.

33 E.g., *Piers Plowman*, B, XII, 16 ff., although Langland, characteristically, is more concerned with the ethics of verse composition than its technique.

34 The most recent edition of the *Owl and the Nightingale* is that of E. G. Stanley (London, 1960), where a discussion of the problems of its authorship and meaning, with full references, will be found.

35 For the dual character of this landscape see **pp. 79–83.**

36 It is possible that his main knowledge of Seneca was derived from a *Florilegium;* see R. A. Pratt 'Chaucer and the Hand that Fed Him', *Speculum*, XLI (1966), pp. 619 ff. The use of such a work, however, does not necessarily exclude the reading of the originals.

37 For details of Chaucer's knowledge of Latin poetry, see E. F. Shannon, *Chaucer and the Roman Poets* (Cambridge, Mass. 1929). For a good summary, see R. L. Hoffman, 'The Influence of the Classics on Chaucer' in Beryl Rowlands, ed., *Companion to Chaucer Studies* (Oxford, 1968), pp. 162 ff.

38 The stories of Aeneas and of Thebes existed in well-known romance versions, and the *Ovide Moralisé* of Bersuire was widely disseminated and extremely popular. This, as its name suggests, adapted Ovid to the beliefs and tastes of its author's own age.

39 See **pp. 164–5.**

40 This is of special importance in relation to the *Troilus* and the *Knight's Tale*. See **pp. 164 ff.** and **II, chapter 1,** *passim.*

41 See especially **II, pp. 48 ff., 139 ff.**

42 The first quotation is from William Webbe, *A Discourse of English Poetrie*, as quoted in Spurgeon, *Chaucer Criticism and Allusion*, I, p. 129. For Webbe, Chaucer was 'the God of English poets' who 'hath left many works both for delight and profitable knowledge, farre exceeding any other that as yet euer since hys time directed theyr studies that way'. Gabriel Harvey is quoted from his manuscript notes in Spurgeon, p. 128. He is especially impressed, in the case of Lydgate as well as Chaucer, by their 'Astronomie, Philosophie, and other parts of profound or cunning art'.

2 The urbane manner

1 See Robinson, ed., *Works of Chaucer*, p. 523. It is, however, possible that the poem was written earlier and provided with a new envoy for this occasion.

2 *Ibid.*, p. 523.

3 *Ibid.*, pp. 422–3. The couplet is in both versions of the Prologue. Unfortunately the dating and order of composition of the two are still uncertain. The first version could have been written as early as 1385, the second, generally assumed to be the revised one, in which the couplet still stands, and is therefore presumably still topical, as late as 1395. See *ibid.*, pp. 839–40, for a summary of the discussion with full references, and R. D. French, *A Chaucer Handbook* (New York, 1947; 2nd ed.,) pp. 126 ff.

4 Agreement on the occasion and date of this poem is general, that is, that it commemorates the death of Blanche, Duchess of Lancaster, in September 1369 and was written very soon after this event. For a dissenting voice (although the date need not necessarily be affected), see Bernard F. Huppé and D. W. Robertson Jr, *Fruyt and Chaf: Studies in Chaucer's Allegories* (Princeton, 1963), pp. 32 ff. The Prologue to the *Legend of Good Women* is, in fact, a fourth love vision, but here the form is only used as a device to introduce the unrelated matter of the tale-collection.

5 The miniature in MS 61, Corpus Christi College, Cambridge (see frontispiece), may even represent his usual method of publication although it is, obviously, an idealized scene. On the relationship of Chaucer to his audience see further J. Lawlor, *Chaucer* (London, 1968).

6 See Clemen, *Chaucer's Early Poetry*, p. 23; Muscatine, *French Tradition*, *passim*. It must be remembered, however, that interest in French poetry does not exclude the possibility of knowledge and enjoyment of earlier works in English.

7 It has often been claimed that the *Pearl*-Poet had first-hand knowledge of Dante. See P. M. Kean, *The Pearl: An Interpretation* (London, 1967), pp. 120 ff. He is, however, the only contemporary of Chaucer for whom such a claim could be made.

8 W. W. Skeat, ed., *The Lay of Havelok the Dane*, revised by K. Sisam (Oxford, 1915), l. 195. This may, of course, mean no more than 'discuss marriage'; but, in the context, it seems to me to have a more precise sense. It is a sign of maturity in a twelve-year-old princess that she 'couþe of curtesye / Don, and speken of luue-drurye'. Though her marriage is certainly contemplated (196–203), this couplet seems to refer to fashionable adult behaviour in general.

9 We cannot, of course, prove that these serious poems were, in fact, intended for the same audience as the love poems, but it is significant that they show exactly the same interest in experimentation with verse forms. It is also true that Chaucer generally mingles moral and philosophical themes with that of love. This is not only the case in his most complex works – the *Parlement of Foules*, the *Troilus* and the *Knight's Tale* – but also of simpler ones like the *Complaint of Mars* and the *Book of the Duchess*.

10 Deschamps' short moral poems tend to use the same abrupt, familiar openings addressing the reader as do Chaucer's, and usually continue in the same half argumentative, half exhortatory style. His metrical virtuosity is not so great as the English poet's, but the same basic way of writing is used by both. See the 'Balades de Moralitez', *Œuvres Complètes d'Eustache Deschamps*, I and II, SATF (Paris, 1880).

11 This is not, of course, to say that either Deschamps or Chaucer would not have regarded Seneca as a Christian author.

12 Cf., e.g., Balade cxci, 12–14; Balade clxxxvii, 19–20. The only specifically Christian note introduced by Chaucer is in *Truth*, 18–19, on the pilgrimage of life and the duty of thanking God for all – and this is distinctly less specific than most of Deschamps' references.

13 See Robinson, notes to lines 7, 11, 17.

14 See **p. 61.**

15 See, e.g., R. M. Gummere, ed., *Seneca ad Lucilium: Epistulae Morales* (Cambridge, Mass. 1961, Loeb edition), xxiv, 4; xxviii, 8; lxx, 9; lxxi, 17; xcviii, 12.

16 *Ibid.*, vii, 1. All quotations are from the text and translation of the three-volume Loeb edition.

17 See Robinson, note to *Truth*, 2.

18 For this idea cf., e.g., Epistles vii, xiv, xix, xxvii, all on the same theme of worldly business and the need to avoid it.

19 It is also possible that it has an allegorical meaning of a topical kind and refers to current events and personalities (see Robinson, notes, for references). J. D. North, 'Kalenderes Enlumyned ben They: Some Astronomical Themes in Chaucer', *RES*, N.S. XX (1969), pp. 137 ff., considers that the poem reflects the state of the heavens in 1385–1386.

20 Elias Ashmole, *Theatrum Chemicum Britannicum* (London, 1652; reprinted New York, 1967), pp. 415 ff.

21 Muscatine, *French Tradition*, p. 107. For a full discussion of the *Book of the Duchess*, see Clemen, *Chaucer's Early Poetry*, pp. 23 ff. and the references there given.

22 Most successfully, no doubt, by the Scottish Chaucerians; but cf., e.g., a passage like lines 372 ff. of the *Flower and the Leaf*, in which the company that has been drenched by the storm is rescued by the good offices of their rivals, or the dialogue of the *Assembly of Ladies*, to which the poem owes most of its charm.

23 See Martin M. Crow and Clair C. Olson, eds, *Chaucer Life-Records* (Oxford, 1966), pp. 13 ff.

24 On the themes of the *House of Fame*, see **pp. 85 ff.**

25 For accounts of the French love vision literature in relation to Chaucer see Clemen, *Chaucer's Early Poetry*, chs 1, 2 and 3, Muscatine, *French Tradition*, ch. 4. Robinson, notes, contains reasonably complete references to the individual poems Chaucer is likely to have known and used.

26 E. Hoepffner, ed., *Œuvres de Guillaume de Machaut* SATF (Paris, 1908), I, pp. 57 ff.

27 *Book of the Duchess*, l. 531. Both phrases can be translated 'acting, speaking proudly', but the alternative senses of 'over-elaborate' for 'quaint' and 'brusque' or 'rude' for 'tough' seem to fit the context better. Both are well evidenced.

28 *Œuvres de Machaut*, I, pp. 11 ff.

29 M. A. Scheler, ed., *Œuvres de Froissart* (Brussels, 1870), I, 1 ff.

30 The same stylistic device is used by Froissart when, in lines 1–12 of the *Paradys d'Amour*, the rhyme-scheme involves the repetition of parts of the verb 'veiller'. The effect is thus the opposite of Chaucer's, with the emphasis on wakefulness. Lines 13 ff. of the *Paradys* do contain numerous repetitions of parts of the verb 'dormir', but this material is not used by Chaucer until he reaches line 240 of his own poem.

31 Deities or allegorical personages, especially female ones, are often somewhat arbitrary in their commands – but it seems to me that, just as Fame, in the *House of Fame*, is exceptionally free in her language, so here the colloquialism goes further than it could do in the more consistent language of Chaucer's French prototypes. Compare, for example, a similar command in the *Jugement dou Roy de Navarre*, where the general level of style is lower than in some French love visions:

> Lors un escuier appealla
> Et li dist: 'Vois tu celui la
> Qui bel se deduit et deporte?
> Va a lui, et si me raporte
> Qui il est, et revien en l'eure,
> Sans la faire point de demeure.'
> (559–64)

32 It is used in the *Troilus* by Pandarus, for example:

> His nece awook, and axed, 'Who goth there?'
> 'My dere nece,' quod he 'it am I.'
> (III, 751–2)

In the *Legend of Good Women* the context is one of even more formal politeness:

> This god of Love on me hys eyen caste,
> And seyde, 'Who kneleth there?' and I answerde
> Unto his askynge, whan that I it herde,
> And seyde, 'Sir, it am I,' and com him ner,
> And salwed him.
>
> (F, Prologue, 311–15)

33 Although I would agree with Huppé and Robertson that 'the hart is symbolically complex' (*Fruyt and Chaf*, p. 54, n. 26), I can see no sign of the 'allegorization of God as the Hunter-King hunting after the human soul' (*ibid.*, p. 49).

34 On the relationship of the Dreamer and the Man in Black, see Clemen, *Chaucer's Early Poetry*, pp. 42 ff. and the references there given, especially in n. 1, p. 43.

35 For Chaucer the heart is the location of the rational soul. In his description of Arcite's death (*Knight's Tale, CT* I, 2797 ff.), first the 'vital strength' is lost, to the accompaniment of coldness; then, when death affects the heart, in which the intellect dwells, the process is complete and his spirit leaves his body. The 'vital strength' seems equivalent to the 'spirits' here – the means by which body and soul are normally held together. Their failure produces at first paralysis and unconsciousness, and then, if it is continued, death. For a good short account of the spirits in this sense, see C. S. Lewis, *The Discarded Image* (Cambridge, 1964), pp. 166 ff. On Arcite's death, with particular reference to the heart as the seat of the rational soul, see W. C. Curry, *Chaucer and the Medieval Sciences* (London, 1960; 2nd ed., pp. 299 ff.) and J. A. W. Bennett, *Chaucer: The Knight's Tale* (London, 1954, pp. 141–4). It is clear that the state of the Man in Black is a potentially serious one. The idea that Nature is opposed to grief is Senecan (see *Consolatio ad Marciam*, vii, 3; *Epistulae Morales*, ii).

36 There are signs that for the Middle Ages this might have a more sinister sense than it would for us. The unsuccessful lover who wanders in the wood is often depicted as not merely sad but also mad. This is the case with Lancelot, Tristram, Ywain and Amades. Similarly, the speaker in a Middle English lyric swears that, if his lady does not satisfy his desires he will 'wyht in wode be fleme', where something more damaging than a country ramble is clearly meant ('Lenten ys come wiþ loue to toune', line 36, in Carleton Brown, ed., *English Lyrics of the Thirteenth Century* [Oxford, 1932]).

37 C. S. Lewis, *The Allegory of Love* (Oxford, 1948), p. 164.

3 New themes in the love vision

1 The *Parlement* has been treated at length by several scholars comparatively recently, and it will be obvious that the present discussion owes much to their work, while, I hope, it still offers its own approach. The most important books and papers on the subject are: J. A. W. Bennett, *The Parlement of Foules: An Interpretation* (Oxford, 1957); D. S. Brewer, ed., *The Parlement of Foulys* (London, 1960); D. Everett, 'Chaucer's Love Visions with particular reference to the *Parlement of Foules*', in *Essays on Middle English Literature*, ch. 4; Clemen, 'The Parliament of Fowls', *Chaucer's Early Poetry*, ch. 3. Here, as elsewhere in this book, I must ask for the acceptance of a general acknowledgement of my very great debt to earlier critics, in order not to burden the reader with too many notes containing detailed references to agreements and disagreements with other writers.

2 Chaucer would certainly have regarded this as one of the most important sources of poetic material, since – English poetry apart, in which love lyric and romantic love story were already flourishing – his fashionable French and Italian models made so much use of it. As we have seen, however, moral-philosophical and purely religious poetry were also demanded of a poet who aimed at a sophisticated audience in the fourteenth century.

3 See Bennett, *Parlement*, pp. 45 ff.; Brewer, ed., 26 ff.

4 Cicero writes of the fate of the souls of those 'qui se corporis voluptatibus dediderunt' (*Somnium*, II, xvii) and uses the term 'libido' for the passion which rules them. As Bennett points out (*Parlement*, pp. 41–2), in Classical Latin 'libido' meant 'sensual passion'. It later, however, came to mean 'sodomy', i.e., the perversion which is castigated in the *de Planctu Naturae*. Chaucer's use of 'likerous' suggests that he may have preferred the more general sense and had in mind the medieval vice of *luxuria*, which, although it might include sodomy, is generally contrasted with the productive and virtuous love of marriage.

5 On this phrase see **pp. 160–2.**

6 See H. Rackham, ed., *de Natura Deorum* (Cambridge, Mass., 1951; Loeb ed.), II, xxiv: 'Suscepit autem vita hominum consuetudoque communis ut beneficiis excellentis viros in caelum fama ac voluntate tollerent.' ('Human experience, moreover, and general custom have made it a practice to confer the deification of renown and gratitude upon distinguished benefactors.') Cf. *Tusculan Disputations*, I, xii. On this view of the gods in the Classical and medieval period see J. Seznec, *La Survivance des Dieux Antiques* (London, 1940).

7 For Plato's account of the creation see A. E. Taylor, *A Commentary on Plato's Timaeus* (Oxford, 1928). Macrobius's use of the *Timaeus* and

its neo-Platonic commentators is discussed, with full bibliographical references, by W. H. Stahl in the introduction to his translation of the *Somnium Scipionis* (*Macrobius: Commentary on the Dream of Scipio*, Records of Civilization, Sources and Studies, XLVIII [New York, 1952]). See also the footnotes to this translation. A. O. Lovejoy, *The Great Chain of Being* (Harvard, 1936), chs. 2 and 3, discusses many of the ideas involved, in relation to both Greek and medieval philosophy.

8 See **pp. 175 ff.** and **II, pp. 41 ff.**

9 See **pp. 175 ff.**

10 Chaucer could have taken this term from either the *de Planctu* (cols. 453, 476, 479) or the *Roman* (16782, 19507) or both. He uses it in a more restricted sense of Nature's power to make and adorn (*'forme and peynten'*) earthly creatures in the *Physician's Tale* (*CT* VI, 21). Here he is careful to state that God is the ultimate source of all forms ('formere principal', line 19). When Chaucer addresses the Blessed Virgin Mary as 'vicaire and maistresse / Of al this world' (*ABC*, 140–1), he is presumably thinking of her in relation to grace, and so to reformation, not formation.

11 I. P. Sheldon-Williams and Ludwig Bieler, eds., *Iohannis Scotii Eriugenae Peryphyseon* (*De Divisione Naturae, Liber Primus*) *Scriptores Latini Hiberniae*, VII (Dublin, 1968). All quotations are from the text and translation of this edition.

12 See **II, pp. 41 ff.**

13 *Man of Law's Tale* (*CT* II, 1131); *Clerk's Tale* (*CT* IV, 1129, 1132, 1136); *Franklin's Tale* (*CT* V, 760). In all these, married love and its results are in question.

14 *De Planctu Naturae*, in Thomas Wright, ed., *The Anglo-Latin Satirical Poets*, II (London, 1872), p. 451. This echoes the 'rerum concordia discors' of Horace, *Epistles* xii, 19 (of the Empedoclian doctrine of nature as a perpetual conflict of love and strife).

15 *Somnium*, I, vi: 'Nam impar numerus mas, et par foemina vocatur. Item arithmetici imparem patris, et parem matris apellatione venerantur. Hinc et Timaeus Platonis, fabricatorem mundanae animae Deum partes eius ex pari et impari, id est, duplari et triplari numero, intertexuisse memoravit; ita ut a duplari usque ad octo, a triplari usque ad viginti septem staret alternatio mutandi.' ('An odd number is called male and an even female; mathematicians, moreover, honour odd numbers with the name of Father and even numbers with the name of Mother. Hence Timaeus, in Plato's dialogue by the same name, says that the God who made the World-Soul intertwined even and odd in its make-up; that is, using the numbers two and three as a basis, he alternated the odd and even numbers from three to twenty-seven.')

16 *Ibid.*, I, vi: 'Ita enim elementa inter se diversissima, opifex tamen Deus ordinis opportunitate connexuit, ut facile iungerentur. Nam cum binae in singulis qualitates essent: talem unicuique de duabus

alteram dedit, ut in eo cui adhaereret cognatam sibi et similem reperiret. Terra est sicca, et frigida: aqua vero frigida, et humida est. Haec duo elementa licet sibi per siccum, humectumque, contraria sint, per frigidum tamen commune iunguntur. Aer humectus, et calidus est: et cum aquae frigidae contrarius sit calore, conciliatione tamen socii copulatur humoris. Super hunc ignis cum sit calidus, et siccus, humorem quidem aeris respuit, siccitate; sed connectitur, societate caloris. Et ita sit, ut singula quaeque elementorum, duo sibi hinc inde vicina singulis qualitatibus velut quibusdam amplectantur ulnis.' ('Thus, in spite of the complete unlikeness of the elements, the Creator harmonized them so skilfully that they could easily be united. He gave two qualities to each, one of which was of such a kind that each element could find this quality related to and similar to itself in the element to which it adhered. Earth is dry and cold, water cold and moist; but although these two elements are opposed, the dry to the wet, yet they have a common bond in their coldness. Air is moist and warm, and, although opposed to water, the cold to the warm, nevertheless they have the common bond of moisture. Moreover, fire, being hot and dry, spurns the moisture of the air, but yet adheres to it because of the warmth in both. And so it happens that every element appears to embrace the two elements on each side of it by single qualities.')

17 *Ibid.*, I, vi: After speaking of the difference in 'density and weight' between the four elements, which, since it exists in the same proportions between the different pairs, is also a linking factor – 'ita ex ipso quo inter se sunt aequaliter, diversa sociantur' – Macrobius goes on to describe the three interstices which link the elements in this version of the chain: 'Et a terra quidem usque ad aquam spatium, necessitas a Physicis dicitur: quia vincire et solidare creditur, quod est in corporis lutulentum. . . . Illud vero quod inter aquam et aerem, harmonia dicitur, id est, apta et consonans convenientia: quia hoc spatium est, quod superioribus inferiora conciliat, et facit dissona convenire. Inter aerem vero et ignem obedientia dicitur: quia sicut lutulenta et gravia superioribus necessitate iunguntur; ita superiora lutulentis obedientia copulantur, harmonia media, coniunctionem utriusque praestante.' ('The demarcation between earth and water is called Necessity by natural philosophers because it is believed to bind and solidify the clay of which bodies are made. . . . The demarcation between water and air is called Harmony, that is a compatible and harmonious union: for this is the interval which unites the lower with the upper, reconciling what is incongruent. The demarcation between air and fire is called Obedience; for whereas the muddy and heavy bodies are joined to the things above by Necessity, the things above associate with what is muddy by Obedience, with Harmony in the middle promoting a union of both.' That the chain of the elements was thought of as a process, not a state, is shown by a passage like the following (Cicero, *de Natura Deorem*, II, xxxiii): 'Et cum

quattuor genera sint corporum, vicissitudine eorum mundi continuata natura est. Nam ex terra aqua ex aqua oritur aer ex aere aether, deinde retrorsum vicissim ex aethere aer, inde aqua, ex aqua terra infima. Sic naturis his ex quibus omnia constant sursus deorsus ultro citro commeantibus mundi partium coniunctio continetur.' ('Again, the continuum of the world's nature is constituted by the cyclic transmutations of the four kinds of matter. For earth turns into water, water into air, air into aether, and then the process is reversed, and aether becomes air, air water, and water earth, the lowest of the four. Thus the parts of the world are held in union by the constant passage up and down, to and fro, of these four elements of which all things are constructed.') The idea of transmutation and cyclic movement, which does not appear in the *Parlement*, is important in the *Knight's Tale* (see **II, pp. 46–7**). If Chaucer did not know it from any other source, he would still be familiar with Boethius's 'entre-chaungeable mutacioun' (*de Consolatione Philosophiae*, Book IV, pr. vi).

18 (*Parlement*, 381). As Bennett points out, the normal meaning of 'even' in the phrase 'even number' in the fourteenth century would be 'exact' (p. 133). The only support for the sense 'not odd' comes from *Piers Plowman*, B, XX, 268: 'Heuene hath euene noumbre, and helle is with-out noumbre.' It is true that, according to Revelation, the number of the blessed is even, in the modern sense – *viz.* 144,000; but, in the context, Langland means that a definite, exact number is given for heaven, while hell, on the authority of Job 10:22, has 'nullus ordo' (cf. *Parson's Tale*, *CT* X, 218, where this is associated with number). This enables Langland to make a jibe against the Friars: they have no fixed number of members, in keeping with their ability to support them, and in this respect they resemble Hell, not Heaven. See R. W. Frank Jr, *Piers Plowman and the Scheme of Salvation* (New Haven and London, 1957), pp. 112 ff.

19 The whole of chapter vi in Book I of the *Somnium* is relevant. It will be enough to quote the conclusion to the passage on the interstices: 'Ex quatuor igitur elementis, et tribus eorum interstitiis absolutionem corporum constare manifestum est. Ergo hi duo numeri, tria dico et quatuor, tam multiplici inter se cognationis necessitate sociati, efficiendis utriusque corporibus, consensu ministri foederis obsequuntur.' ('Complete bodies clearly consist, therefore, of four elements and their three interstices. And, you see, these two numbers, three and four, united by so many relationships, lend themselves to making both kinds of bodies [plane and solid] by reciprocal agreement.') This passage contains the idea expressed by Chaucer's phrase 'of accord', although he was probably also thinking of the wording of Alanus: 'quatuor elementorum concors discordia' (*de Planctu*, in Wright, ed., *Anglo-Latin Poets*, II, p. 451). Boethius's 'noumbres proporcionables' (in Chaucer's translation of *de Consolatione Philosophiae*, III, m. ix, 18–19) are also three and four: the four elements and 'the mene soule of treble kynde'.

20 According to all Classical and medieval musical theory, musical harmony depended on numerical relationships which reproduced those of the music of the spheres. See E. Wellesz, *A History of Byzantine Music and Hymnography* (Oxford, 1962, 2nd ed.), ch. 2.

21 See *de Planctu*, in Wright, ed., *Anglo-Latin Poets*, II, pp. 475 ff. It is significant that in the *Parlement* Chaucer combines in one figure Venus with the flaming torch (the Venus of sexual passion from the *Roman de la Rose*) and the 'blysful lady swete', Cytherea, corresponding to the Venus to whom he elsewhere (notably in the *Troilus*, III, 1 ff.) appeals as a cosmic force.

22 *De Planctu* in Wright, ed., *Anglo-Latin Poets*, II, 445 ff. Chastity, as well as Hymen, is a member of Nature's following.

23 See *Roman de la Rose*, especially 18947 ff. Nature, however, first appears at 15891 ff. Jean de Meun's treatment of the material is extremely diffuse.

24 *Ibid.*, 19021 ff.

25 For their stories see Robinson, notes. Hercules' love was a criminal one insofar as it was adulterous; and his death was the result of Deianira's jealous action. Chaucer nowhere shows any tendency to regard adulterous love as justifiable. In his one comparatively sympathetic treatment of love outside marriage, the *Troilus*, the lovers are, respectively, widowed and unmarried.

26 The vestal virgin breaks a deliberate vow to serve the gods in a certain way. Diana's nymphs pass from her service to that of Venus as part of a natural process in which virginity is converted to fruition. For Chaucer, Diana was a goddess of fruitfulness as well as Venus (see **II, p. 28**).

27 It is true that the phrase 'serve Venus ne Cupide' can be taken as a mere formula, meaning no more than 'love' (see Brewer, ed., *Parlement*, note to 652); but its position is emphatic, and in a poem which, as I believe, turns on the relations of Venus and Nature, it is appropriate that Nature's favourite bird should refer to her relationship to the other goddess.

28 Chaucer has combined the single gate and single inscription of the *Inferno*, III, 1–3 (whose cadence his own inscription echoes), with the two gates from which issued the true and false dreams of the *Aeneid*, VI, 893 ff. These have no inscriptions, but do have the contrary import of the gate of the *Parlement*.

29 Two recent full-length studies of the poem are J. A. W. Bennett, *Chaucer's Book of Fame: An Exposition of 'The House of Fame'* (Oxford, 1968), and B. G. Koonce, *Chaucer and the Tradition of Fame: Symbolism in the House of Fame* (Princeton, 1966). To the first of these books I must acknowledge a general debt, although, once again I have not noted every agreement or disagreement in the course of this chapter. I do not think that I owe much to the second, which takes a totally different viewpoint.

30 It is, however, nearer to the style of Ovid than of Virgil. The emphasis

falls on the unhappy figure of Dido and her long complaint. For a detailed analysis of Chaucer's rehandling of the *Aeneid*, IV, see Bennett, 'Venus and Virgil', *Chaucer's Book of Fame*, ch. 1.

31 *Ibid.*, ch. 1, and see further **pp. 102–4.**

32 Even the grotesque and comic rumours are, like the eagle, 'wynged wondres' (*House of Fame*, 2118).

33 As, for example, Muscatine seems to do when he criticizes the 'grotesque stylistic disharmony with its narrative context' of parts of the *House of Fame* (*French Tradition*, p. 109).

34 The *descriptio* of Fame is analysed at length by Bennett, *Chaucer's Book of Fame*, pp. 128 ff. On the linking of Fame with poetry, see pp. 136 ff. Koonce's statement (*Chaucer and the Tradition of Fame*, p. 5) that 'in its simplest reduction, the theme of the *House of Fame* is the vanity of worldly fame' seems to oversimplify this passage.

35 Chaucer's attitude to Homer in the *House of Fame* (1475 ff.) is a little doubtful; although he attributes criticism of him to envy, he is obviously well aware of the tradition that, as the translator of the *Destruction of Troy* puts it, placed all 'poyetis of prise' among those who 'dampnet his dedys and for dull holdyn' (47 ff.). His opinion of Homer seems to have changed for the better by the time he wrote the *Troilus*, since he mentions him with respect at the end.

36 Skeat–Sisam, ed., *Havelok*. There is no positive evidence to show whether or not Chaucer knew this romance. The story, perhaps in the version we know, perhaps in another or others, seems to have been popular and well known, to judge from Robert Manning's reference to it and from the existence both of a fragment of another MS and a résumé in the Lambeth interpolation of Manning. This, however, on the evidence of the names of the characters, has more affinity with the extant French version than the English Lay. See Skeat–Sisam, Introduction, paragraphs 8–9, for details.

37 Smithers, ed., *Kyng Alisaunder*, EETS, O.S., 227 (1952 for 1947) and O.S., 237 (1957 for 1953). On the lyrical 'headpieces' of this poem, see O.S., 237, pp. 35 ff. Such passages, at least as far as content is concerned, are to be found in Old French and medieval Latin narrative poems.

38 Bliss, ed., *Sir Orfeo*. I quote from the Auchinleck text, which may have been known to Chaucer. See Laura H. Loomis, 'The Tale of Sir Thopas', in *Sources and Analogues*, pp. 486 ff. and the references there given.

39 The nearest to Chaucer's own day is Guido delle Colonne, who made a Latin prose redaction of the much more important work in French of Benoît de Sainte-Maure, the *Roman de Troie*. Chaucer evidently considers the use of the two great languages of the Classical past important in the selection of the basic upholders of fame. 'Englyssh Gaufride' is unlikely to break this series. He is, almost certainly, Geoffrey of Monmouth, who, of course, wrote in Latin.

40 This structure is not dictated by the French love vision. The opening

on sleep and dreams can be found there – that of the *House of Fame* is, in fact, closely imitated from a poem of Froissart (for details see Robinson, notes). The device of a tale told at length is not developed by French writers, although they do make use of *exempla*. Since the core of the love vision in French is the didactic speeches, which give instruction concerning Love at length, the descriptions and settings are necessarily subordinate, and there is nothing to compare with Chaucer's thematic use of these parts of his work. It might even be possible to see an element of literary satire in Chaucer's insistence on the elusive love-tidings which are never actually spoken. Such reticence is, at any rate, markedly unlike the normal practice of the French poets.

41 The tablet of brass seems to have an inscription on it consisting of, at least, the opening lines of the *Aeneid* (the 'Thus writen' of line 142 is, clearly, followed by a quotation). What happens next is not so clear, but line 149, 'And tho began the story anoon', could indicate a different method of representation, and the repeated use of 'saw' (lines 151, 162, 174, 193, etc.) suggests pictures. 'Graven' (e.g. line 193) is ambiguous and could mean either 'drawn' (sculpted or incised) or 'inscribed', but at line 211 the unambiguous 'peynted' is used. I think that the tablet of brass is either to be taken as providing the title lines for the series of paintings that accompanies it, or, in the manner of a dream, as dissolving and giving way to the more vivid method of painting. For a discussion of the passage and its various possibilities see Bennett, *Chaucer's Book of Fame*, pp. 13–14.

42 I do not, therefore, think that the iconography, typical and untypical (in the case of the comb), of Chaucer's treatment has much significance for the rest of the work. He seems to me merely to take over a set piece found in convenient form in the *Teseida* and to treat it cursorily. More emphasis is placed on the function of Venus in the poem in Bennett, 'Venus and Virgil', *Chaucer's Book of Fame*, ch. 1.

43 For Chaucer's use of the machinery of the gods in the *Troilus*, see **pp. 165 ff.**, and in the *Knight's Tale*, see **II, chapter 1.**

44 The implication and Chaucerian associations of the desert are discussed at length by Bennett, *Chaucer's Book of Fame*, pp. 47 ff.

45 See **pp. 169 ff.**

46 The same idea is implied in lines 1209–13. 'Craft', 'skill in art', counterfeits or copies nature; 'smale harpers', on the contrary, can only imitate other artists 'as an ape'. According to a common conceit, any artist, however great, is of course 'the ape of Nature' – *simia naturae*.

47 Virgil, *Aeneid*, IV, 188–90:

> tam ficti pravique tenax quam nuntia veri.
> haec tum multiplici populos sermone replebat
> gaudens, et pariter facta atque infecta canebat,

is the basis of the description of the flying rumours ('nocte volat caeli medio, terraeque per umbram / stridens'. *Aeneid*, IV, 184–5) in the third book of the *House of Fame*.

48 Cf., e.g., *Havelok*, lines 886–94;

> Havelok it herde, and was ful blithe
> That he herde 'bermen' calle.
> Alle he made hem dune falle
> That in his gate yeden and stode,
> Wel sixtene laddes gode.
> Als he lep the kok [un-]til,
> He shof hem alle upon an hyl;
> Astirte til him with his rippe,
> And bigan þe fish to kippe.

And cf., e.g., lines 909 ff.

49 The only deficiency seems to be that there is no description of the goddess to whom the House of Rumour belongs. One would expect a set piece parallel to the *descriptio* of Fame. This would, of course, present difficulties, since much of the material belonging to *Fama* = Rumour has been used in the description of *Fama* = Renown, and what is left has been used for the flying rumours. The 'lytel laste bok', too, has run into considerable length already, and there would seem little space for another full-scale *descriptio*. If, however, this was the conclusion Chaucer had in mind, it would account for his failure to finish, in that it was a difficult and exacting task, worth the putting off. It is hard to see why even as confirmed a non-finisher as Chaucer should have postponed the writing of a few concluding lines of the sort proposed by Caxton.

4 *Troilus and Criseyde*

1 The relative dates of the two poems are, of course, uncertain. A date for the *Parlement* of 1393, which is definitely later than the *Troilus*, has recently been suggested by North, 'Kalenderes Enlumyned', pp. 270 ff. This depends on the interpretation of the description of Venus's temple and its attendant figures in astronomical terms. The argument, however, seems of dubious validity in view of the fact that most of these details are taken over from the *Teseida* or the *Roman de la Rose*. As far as our understanding of Chaucer's thought is concerned, the question of which poem came first is not really crucial. The *Parlement* undoubtedly gives in summary form ideas that are more fully developed in the *Troilus*, whether Chaucer proceeded from a brief statement to a fuller one or *vice versa*.

2 See K. Young, *The Origin and Development of the Story of Troilus and Criseyde*, Chaucer Society, 2nd series, 40 (1908); C. S. Lewis, 'What

Chaucer Really did to *Il Filostrato*', *Essays and Studies*, XVII (1932), pp. 56 ff.; Sanford B. Meech, *Design in Chaucer's Troilus* (Syracuse, 1959). Ida L. Gordon's study *The Double Sorrow of Troilus* (Oxford, 1970) came to hand too late for reference here; I am glad to find much agreement between us, though I think our main theses differ a little.

3 *The Filostrato of Giovanni Boccaccio* text and trans. by N. E. Griffin and A. B. Myrick (Philadelphia and London, 1929), pp. 114 ff. All quotations are from this edition.

4 *Ibid.*, iii, st. 28 ff.

5 *Ibid.*, pp. 126–7.

6 At II, 606, she considers the possibility 'of peril, why she ought afered be'. In lines 708–14 she seriously contemplates the fear of standing 'in worse plit' if she were to earn the hatred instead of the favour of such a powerful man as Troilus. At III, 76, it is, thus, his 'lordshipe' that she comes to beg for. Even in the consummation scene, Pandarus harps on the same string: 'Nece, se how this *lord* kan knele!' (III, 962).

7 Cf. III, 1210–11. Her reproaches to Pandarus next morning are hardly serious. She answers his enquiry as to how she is, with a colloquialism typical of their friendly exchanges: 'Nevere the bet for yow, / Fox that ye ben!' (III, 1564–5).

8 V, 956 ff. See further **p. 135.**

9 Pandarus the ready-tongued is finally completely silenced: 'Astoned', 'as stille as ston; a word ne kowde he seye' (V, 1728–9). His attempts to convert Troilus to his own way of thinking are unsuccessful (IV, 393 ff., and V, 330 ff.).

10 IV, 547 ff.; V, 43 ff.

11 The phrase 'make in som comedye' suggests that the term does not refer to a literary kind, but to the nature of the subject.

12 *CT* VII, 1973–81, 1991–6, 2761–6. For parallels and possible sources, see Robinson, notes.

13 For a somewhat different idea of the meaning of tragedy for Chaucer see D. W. Robertson Jr, 'Chaucerian Tragedy', *ELH* XIX (1952), pp. 1–37. This article also emphasizes the link between tragedy and Fortune.

14 See Howard R. Patch, *The Goddess Fortuna in Medieval Literature* (Cambridge, Mass. 1927; reprinted London, 1967: my references are to the reprint), pp. 10–14 give a brief account of Classical ideas.

15 See **II, pp. 41 ff.**

16 The concepts of Fortune and Nature, and even of Love, are very nearly related when they are used with reference to the results brought about by God's creative providence in the world. Thus Boethius, writing of Love, speaks (in Chaucer's version) of the 'atempraunce' which 'norysscheth and bryngeth forth alle thinges that brethith lif in this world; and thilke same atempraunce, ravysschynge, hideth and bynymeth and drencheth undir the laste deth, alle thinges

iborn' (IV, m. 6, 34 ff.). This 'atempraunce' is the same as that by which Nature, in the *Parlement*, controls the elements. See Patch, *The Goddess Fortune*, pp. 75 ff., on Nature and Fortune, and 90 ff., on Fortune and Love.

17 *de Consolatione*, II, pr. viii, 11 ff.

18 In the *Divina Commedia*, the tour of heaven is ordered as a progression through the spheres, starting from that of the moon. In both the *Troilus* and the *Parlement*, Chaucer makes use of the clearer view afforded to the soul which mounts above the sphere of change. In the *House of Fame*, the Eagle's flight does not take him so far – Fame operates in the delusive sphere of Nature. For living men such flights are, of course, made 'wyth fetheres of Philosophye' (*House of Fame*, 974), that is, Reason is not subject to Fortune and change (cf. *de Consolatione*, IV, m. i).

19 *CT* I, 3072 (see further **II, 48 ff.**); cf. *de Consolatione*, II, m. viii 21 ff.

20 See **pp. 148 ff.**

21 *de Consolatione*, IV, pr. vi and m. vi, *Inferno*, VII, 67 ff.; Chaucer, *Fortune*, 57–72.

22 For the implications of this passage in Chaucer's hands, see also **pp. 175–7.**

23 E.g., at I, 968; and cf. I, 986; II, 316 ff. Criseyde echoes this praise at II, 703 ff. (and it is notable that Antigone's song develops the same theme, i.e., of a lover who is 'welle of worthynesse' at II, 841). Cf. III, 474 ff.; III, 1550 ff.

24 As described, e.g., in the very popular *Legenda Aurea*.

25 This dream, like that of Troilus concerning the boar at V, 1232 ff., could be intended as a true prophetic dream, in which future events are shown under allegorical disguise (one of Macrobius's categories); or we could take it as showing psychological insight on Chaucer's part – the dreaming mind, in both cases, admits as a *fait accompli* what the waking mind is not yet prepared to admit. The case for 'realism' in the depiction of dreams in Chaucer and other medieval authors has recently been discussed by Constance B. Hieatt, *The Realism of Dream Visions* (The Hague and Paris, 1967).

26 North, 'Kalenderes Enlumyned' pp. 142–3.

27 See Curry, *Chaucer and the Medieval Sciences*, ch. 10. 'Destiny in Troilus and Criseyde', North ('Kalenderes Enlumyned'), points out that Skeat's notes are usually a more reliable source than Curry's book for the analysis and interpretation of astronomical references.

28 For a contrary view see D. W. Robertson Jr, *A Preface to Chaucer* (Princeton and London, 1963) pp. 251 ff.

29 See **II, pp. 11–14.**

30 A. C. Cawley, ed., *Everyman* (Manchester, 1961).

31 *Piers Plowman*, B, XI, 60 ff.

32 E.g., I, 582; II, 323 ff.; II, 1355–8; IV, 344 ff.; IV, 427–31; IV, 872 ff.

33 Book II, 78 ff. and 1093 ff.

34 All mentioned in Book II; and cf. III, 614: 'He song; she pleyde; he tolde tale of Wade'.

35 IV, 680 ff. Throughout 'tho wordes and tho wommanyshe thynges . . . Hire advertence is alwey elleswhere' (694–8).

36 For this characteristic of the *fabliau* see Muscatine, *French Tradition*, p. 60.

37 This is Macrobius's order in the *Somnium*. The reading 'eighthe' is not that of the majority of MSS (most have 'seventhe'), but it agrees with Boccaccio's 'ottava'. For various interpretations of this passage see Robinson, notes and the references there given.

38 The middle pair, however, can change places. Boethius, for example (*de Consolatione*, IV, m. i), has the order earth–air–water (clouds)–fire in a space-flight of the mind; Macrobius (*Somnium* II, vi) prefers earth–water–air–fire.

39 The conquest of the passions is a major theme in all Stoic or Stoic-derived authors. On the death of epic heroes, see **pp. 172 ff.**

40 See *OED* 'World', sb., I. 3; and cf. the phrase 'as the world asks', e.g., *Piers Plowman*, B, Prologue 19; *Sir Gawain and the Green Knight*, 530. Dante's phrase 'cieco mondo' may also have been echoing in Chaucer's mind. Generally used of a dark place (e.g., *Inferno* XXVII, 25), it is figurative in *Purgatorio* XVI, 66, in a passage dealing with fate and freewill.

41 See *OED* 'Intention', sb., I. 1.

42 Cf. Chaucer's use of the proverb 'A blynd man kan nat juggen wel in hewis' (II, 21) to excuse his own inability to speak 'feelingly' of love. As a proverb it was, no doubt, a commonplace, but it nevertheless helps to establish the theme.

43 For Chaucer the God of Love is not necessarily blind. Cf. the description in the Prologue to the *Legend of Good Women*, F. 226 (based on the *Roman de la Rose*; the Chaucerian version, A, 885 ff.). On the variety of the treatments and attributes of Cupid as God of Love, see Seznec, *La Survivance des Dieux Antiques*, pp. 93 ff.

44 *De Consolatione*, Book V, m. iii, 29. For a similar blending of two separate sources in a passage of apparently straight translation see J. A. W. Bennett, 'Chaucer, Dante and Boccaccio', *Medium Aevum*, XXII (1952), pp. 114 ff.

45 It is generally accepted that Chaucer must have made his translation of the *de Consolatione* at about the time when he was writing the *Troilus*, and that he was profoundly influenced by it in this poem. See Robinson, p. 811, and R. K. Root, *The Book of Troilus and Criseyde by Geoffrey Chaucer* (Princeton, 1945), p. xli.

46 Roncaglia, ed., *Teseida*.

47 Boccaccio also drew on the *Pharsalia*, IX, 1.

48 See above, note 18 of this chapter.

49 See *OED* 'Lust', sb., 2. c.

50 *Ibid.*, 4.

51 Gower also uses this phrase, in similar contexts, e.g., in the tale of

Virginia, *Confessio Amantis*, VII, 5147, 5219. If Chaucer derived it from Dante, as I have suggested, it seems likely that Gower borrowed it from Chaucer.

52 A common phrase with St Bernard, and (for the idea) cf. the title of an anonymous treatise *de Quattuor Gradibus Violentiae Amoris*, PL, 196, 1207 ff. (attributed to Richard of St Victor).

53 See also **pp. 70–1.** The relation of this passage to the *Parlement* is fully discussed by Bennett, *Parlement*, pp. 41 ff.

54 For the convention of the list of past poets, and Chaucer's use of it, see Robinson, notes, p. 837.

55 There is no complete history of medieval astrology. It is discussed by Lynn Thorndike, *A History of Magic and Experimental Science*, 6 vols. (London, 1929; 2nd ed.). See also C. H. Haskins, *Studies in the History of Medieval Science* (Harvard, 1927; 2nd ed.), and T. O. Wedel, *The Medieval Attitude toward Astrology* (Yale, 1920). North's article 'Kalenderes Enlumyned' is also useful on special points; and I am indebted here, and in **II, chapter 1,** to Raymond Klibansky, Erwin Panofsky and Fritz Saxl, *Saturn and Melancholy* (London, 1964). Chauncey Wood, *Chaucer and the Country of the Stars* (Princeton, 1970), reached me too late for reference here.

56 St Thomas Aquinas sums up in favour of free will in *Summa Theologica*, I, qu. cxv, art. 4, and in *Opusculum XVII* (P. Mandonnet, ed. [Paris, 1927], III, pp. 142 ff.). Contrary opinions, however, were held. Daniel of Morley, for example, who based his work on Adelard of Bath, took up an almost completely fatalistic position in *Liber de Naturis Inferiorum et Superiorum* (K. Sudhoff, ed. [Leipzig, 1917], VIII). Such popular authors as Jean de Meun (*Roman*, 17059 ff.) and Gower, however, are in agreement with Thomas Aquinas (*Confessio Amantis*, VII, 633 ff., a section introduced by Latin verses containing the significant line: 'Vir mediante deo sapiens dominabitur astris').

57 North, 'Kalenderes Enlumyned,' p. 437, suggests that the Astrolabe here represents a change of heart. If the present interpretation of the *Troilus* passage is accepted, however, Chaucer's view is a consistent one. We could also compare the attitude to natural magic (also involving astrology) in the *Franklin's Tale*. This is dismissed in similar terms as 'supersticious cursednesse' (*CT* V, 1272) and as what 'hethen folk useden in thilke dayes' (1293).

58 J. H. Mozeley, ed. and trans. *Statius* (London and Cambridge, Mass., 1961, Loeb ed.). All references are to this edition. The condemnation of belief in auguries and omens was a common homiletic theme in the Middle Ages. Cf., e.g., the *Parson's Tale*, *CT* X, 603 ff. and J. R. R. Tolkien, ed., *Ancrene Wisse*, EETS, 249 (1962), p. 108, lines 25–6.

59 These two passages are compared by Bennett in *Chaucer's Book of Fame*, p. 90. He concludes that the attributes of God shown forth in the creation inhere in Adam, since he was made in God's image. The *Second Nun's Prologue* has material similar to that used at the end of the *Troilus* (cf., e.g., lines 71–4). Its date is uncertain, but it is not a very

early work, since it has many echoes of Dante. Nor was it originally written for the *Canterbury Tales*, since it has references to translating, to writing and to readers. There is, in fact, nothing against the assumption that it was in hand at about the time when Chaucer was finishing the *Troilus* and ideas of this kind were in the fore-front of his mind.

60 Hilton, however, in the *Scale of Perfection* (written during Chaucer's working life), places the divine likeness in an Augustinian resemblance of the soul to the Trinity and sees this as the source of human dignity: 'So man's soul which may be called a created trinity, was perfected in the memory, sight, and love of the uncreated Blessed Trinity. This is the dignity and nobility which belong to a man's soul naturally at its creation. You possessed this state in Adam before man's first sin' (*The Scale of Perfection*, Dom Gerard Sitwell, O.S.B., trans. [London, 1953]). See also E. Gavin, 'La *dignitas hominis* e la letteratura patristica', *La Rinascita* (1938), I, iv.

61 Cf. Pseudo-Ptolemy, *Centiloquium*, 8: 'Anima sapiens adiuvat opus stellarum', that is, the wise astrologer can observe the nature of the planetary influences and take advantage of them. St Thomas's 'dominatur' alters the meaning of the proposition and places the wise man in a much more independent position. That some form of this proposition was widespread is shown by the references to the *Roman de la Rose* and the *Confessio Amantis* given above (note 56).

62 The material in Chaucer's *Troilus*, Book V, covered much more briefly by Boccaccio, is greatly rearranged. Chaucer omits Troilo's attempted suicide (*Filistrato*, VII, 33). This passage would seem to serve as a substitute.

63 For the story of his death see *Thebaid*, Books X–XI.

64 'To recount all the guilty tale of Thebes'. The opening of the first book of the *Thebaid* is designed to emphasize the evil which begins with the origin of the race (lines 4 ff.) and is continued in the history of the house of Oedipus.

65   ast illum amplexae Pietas Virtusque ferebant
            leniter ad terras corpus; nam spiritus olim
            ante Iovem summis apicem sibi poscit in astris.
                      (*Thebaid*, X, 780–2)

66 'Sator astrorum' (*Thebaid*, III, 218); 'Summe sator terraeque deumque' (*Thebaid*, III, 488).

67 *Purgatorio*, XXI, XXII. It is possible that Dante's reasons were unconnected with the subject matter of the *Thebaid*. See the Loeb *Statius*, pp. xxvi–xxviii, where references to various discussions of the problem are given.

68 Cf., e.g., *Thebaid*, IV, 691, where Bacchus appeals to the influence of the stars (just as Pandarus does) to help him bring about a result dependent on weather – in this case drought.

69   quae saeva repente / victores agitat leto Iovis ira sinistra,

                                         (*Thebaid*, III, 537–8)

For Jupiter as a Creative Providence see **II, chapter 1,** and cf. Plate II, where he is represented through the purely Christian iconography of the hand of Providence coming through the cloud. Although this illustration is a late one, it represents the figures of the gods in a medieval, not a Renaissance way.

70 Cf. *Filostrato*, III, st. 75. Boccaccio merely adds 'men and gods', in the plural ('E gli uomini e gli dei'), to the list of the parts of the world affected by love. Chaucer's change to 'God', singular, and the commanding position he gives to the phrase 'God loveth', by placing it at the beginning of the line with inversion of the stress, completely alters the implications of the passage.

71 *Profuit Ignaris*, 55–9 (text and trans. in Peter Dronke, *Mediaeval Latin and the Rise of European Love-Lyric*, II [Oxford, 1966] pp. 452 ff.). The idea of the *amours* of Jupiter as an example and excuse for human love goes back to Roman comedy, and before it to Greek (Aristophanes, *Clouds*, 1033–4). The important passage for the later Middle Ages was probably Terence, *Eunuchus*, III, v, 36. Terence was a curriculum author during the Middle Ages – see E. R. Curtius, *European Literature and the Latin Middle Ages*, W. R. Trask, trans. (New York and London, 1953) pp. 49, 260 – but this particular passage was, oddly enough, handed on by St Augustine's use of it in the *de Civitate Dei*, II, vii:

Hinc apud Terentium flagitiosus adulescens spectat tabulam quandam pictam in pariete 'ubi inerat pictura haec, Iovem / Quo pacto Danae misisse aiunt quondam in gremium imbrem aureum,' atque ab hac tanta auctoritate adhibet patrocinium turpitudini suae, cum in ea se iactat imitari deum – 'At quem deum!' inquit, 'qui templa caeli summo sonitu concutit. / Ego homuncio id non facerem? Ego vero illud feci ac libens.'

(Thus, when the young profligate in Terence sees a painting on the wall 'which shows Jupiter descending in a golden shower into Danae's lap', he takes this as an authoritative precedent for his own licentiousness, and boasts that he is imitating a god: 'And what a god!' he says, 'the one who shakes with his thunder the temples of heaven. And am I, poor creature, not to do the same as him? No, I did it, and with a will!')

Although Chaucer is far from the spirit of this passage, and even the *Profuit Ignaris* has its serious aspects, the fact that this topic was transmitted in a comic setting needs to be taken into account.

Index

Index

Index

Index

Index

Index

Index